The Proverbs 31
Ministry ™

Encouragement and Inspiration
For Women

TOUCHING WOMEN'S HEARTS, BUILDING GODLY HOMES

The Proverbs 31 Ministry ™

The Best of The Proverbs 31 Ministry
First printing 1999
Second printing 2000

International Standard Book Number: 0-9649507-0-7
Library of Congress Catalog Card Number: 99-96034

Credits: Editor: **Glynnis A. Whitwer**
Graphic Design: **Harriet McDowall, PageCreations**
Cover Design: **www.Valentinedesign.com**

To order additional books or request information about the ministry, please call or write:

The Proverbs 31 Ministry
P.O. Box 17155
Charlotte, NC 28227
(704) 849-2270
www.proverbs31.org
e-mail: P31Home@proverbs31.org

About The Proverbs 31 Ministry

The Proverbs 31 Ministry is a non-denominational organization dedicated to glorifying God by touching women's hearts to build godly homes. Through Jesus Christ, we shed light on God's distinctive design for women and the great responsibilities we have been given. With Proverbs 31:10-31 as a guide, we encourage and equip women to practice living out their faith as wives, mothers, friends and neighbors.

What began in 1992 as a monthly newsletter has now grown into a multi-faceted ministry reaching women across the country and around the globe. The ministry has been featured on "The 700 Club" television program, the BBC in England, Larry Burkett's "How to Manage Your Money" and "Money Watch," Focus on the Family's "Renewing the Heart" radio program, and in various newspapers across the country.

Proverbs 31 Ministry offers the following:

Monthly Publication: The Proverbs 31 Woman is a 16-page publication. This storehouse of inspiration and information gives women helpful ideas on spiritual growth, family activities, relationship building, and much, much more.

Radio Program: The Proverbs 31 Radio Ministry airs a daily two-minute program offering encouragement and inspiration for women by women. This program is now heard on over 350 national and overseas networks.

Speaking Ministry: Our ministry features dynamic speakers who share life-changing and inspirational messages at women's conferences, banquets and retreats.

Prayer Team: A team of prayer warriors takes the prayer requests from conferences, radio call-ins and letters, and brings them before the Lord.

Encouragement Groups Bible Studies: A curriculum for church or community groups that help cultivate mutual support, prayer and fellowship.

On-line Support Groups: Through the Internet, there are several types of support groups that include on-line Bible studies for women who may not otherwise have an opportunity for fellowship. Make sure you visit The Proverbs 31 Ministry website at www.proverbs31.org.

The Proverbs 31 Ministry
PO Box 17155
Charlotte, NC 28227
Toll free 1-877-P31-HOME
www.proverbs31.org
e-mail: P31Home@proverbs31.org

We feel very honored that you have chosen to read this book. As you embark on this journey it is our prayer that your heart will be filled with love and inspiration along the way. We know first hand that being like the Proverbs 31 woman is not easy so we have compiled the best articles of our newsletter written by women all over the country with the hope of encouraging and equipping you to become the woman God intends for you to be.

Proverbs chapter 31 examines a woman's life through many seasons. Whether you are a newlywed, mother of young children, mother of teenagers, or empty nester you will find articles that will touch your heart and stir your soul. So, go curl up in your favorite reading spot and enjoy a few quiet moments reading our book. It is our prayer that God will use this book to draw you closer to Himself, fall even deeper in love with your husband, and learn new ways to nurture your children.

From our heart to yours,

Sharon Jaynes   **Lysa TerKeurst**
President   *Vice President*

wife of noble character who can find? She is worth far more than rubies. Her husband has full confidence in her and lacks nothing of value. She brings him good, not harm, all the days of her life. She selects wool and flax and works with eager hands. She is like the merchant ships, bringing her food from afar. She gets up while it is still dark; she provides food for her family and portions for her servant girls.

She considers a field and buys it; out of her earnings she plants a vineyard. She sets about her work vigorously; her arms are strong for her tasks. She sees that her trading is profitable, and her lamp does not go out at night. In her hand she holds the distaff and grasps the spindle with her fingers.

She opens her arms to the poor and extends her hands to the needy. When it snows, she has no fear for her household; for all of them are clothed in scarlet. She makes coverings for her bed; she is clothed in fine linen and purple. Her husband is respected at the city gate, where he takes his seat among the elders of the land. She makes linen garments and sells them, and supplies the merchants with sashes. She is clothed with strength and dignity; she can laugh at the days to come.

She speaks with wisdom, and faithful instruction is on her tongue. She watches over the affairs of her household and does not eat the bread of idleness. Her children arise and call her blessed; her husband also, and he praises her: "Many women do noble things, but you surpass them all."

Charm is deceptive, and beauty is fleeting; but a woman who fears the Lord is to be praised. Give her the reward she has earned, and let her works bring her praise at the city gate.

A Special Thanks to our Editor

An editor of noble character who can find?
She is worth far more than rubies.

A special thanks to Glynnis Whitwer, a true Proverbs 31 woman who
has donated many hours of hard work to
put this book together. We love you Glynnis!

The Staff of The Proverbs 31 Ministry

♡

Dedication

To the women in my life who have modeled
the characteristics of a Proverbs 31 woman for me:
My grandmothers, my mother and my three sisters.

To the three women, whom I don't know yet,
but who will someday claim my
sons' hearts and hands in marriage.
May the Lord write His name on your hearts
and may you grow up to be godly women.

To my beloved husband Tod,
and my amazing three sons Joshua, Dylan & Robert.
I love you beyond words.

G.A.W.

TABLE OF *Contents*

Chapter One

GROWING IN GRACE

Chapter Two

THEY ARE NO LONGER TWO, BUT ONE

Chapter Three

CHILDREN ARE A GIFT

Chapter Four

PRACTICING SERVANTHOOD

Chapter Five

THE REFINER'S FIRE

Chapter Six

CREATING A HAVEN OF PEACE

Chapter Seven

THE BEAUTY OF MOTHERHOOD

Chapter Eight

HOLIDAYS AND EVERYDAYS

Chapter Eight (continued)

Chapter Nine

CHAPTER

Growing in Grace

"CHARM IS DECEPTIVE, AND BEAUTY IS FLEETING;

BUT A WOMAN WHO FEARS THE LORD IS TO BE PRAISED."

PROVERBS 31:30

My Name Was Called

LYSA TERKEURST

My heart raced with excitement as we approached the tall gray-haired man with the large black book. Everyone standing in line was focused on what they would say when it was finally their turn. My turn came and went and I wondered with great anticipation if my name was one of the few written in the man's book. I filed into the row my group was directed toward, took my seat, and waited.

Suddenly, huge spotlights flashed and their beams started turning somersaults all around us. Large cameras came to life as the crowd was directed to cheer and show our excitement over being there. I held my breath as the first four names were called. My heart leapt as I heard my first name only to sink when it was called with the wrong last name. A game was played, then a commercial, and then it was time for another name. "Lysa TerKeurst come on down! You're the next contestant on The Price Is Right!" I screamed, jumped up and down, hugged half the people around me, and ran to my place in Contestants' Row.

Now I wish I could tell you how I impressed the nation with my great bidding abilities and all about the fabulous prizes I won. Sorry to disappoint you, but I and all my excitement stayed right there on Contestants' Row. However, I did walk away with some nice parting gifts and, even better, a life lesson from God.

The only things lasting and eternal are found through our relationship with Jesus

One day we all will stand in line with great excitement as we approach a tall gray-haired figure with a large black book and we all will want our names to be written there. However, nothing we say or do or have done in the past will be enough to win us a spot in that book. The names written there are all the people who have at one time surrendered their life to God and accepted Jesus Christ as their personal Lord and Savior. And on that day we will not be able to stand as we approach the Almighty for it is written that every knee shall bow and every tongue shall confess that He is Lord. Every one of us will desire with every ounce of our being to hear our name called and then be ushered into the glory of our Father's presence where we are declared to be accepted in the Beloved. And then will our treasures be revealed: the mansion prepared just for us on a street paved with gold; the crowns of glory that we will be able to place at the feet of our Father; the loved ones we grieved that have been awaiting our reunion; and best of all, Jesus. We will be able to see Him in all His glory and talk to Him face to face.

Yes, it was exciting to be on "The Price is Right" but like everything else in this world the thrill was temporary and the glory fleeting. The only things lasting and eternal are found through our relationship with Jesus ... the one who guarantees our name will be called if we confess Him as our Lord and Savior. ♡

Strength Comes From Our Relationship With The Lord

JENNIFER SCHROEDER

*W*ho is this woman described in Proverbs 31:10-31? She is virtuous, a willing worker, a provider, smart, strong, giving, confident, prepared, resourceful and happy. She also fears the Lord, and her husband and children praise her! She sounds like someone who I would love to know ... or better yet, be just like!

Verse 30 says *"Charm is deceptive, and beauty is fleeting; but a woman who fears the Lord is to be praised."* Our relationship with the Lord is to be our crowning virtue. I have tried so many times in my strength to be like this woman — but I always fall short of the mark.

The Lord tells us that *"He who began a good work in you will perfect it until the day of Jesus Christ"* (Philippians 1:6). And in 2 Corinthians 12:9 *"My grace is sufficient for you, for My power is made perfect in weakness."* (NAS)

It is easy to be overwhelmed and discouraged when reading about the Proverbs 31 woman. But remember that GOD IS DOING A GOOD WORK IN YOU! GOD LOVES YOU AND IS PERFECTING YOU BY HIS STRENGTH!

Proverbs 31 women, let's be encouraged by the fact that the Lord knows our weaknesses and is able to make us strong!! Look to the wife of noble character as an example and strive to make your relationship with the Lord your crowning virtue today — He will bless you for it. ♡

Forgive Me Lord; I Mumble Too

NANCY SOUER

TOO OFTEN DURING A FRUSTRATING DAY

I'VE TOLD ONE OF THE KIDS TO QUIT THEIR

"SENSELESS MUMBLING" TO ME.

BUT THEN I'M ASHAMED LATER,

WHEN I STOP TO CONSIDER HOW I'D FEEL

IF SOME NIGHT, DURING MY PRAYER,

THE LORD INTERRUPTED, SAYING,

"CHILD, QUIT MUMBLING." ♡

Getting To The Heart Of The Matter

LYSA TERKEURST

Have you ever asked God for love, joy, peace, patience, kindness, goodness, faithfulness, gentleness or self-control? Chances are that if you are a wife and mother, you have asked for these qualities many times. Recently, God gave me an answer to my many prayers on this subject. I was reading Galatians 5:22-25 that says, "*But the fruit of the spirit is love, joy, peace, patience, kindness, goodness, faithfulness, gentleness and self-control. Against such things there is no law. Those who belong to Christ Jesus have crucified the sinful nature with its passions and desires. Since we live by the Spirit, let us keep in step with the Spirit.*" When I read these scriptures I realized that when I asked Jesus into my life, the Holy Spirit then indwelled my heart. Romans 5:5 tells us that, "*... God has poured out His love into our hearts by the Holy Spirit, whom He has given us.*" The fruit of the Spirit has already been given to us. The problem is that our hearts get so filled with sin that the beautiful fruit gets crowded out.

For many years I carried the guilt of my past sins around with me. I thought I could keep secrets from God. These sins, feelings of guilt, unwillingness to forgive others and secrets so crowded my heart that there was little room for the Spirit, much less the fruit of the Spirit. I was like the little teapot nursery rhyme: "I'm a little teapot, short and stout. Here is my handle, here is my spout. When I get all steamed up, hear me shout. Tip me over and pour me out." When I got steamed up you had better hope I didn't get tipped over because what came out was no cup of tea.

In Luke 6:45, Jesus teaches, "*The good man brings good things out of the good stored up in his heart, and the evil man brings evil things out of the evil stored up in his heart. For out of the overflow of his heart his mouth speaks.*" In order for the overflow of my heart to be good and reflect the Holy Spirit's fruit, I must spend time with God everyday ... praying, confessing and thanking Him. I must also study and memorize His word. Psalm 119:10, 11 instructs to seek God with all your heart and to hide His word in your heart so that you might not sin against Him.

Beware of spiritually dry times. Keep your heart clean, pure and filled with God's word. In doing so on a daily basis, you will have all the love, joy, peace, patience, kindness, goodness, faithfulness, gentleness and self-control that you will ever need. ♡

Only God Is Perfect

FRANCES GREGORY PASCH

I had often heard the scripture about Martha and Mary, but I never fully understood what the Lord meant when He said, *"Martha, Martha ... you are worried and upset about many things, but only one thing is needed. Mary has chosen what is better..."* (Luke 10:41-42).

I was so much like Martha, always rushing around, trying to make everything as perfect as possible. I found it hard to comprehend why it was better for Mary to sit at Christ's feet, listening instead of working. I had to be doing something to feel fulfilled. So I spent most of my life striving to be the perfect wife, mother and homemaker, instead of enjoying life to the fullest. I believed in God, but I made my own plans and goals. I prayed, but most often when things were not going well. I was never taught to read the Bible.

At 50, I accepted Christ as my Lord and Savior. When I started putting Him first, my life changed dramatically. He opened my eyes and showed me that I had made my life a lot harder than it had to be. Now I spend time daily with the Lord, studying the Bible and praying to discover His will for my life. The following has helped me avoid some of the emptiness and unfulfillment I experienced:

Enjoy each day — Don't dwell on the past, especially the bad things that have happened. We all make mistakes, but rather than rehashing them, learn from them and try again. I wasted too many years wishing things had been different.

Don't live for tomorrow — You may only have today. Make plans, but don't waste time concentrating on the future and miss the present.

Don't set impossible goals — I did, and it was frustrating. You'll never be perfect — only God is perfect. Realize we all fall short, but with God, we're not inadequate.

Don't worry about what other people think — I measured my worth by my performance. I felt condemned if my house and my boys were not perfect. I didn't realize my self worth comes from the Lord, not from my accomplishments. Only God is perfect and the Martha in me can rest. ♡

Being Still To Be With God

RENEE SWOPE

Spending time with the Lord each day is a commitment I have to make on a regular basis. I am constantly struggling to find time to sit at His feet ... or should I say "choosing time" to sit at His feet. There is always enough time; it's just a matter of how I choose to spend it.

As soon as I wake up, I start thinking of things to do. There are dishes in the sink, the dog needs to be fed and taken outside, Joshua (my 6-month-old) needs to be fed, changed, bathed and entertained, the bed needs to be made and I need a shower. "Gee, it'd be fun to watch 'Regis & Kathie Lee', and maybe I should start some laundry" are just a few of my thoughts. The list goes on and before I know it the day is half over and it's time to run errands or start dinner. Yet I hear the Lord's voice calling, *"Be still, and know that I am God,"* Psalm 46:10. "Okay Lord," I say, "just let me finish this one thing."

My problem is that I am a "doer". I gain fulfillment by the number of things I can check off my "TO DO" list. He calls me to seek fulfillment in Him; not in how many check marks I have at the end of the day. He cares about my heart and wants me to depend on Him to complete all the things that need to be done. Isaiah 26:12 sums it up, *"Lord, you establish peace for us; all that we have accomplished you have done for us."*

The Lord continues to teach me to come to His feet each day and seek His face. Through prayer and reading the Bible, He is able to direct my path. He wants me to commit whatever I do to Him, so He can make my plans successful (Prov 16:3). It is my responsibility to obey. He promises in Isaiah 1:19, *"If you are willing and obedient, you will eat from the best of the land."* I must admit, on the days that I ignore His call and depend on my own strength, I find myself tired and frustrated. But when I seek Him first and commit my day to Him, I feel more peace because I've left the results to Him.

Being still to be with God is not easy for me and yet I want it to be. My prayer is that the Spirit in me would yearn so deeply for God's fellowship that I couldn't stand to do anything until I've had time with Him. ♡

Spending Time With The Lord

CAROLINE WILKERSON

trive for holiness. It's not easy, but it is what we are called to do. Those three words are my safety net. I think of them often throughout the day as I fulfill my role as wife and mother. As I help my second-grade daughter with homework, or read a story to my 4-year-old son or play peek-a-boo with my 2-year-old daughter, I feel called to become more "Christ like." This means to be a holy woman of God and a living example of one of God's children.

To help me on my road to holiness, I set aside at least 15 minutes a day to talk to the Lord. I seek the silence during nap time, which is about the only time of day I can grab some solitude! I focus on nothing but becoming more aware of God's presence. It is then that my heart opens up and I can communicate my innermost thoughts, fears, hopes and praises to our precious Father. I know He hears me and gives me peace.

If I don't spend this time daily, I feel that my day rushes by me and I've lost a sense of myself. In John 15:5 Jesus says, *"I am the vine; you are the branches. He who abides in Me and I in him, he bears much fruit; for apart from me you can do nothing."* (NAS) This verse speaks volumes to me for it is true. If I make time to spend with the Lord, my day is productive. I feel the Lord's guidance as I drive carpools, do the laundry, play with my children and do all the other tasks God has called me to do in a typical day. If I don't take that time, I feel lost and overwhelmed. I really am "nothing" without my daily connection to God.

Fifteen minutes may not sound like much to some people, but for my crazy schedule, it feels like an hour! Sometimes God gives me 30 minutes or more. I thank Him for any extra time He allows me. Any time at all we can truly spend in silence with the Lord is a special gift not to be taken for granted. ♡

Be Still My Stubborn Heart

CHERYL L. BESSETT

Once again, I find myself waiting on the quietness of the Lord. Once again, I find the wait exhausting. I seem to have to constantly discipline my mind to the quiet of His kingdom. Strange that the Prince of Peace has court jesters that are anything but peaceful at times. I find that, more often than not, the mundane details of my daily life overshadow the glorious lightness of His burden. Why do I choose the weight of my own power, instead of the gentle touch of the Master's hand?

It sounds so simple, to lay back, basking in His word. But we mothers know that those things that sound simple can be difficult to do (getting everyone into the car, getting everyone to church, getting everyone bathed and ready for bed — the list goes on and on). As I consider the times that I have been interrupted while praying by children spilling milk, or disasters in the making, I have a better picture of what Jesus prayed for me in the Garden of Gethsemane. That I would not be taken from the world, but that I would be protected from it. Often I feel caught between a place of spiritual renewal and the crisis that seems to loom around the corner.

I need to come before Him and ask for a peace, for a quiet, for a time set aside to rest in His presence. The blessing comes when I realize that He is there, always waiting for me. He will wait for me as I shower, as I stand in the line at the grocery store, as I vacuum the carpet, as I lie in bed listening for the cry of my baby, as I sort the laundry, even as I sit at the stop light. And alas, I come to the truth: it is not really me waiting for His peace, it is Him waiting on me to partake of His peace. What a joyous revelation: His truth really does set us free. ♡

Spilt Milk

N A N C E E   S K I P P E R

ccording to Webster's Dictionary, hardship is: privation; bodily oppression; that which is difficult to endure. Life is full of hardships; some major, many minor, some short lived, others like the proverbial dripping faucet. Though I have experienced relatively few major hardships, I quite keenly feel the frustration of the "mini hardships" of daily living.

Sounds ridiculous even to classify these little irritations as hardships, but it is indeed these "mini hardships" of everyday life that I allow to weigh me down to a greater or lesser degree every day.

You've heard the saying, "No use crying over spilt milk." Sounds reasonable, but after so many spilt milks I start inwardly and sometimes outwardly whining, "Not again!" What's the result? Joylessness!

What does a "spilt milk" day look like? Well, it starts out when:
the night before you unwittingly set the alarm for 6 p.m. instead of 6 a.m.
staggering to the kitchen to make the morning coffee, your slippers adhere to a floor that feels like it's been waxed with apple juice
the coffee grounds miss the trash
Junior spills his cereal
the sink stops up
the car won't start
your toddler has no vision for potty training
the check you wrote to Wal-Mart bounces (how embarrassing!)
you finally write that long-promised letter and someone lays a popsicle on it while you're getting a stamp
the phone rings and simultaneously the bug man, meter reader and UPS delivery man all appear in your driveway. It is at this moment your toddler decides to go potty.

I could go on. Sound familiar? By 10 a.m. the joy of a new day has evaporated! Despair may set in as the mundane struggles of life overwhelm us. Are these true hardships? No. Inconveniences? Yes. Frustrating? Definitely! Providential opportunities? Huh? Bingo! We are given countless opportunities daily, hourly, even minute by minute to grow in grace, to rest in Him, to stop and pray, to practice what we preach.

Is God sovereign or isn't He? Does He have a purpose for me or am I just bumbling aimlessly along from spill to spill? Is there a rainbow of promise and hope above the puddles or do I give into these despairing feelings of "what's the use?"

The answer to all three is an ear-shattering YES! Yes, God is sovereign. Yes, He has a purpose for me. Yes, I have a future and a hope! But too often I have been surprised by reality. It is a constant challenge to see the mundane as meaningful and the tediousness of life as the testing ground of our faith. To not only realize, but embrace the truth that over such vexing circumstances God is in control. Through such troublesome realities saints are fashioned. Big ones and little ones!

But this precept is impossible to maintain unless we are constantly aware of the sustaining hand of our Savior. He alone redeems our life from the pit. He alone can rearrange our priorities and renew our strength. He alone can restore our joy. Doesn't that put spilt milk days into perspective? ♡

Shining God's Light On My Child

ANNMARIE CASSIDY

*A*s my son entered kindergarten in the fall of 1995, I was determined to take an active role in his education. I wanted to volunteer in the library, art class and everywhere else we moms are needed. What I didn't consider was the imminent birth of our third baby and the demands of my very active 2-year-old, which would make participating in these activities almost impossible! With the benefit of hindsight, I now know that the Spirit found an activity for me — Moms in Touch.

Moms in Touch is an international organization. It is a group of moms who come together in prayer for the needs of the children, school, faculty and administration. It is truly a gift to our children and has become a great gift to me. I can think of no better use of my time than to ask for the Lord's intercession in the lives of our children and our schools. It is very peaceful to sit in the company of other women whose spiritual devotion is so keen and priorities so clear! What we share together is precious and the fruits of this blessed association are spilling into all aspects of my life.

My son (now in first grade) has been surprisingly responsive to this prayerful activity. I have shared with him what we do at our meetings and it has sent a very strong message. Actions do speak louder than words. I see him turning to the Lord for guidance and solutions to his 7-year-old problems. He has even given me prayer requests to take to my meetings! In his own way, he seems to be proud and supportive of what we are doing.

I am grateful that Moms in Touch was already active in my son's school. I would not have wanted to miss this last year in prayer! There's no better way to teach a child that the Lord is part of every aspect of his life than to let him know he is lifted up in prayer. ♡

It's Hard To Be Good

MARJORIE K. EVANS

My 6-year-old son was unusually quiet when he came home one afternoon. "How was school today, David?" I questioned. Reluctantly he replied, "It was all right." Sensing that something had happened to upset David, I didn't query him any further. I had learned that probing tended to make him more reticent than ever. In his own time he would tell me the problem.

David was subdued during supper and throughout the evening. It was only when he had finished praying and was in his bed that he began to talk. "Mommy, on the way home from school today some of my friends said, 'Let's pick pomegranates from the tree across the street. Nobody will know.' I said, 'No, I won't 'cause that's stealing and it's wrong.' And then, Mommy, they yelled, 'Chicken! Chicken!' and chased me down the sidewalk."

With a sob he said, "It's a lot harder to be good than to be bad, isn't it, Mommy?" Indeed it is hard to be good. None of my friends entice me to pick pomegranates, but just the other day a clerk gave me too much change and my friend urged, "Oh, go ahead and keep it, Marge. You can use the money. Besides, it won't come out of the clerk's pocket." For a moment, I was tempted. Also, as I hurried to an appointment last week, I was tempted to exceed the speed limit, rationalizing, "Everyone else does it." I've been asked to teach Sunday school. Instead of telling the superintendent the truth — that I really don't want to teach at this time — I'm tempted to say I'm not feeling well or I'm too busy. So the temptations go on and on.

In Ephesians 6:10 we are told to "... *be strong in the Lord, and in the strength of His might.*" (NAS) So, my prayer is that I will be strong in the Lord and have the strength and courage of my young son so that I, too, will resist temptation. ♡

The Age Of Our Faith

LYSA TERKEURST

At what age do we stop having child-like faith ... child-like imaginations ... child-like dreams? At what age are we no longer fascinated by caterpillars and butterflies? At what age do we leave the magic and wonder of childhood behind?

One day I was standing in the kitchen cooking dinner when I heard my daughters, Hope (3) and Ashley (2), yelling their names over and over again at our dog, Major. With my curiosity piqued, I walked out to the garage to see what they were up to. I asked, "Hope, what are you girls doing?" She put her tiny hands on her hips and replied, "Mom, we are teaching Major to talk!" My initial thought was to tell them how silly their attempt was and that dogs don't talk. Then it hit me. I had lost my child-like faith, imagination and dreams and I was about to push my adult cynicism into their world of wonder. In my adult wisdom I knew Major could not talk in human words, but child-like faith believes that all things are possible. After all, Numbers 22:28 tells us that God made a donkey talk!

One of the greatest biblical principles we can teach our children is that with God all things are possible. Not that we should spend our time teaching dogs to talk, but we should be careful not to put God in a box and only ask Him for things that we can make happen in our own human strength. Miracles still happen and if we would look at Jesus through child-like eyes we would see just how amazing He is.

One of the greatest examples of the incredible power of child-like faith is found in the story of Wilma Rudolph. Doctors said she would never be able to walk without braces but her parents told her that God can make anything happen if we just believe. Wilma did believe and God answered her prayers. Not only did she learn to walk without braces but she learned to run! And with a lot of hard work, she ran all the way to the Olympics where she captured many medals including a gold!

Let me encourage you today not to get caught up in grown-up wisdom so much that you loose sight of being a child of God. Rediscover His miraculous ways and beautiful creation. Rediscover your child-like faith, child-like dreams and child-like imagination.

Oh, I've got to go. Major is calling my name! ♡

You'll Meet An Old Lady

AUTHOR UNKNOWN

You are going to meet an old lady someday. Down the road, ten, twenty, thirty years; she's waiting for you. You will catch up to her. What kind of old lady are you going to meet?

That is a rather significant question. She may be a seasoned, soft and gracious lady. A lady who has grown old gracefully, surrounded by a host of friends — friends who call her blessed because of what her life has meant to them. She may be a bitter, disillusioned, dried-up, cynical old buzzard, without a good word for anyone or anything — soured, friendless, alone. The kind of old lady you will meet will depend entirely upon you.

She will be exactly what you make of her, nothing more, nothing less. It is up to you. You will have no one else to credit or blame. Every day, in every way, you are becoming more and more like that old lady. Amazing but true. You are getting to look more like her, think more like her and talk more like her. You are becoming her. If you live only in terms of what you are getting out of life, the old lady gets smaller, drier, harder, crabbier, more self-centered. Open your life to others, think in terms of what you can give and your contribution to life, and the old lady grows larger, softer, kinder, greater.

These little things, seemingly so unimportant now — attitudes, goals, ambitions, desires — are adding up inside, where you cannot see them, crystallizing in your heart and mind. The point is these things don't always show up immediately. But they will — sooner than you think. Some day they will harden into that old lady; nothing will be able to soften or change them then.

The time to take care of that old lady is right now, today. Examine your motives, attitudes, goals. Check up on her. Work her over now while she is still pliable, still in a formative condition. The day when it is too late comes swiftly. The hardness sets in, worse than paralysis. Character crystallizes, sets, gels. Any wise business person takes an inventory regularly. Merchandise is not half as important as the person. You had better take a bit of a personal inventory, too. Then you will be much more likely to meet a lovely, gracious old lady at the proper time. ♡

A Dishwasher's Prayer

ELIZABETH A. CYDERS

LORD, WHILE I WASH AND RINSE THE GLASSES,

HELP ME TO SHINE AND SPARKLE FOR YOU.

JUST AS I USE SCOURING PADS TO REMOVE STAINS

FROM MY POTS AND SKILLETS,

CLEANSE MY SOUL FROM ALL TARNISH OF SIN.

SOMETIMES I HAVE TO LET THE SOILED DISHES SOAK FOR A WHILE

IN HOT SUDSY WATER BEFORE THE FINAL WASHING.

AND LIKEWISE, LORD, THERE ARE TIMES YOU HAVE LET ME

BE PERMEATED BY AFFLICTION IN ORDER TO SOFTEN MY SPIRIT.

LIKE THE DISHES WHICH HAVE BEEN SOAKED,

SCOURED, RINSED AND DRIED,

READY FOR THE NEXT MEAL, SO, LORD, SHALL I BE READY

FOR THE NEXT AREA WHERE YOU WANT ME TO SERVE.

IN JESUS' NAME, AMEN.

A Slip Of The Lip

FRANCES GREGORY PASCH

I DID IT AGAIN, LORD,

OPENED MY MOUTH

AT THE WRONG TIME ...

NOT ONCE,

BUT THREE TIMES.

WHY DID I HAVE TO SAY

"COMB YOUR HAIR"?

WHY WASN'T I JUST HAPPY

THAT HE WAS GOING TO CHURCH WITH ME?

AM I STILL WORRIED ABOUT

WHAT OTHERS THINK?

I THOUGHT I HAD OVERCOME THAT.

IN RETROSPECT,

MY HEART

WAS MORE DISHEVELED

THAN HIS HAIR. ♡

Why God?

FRANCES GREGORY PASCH

WHY DO I THINK

THAT IF OTHERS CHANGE

LIFE WILL BE HAPPIER FOR ME?

WHY DO I ALWAYS

JUDGE THEIR FAULTS,

BUT MY OWN SOMEHOW

DON'T SEE?

WHY DON'T I EVER STOP TO THINK

THAT IF I'D CHANGE

PERHAPS THEY MIGHT TOO?

WHY DON'T I FIRST

TAKE A LOOK AT MYSELF,

AND THEN LEAVE CHANGING THEM

UP TO YOU!♡

Reflections

SANDRA PALMER CARR

*"Keep me as the apple of
your eye; hide me in the shadow of your wings." PSALM 17:8*

When my sons were small, we spent a great deal of time in our high-backed wooden rocking chair. One day I held my younger son, Boyd, then 4 years old, facing me as we rocked, his legs folded at the knee.

Suddenly he lifted his head, stared straight at me and became very still. Then he cupped my face in his tender little hands and said almost in a whisper, "Mommy, I'm in your eyes." We stayed that way for several long moments as the rocking stopped and the room grew quiet. "And I'm in yours," I said. Then he leaned his head against me contentedly, and I resumed rocking and singing.

Occasionally in the days that followed, he would check to see if his discovery was lasting. "Am I still in your eyes, Mommy?" he would ask as he reached up for me.

In life's uncertain moments it is comforting to know I am still in my heavenly Father's eyes. And besides watching me, God listens to my cry for reassurance. ♡

Insights From A Mover Who Is Still Shaking

RACHAEL CARMAN

We are moving. What feelings to those three words conjure up in you? Relief, frustration, excitement, hope, joy, peace, anger, sadness, depression, anxiety? How do those feelings change when you hear them from your husband or your best friend? Moving is an inescapable fact of our fast-paced, mobile society. Living in one town, much less one house, your whole life well, it just doesn't happen anymore.

So how do you face another move? The challenges of moving are obvious. Facing the unknowns like friends, church, neighbors, schools, hair dressers and the like; dealing with the loss of the same; the hassles of packing, the logistics of timing — closings, start dates, first day of school, etc.; how to prepare yourself, your children, your friends; the financial implications of it all. These important details can be overwhelming in the best of situations.

The blessings of a move are less obvious and sometimes go unrealized until you are in the middle of the move or the move is years past. Often God works through a move whether we like it or not to shake us up to rearrange our schedules, priorities and focus as only a move can do. As we shake our fists at God and ask, why? Where do you want us? How can we do this? Who will be our friends, children's teachers, neighbors, pastor? Knowing the end result, He smiles a knowing parental smile and sheds a compassionate parental tear as we face the challenge.

Facing a particularly unappealing move, I questioned the God of the universe. I wondered if He could make sense of it all. And in His grace He taught me about both of us. Through scriptures the Holy Spirit guided me to passages that recounted, reminded and retaught me of His faithfulness, provision, love, gentleness, grace, character and truth. I came face to face with the ugliness of the fallen world and the beauty of Christ's redemption. The Holy Spirit spoke to my heart in songs as I realized the questions I'd asked God, He'd answered and now there were some I needed to consider. Like, who was I really depending on? What things did I really need to live here?

Where was my focus? Why was I running around doing what I was doing? Could I have been so blind to His love, so stubborn toward His will?

In the end, my tight fists of frustration relaxed into hands lifted high in praise of His faithfulness. I'm so grateful, for all that I learned during that time. He gave me a new perspective, a fresh assurance and a hope for a future with Him as the center. As He says in Jeremiah 29:11, *"For I know the plans I have for you, declares the Lord, plans to prosper you and not to harm you, plans to give you a hope and a future."* ♡

Pray About What?

JENNIFER McHUGH

Are you guilty of telling someone you will pray about something and then forgetting that promise by prayer time? You're not alone.

Organizing my prayer life was difficult. I wanted to pray for people, but I could never remember everything. Finally I figured out that I never would remember unless I kept some type of record. I do not like to write, so a journal is something I knew I would never maintain.

After considering the possibilities, I decided on note cards. I keep my cards in a box with a rubber band around them. Each note card has one name at the top. On the left-hand side of the card is the date that I began praying for that request. After the prayer is answered, I highlight it.

After some time, I had so many cards that I was having difficulty praying for everything every day, so I divided the cards into days of the week. For instance, on Mondays I pray for my friends who do not know Jesus Christ as their savior. On Tuesdays, I pray for friends in the ministry (in missions, as pastors, etc.) I also have a stack of cards I refer to daily — for family and friends I have committed to praying for on a regular basis.

This system has worked well for me. The most exciting part is that I can look back and see how God has worked in people's lives! The system is concise and does not require a lot of writing. I have maintained my prayer cards for two years now (longer than I have maintained any other kind of organization).

You can add a picture to your card if it will help you to pray. I have a picture of a couple my husband and I have never met, whom we support financially. This visual aid helps me to focus on them and their needs.

You can set up your own system for quiet time. This note-card system is a way for me to remember to pray about things that I would otherwise forget. ♡

Neighborhood Prayer Group Provides Support

MARY ELLEN BIANCO

Two years ago my neighbor, Hope, invited me to join a weekly prayer group that met at her house. I had some reservations about praying with other women whom I didn't know. What would I pray for? Would the others think I had silly requests of God? It took me several months to finally accept Hope's invitation, but even then I was nervous about praying in front of others. To my surprise the prayer group became my inspiration and source of support during a challenging time in my life.

Four women had been meeting before I joined the group. I was very quickly introduced to Hope's friends Cynthia, Carol and Angela before we started praying. They had been following Evelyn Christenson's book "What Happens When Women Pray" as a simple model for prayer. During the prayer session, a verse from the Bible was read on praise and thanksgiving, then we took turns thanking God for all that was good in our lives. Another verse was read on forgiveness and we asked God to forgive us for the sins we committed. The final verse was for intercession and we prayed for each person we knew who needed help from God. We exchanged prayer requests so we could continue to pray at home between meetings.

The first meeting I attend felt pretty awkward, but soon I was looking forward to praying with these women who had so much faith it God. All of us were homemakers with young children, so we had a lot in common. We would report on answered prayers and continued to pray for those who needed intercession. As the weeks passed and my prayer journal quickly filled, I realized that God was using the five of us to help others. He was also helping me see how powerful prayer can be. Matthew 7:7 became a favorite verse when it was my turn to lead the prayer group: *"Ask and it will be given to you; seek and you will find; knock and the door will be opened to you."* I was able to ask God for anything, knowing that He would answer the prayers in His time.

When my husband took a new job that required constant travel, I asked my prayer partners to help me get through the separations. It was comforting to know that I was being prayed for during such a difficult time. Hope and Cynthia faced the same challenges several months later when their husbands were transferred out of state and they stayed behind with their children for the first few months. We were amazed at how God brought us together to support and encourage each other at a time we needed it the most. Although the weekly meetings stopped last year, we continue to call each other to exchange prayer requests. Many times I'm able to tell others that I'll pray for them, too. It's amazing how it comes as second nature to verbalize my prayer intentions now! I'm grateful that Hope reached out to me because I now have such wonderful friends with whom to share my life and prayers. ♡

Giving God The Glory

WANDA SMITH

*I*n July of 1994 I was diagnosed with a disease that affected the nerves in my face. The pain was so severe it felt like an ice-pick being jammed into my jaw. Nothing would stop it! Finally, after a few weeks of medication, the pain went away, but I was told that it would possibly come back. After reading information about this disease, the prognosis was not good. I talked to people who suffered with it for years and their experiences put fear in me. I kept wondering when and if it would come upon me again.

In 1996 I began to feel small bits of pain again in my jaw. It was a horrible feeling to know that something so painful was returning again. It was much worse than the first episode and lasted two-and-a-half months. I couldn't chew, speak or even swallow without incredible pain in my jaw. My family was watching me slowly lose weight — I was down to 100 pounds. The doctor gave me one medication after the other. Nothing seemed to cut the pain. The heavy medication affected my speech and my mind became more and more fuzzy. It was extremely difficult on my sweet husband Steve, who felt very helpless watching me become weaker and more depressed over the long weeks of pain. I was unable to seek the Lord, but thank God family members and friends were holding me up to the Father in prayer.

One day a friend from church brought a casserole over along with a cassette tape that was made to give hope to people. The tape had verses from the Bible. It gave me hope that God could see me and knew me by name. All I needed to do was spend some time with Him and He would hear my plea for help. Many nights I couldn't sleep very well, so I would get up around 4 a.m. to lie on the floor under a skylight. I would put the tape on and listen with earphones to the very words of God. The words would minister to my spirit and the process of spiritual healing began. I began to experience a closeness with God and a fresh new faith that I hadn't felt in years.

For my sanity I began to slowly ease off the medication. I then began walking through the valley of depression. It was a horrible thing to go through, and yet I wasn't alone. The prayers of others sustained me. Most precious of all was having my husband there with me. We cried together and he held me in his arms as I walked through the darkness. Finally, my doctor recommended that I talk to a surgeon to see what could be done to stop the pain. Surgery that would cost us $20,000 could not even guarantee that I would be free of the agony I felt. Steve and I told the doctor that we would pray about the surgery before we made a final decision, but tentatively scheduled surgery for June 3.

On Sunday, June 2, I got ready to go to church. Steve listened to the answering machine before we left. On it was a message from our adult Bible School teacher asking me to lead our class in song before the lesson. Before I left the house that morning, the Lord very clearly said to me, "I want you to lead the class in a song this morning and I will help you." He told me what song to sing, so I took the sheet of music and placed it in my Bible. Steve didn't know what I was doing, but he said nothing. When we got to class, our teacher explained to visitors that the class had been praying for me for over two months, because I had been very ill. Before I began singing I told everyone that I was still in pain, but that I would sing out of love for God and obedience to Him. I began to sing the words, "Jesus, Jesus Lord to me, Master, Savior, Prince of Peace. Ruler of my heart today, Jesus Lord to me." As I got halfway through the song, I felt a great heat all over the left side of my face where the pain was. The heat just kept getting more intense as I stood there and sang. All of a sudden the feeling went away and I realized that for the first time in months, I had <u>no pain</u>!

No one else knew what was happening to me, but I knew I had just been healed! I dropped to my knees and said to the class, "I have no more pain!" Everyone in the room rejoiced with me. My close girlfriends hugged me and cried with me, feeling the presence of God. I then looked at Steve in the second row. He was sitting there crying, finding it hard to believe that it was all over. I ran to him and said, "Honey, I don't have any more pain!" He jumped up, held me in his arms and we kissed. For a long time we stood there, holding each other and crying with great joy for what God had done. Needless to say, I canceled the MRI and surgery. We then took a trip to the mountains to celebrate our 30th anniversary.

Since that special day I have walked in the joy of the Lord, having so much to thank Him for. I now enjoy talking, eating, laughing and yes, even kissing, without any pain. God gets all of the glory! He is still alive and in the business of healing today. I will forever be grateful for His mercy to me. Proverbs 4:21-22 says, *"Keep these thoughts ever in mind; let them penetrate deep within your heart, for they will mean real life for you, and radiant health."* (TLB) My hope is that you will allow God to be all that He wants to be in your life. May you live in His ways that are written so clearly in His word. ♡

How To Spend An Hour In Prayer

LYDIA HARRIS

"I urge, then, first of all, that requests, prayers, intercession and thanksgiving be made for everyone — for kings and all those in authority, that we may live peaceful and quiet lives in all godliness and holiness. This is good, and pleases God our Savior, who wants all men to be saved and to come to a knowledge of the truth."
I Timothy 2:1-4

Praise God. Read I Chronicles 29:10-13 or Psalm 95:3-8 and praise God for His sovereignty and control. Acknowledge our dependence on God. (5-10 minutes)

Confess Sins. Read II Chronicles 7:14. Follow with silent confession for personal and national sins. (2-5 minutes)

Thank God for personal and national blessings. (10-15 minutes)

Intercede for our nation and leaders. (30-40 minutes) Pray for: government leaders, churches and ministry organizations, imprisoned and persecuted, mass media, schools and youth, families, moral awakening and personal needs.

Close with a patriotic song (e.g. "God Bless America," "America, the Beautiful," or "Battle Hymn of the Republic").

"Men may spurn our appeals, reject our message, oppose our arguments, despise our persons, but they are helpless against our prayers."

J. Sidlow Baxter

41

Praying Using Scripture

God's Word is powerful. Meditate on these Scriptures and use them to guide you in your prayers.

Government leaders: 1 Timothy 2:1-4, Proverbs 2:6, 2 Samuel 23:3,4, Proverbs 3:6,7, Joshua 1:7, 8

Churches and ministry organizations: Proverbs 3:5, Romans 15:5, James 1:5,6, Colossians 1:10-12, Galatians 6:9

Imprisoned and persecuted: Psalm 9:9, Psalm 91:14-16, John 8:36, Hebrews 13:3, Deuteronomy 31:6

Mass media: Proverbs 1:7, Ephesians 5:8-13, 2 Timothy 2:15, Philippians 4:8,9

Schools and youth: Proverbs 4:23-27, Exodus 20:12, Proverbs 3:1-12

Families: Joshua 24:15, Deuteronomy 30:19, 20, Ephesians 6:1-4, Romans 12:10-12

Moral awakening: Psalm 85:6, Matthew 7:3, Romans 13:12-14, Isaiah 55:7, Lamentations 3:40, 1 Peter 1:13-15

Personal Needs: Deuteronomy 6:5, Philippians 4:19, I Peter 5:7, Jeremiah 29:11-13

"Satan trembles when he sees the weakest saint on his knees, for he knows he has no power against our prayers."

Fern Nichols, Founder of Moms In Touch International ♡

Wake-Up Call

JANE STANFORD

My Aunt Helen woke up and looked at the clock. It was 2 a.m. Getting along in years, she knew from experience that sometimes the Lord wanted her awake for a specific reason. So she crawled out of bed, turned on the lights, and reached for her Bible. Almost immediately her grandson's name came to mind. She began praying for him while her fingers flipped through the Bible, searching for an applicable verse.

Later that morning, Helen learned that while she was praying, her grandson was ending his relationship with a young woman. After an emotional struggle, he found inner strength to do the right thing.

When my aunt related her story, I remembered how King Xerxes couldn't get to sleep one night. Instead of tossing and turning, he *"ordered the book of the chronicles, the record of his reign, to be brought in and read to him"* (Esther 6:1). Only through reviewing the records was it discovered that Mordecai, Esther's relative, hadn't received honor for saving the king's life.

Have you had a sleepless night recently? Next time, see if the Lord is calling you for a reason. King Xerxes was awake because God wanted to convey some important information. Helen was called to intercede in prayer. What is the Lord wanting of you? ♡

Babies Milk And Spiritual Growth

DOROTHY R. RUHWALD

*"Like newborn babies, crave pure spiritual milk, so that by it you may
grow up in your salvation, now that you have tasted that the Lord is good."*
1 PETER 2:2-3

Since my baby Sonja was born, I Peter 2:2-3 has taken on a
whole new meaning. Every three hours or so, a baby's crav-
ing for milk is very clearly and definitely expressed: a wide
open mouth, flailing arms, kicking legs, and if the milk is not quick to
appear, an incredibly loud caterwauling! In short, Sonja will do everything
in her power to see that her need for physical nourishment is met. Clearly
she enjoys it; a calming of the previously churning body parts and contented
little noises give proof to that.

If the above Bible verses are taken at face value, as Christians we are to
crave spiritual milk — God's word — in the same way. We should be doing
everything in our power to see that we get fed spiritually through Bible reading, scripture memory and prayer. Soon we will begin to crave spiritual
milk, not just in order to survive, but because, having *"tasted that the Lord is
good"*, we find that we desire Him and enjoy spending time with Him. Thus
spiritual growth continues and increases, and as with a baby, our churning
inner selves find rest as we are filled with contentment and peace.

If Sonja doesn't get milk when it's time to be fed she sometimes reaches
for a substitute — perhaps sucking on her fist, pacifier, blanket or whatever
is in reach of that gaping hole. Such superficial solutions work only for a
short time. They may temporarily soothe her emotional feelings, but they
don't deal with her real need for physical nourishment. In the same way, if
hungry Christians don't get spiritual milk it is all too easy to opt for substi-
tutes in an effort to fill that hole. It may be TV, reading a novel or my all-
time favorite soother, chocolate (which although it makes me grow in other
ways, has never done much for my spiritual growth). We also may water
down our spiritual milk by trying to feed exclusively upon each Sunday's
sermon. None of these activities are bad in their place — and the sermons
are a necessary appetizer — but it is a mistake to try to substitute them for
spending personal time alone with God. The temporary feeling of satisfac-

tion they provide is quickly gone, still leaving us longing for "real food."

Do we need spiritual food to the same extent that a baby needs physical nourishment, i.e. on a very regular basis? Yes, we do; without it we will begin to weaken spiritually. As a baby cannot grow and be healthy without being continuously fed, so we cannot expect to grow without consistently consuming spiritual food. In the same way a person who goes without physical food for too long may no longer experience hunger pangs, we may eventually become so weak spiritually that we may lose our desire for spiritual food.

Lastly, for a baby, just drinking the milk is not necessarily enough. Sonja has no problem with swallowing the milk; the problem is having it stay there. She is not getting any nourishment from the milk that she spits up. In the same way, adults all too often chew on a biblical truth and then spit it back out, which doesn't do a whole lot of good. For us to grow spiritually, we need to digest our spiritual food and allow it to nourish every area of our lives. Only then will we experience real spiritual growth. As we experience this growth in our lives, our desire for spiritual food will increase and we will find ourselves saying with the psalmist: *"O God, you are my God, earnestly I seek you; my soul thirsts for you, my body longs for you ... "* (Psalm 63:1). ♡

Empty Handed

L Y S A   T E R K E U R S T

*A*s we once again resolve to lose that last ten pounds, alphabetize our spices, and make our fortune by cleaning out our attics and finally having that big garage sale, I want to encourage you to add one more resolution: Make this the year that your relationship with the Lord grows deeper and more intimate than ever before. My heart's desire for this year is for it to be a spiritual milestone, especially in the area of my times with Him.

This resolution came about through one of my not-so-Proverbs 31 experiences. One of our volunteers, Kristyn Keen, gave birth to a baby girl recently, so I offered to take her a meal. I had it all planned out. I made a big pot of homemade vegetable soup, corn muffins and brownies. I arranged to deliver the meal on my way to Bible study, knowing I would be headed in her direction. I loaded the van and cheerfully headed off to deliver my goodies. During the drive I had plenty of time to think about the lesson I would teach that night, part of which centered around Ephesians 6 and how to prepare ourselves for the daily spiritual battles in our lives.

As I pulled into Kristyn's driveway I glanced at the clock and saw I was right on schedule. I reached in the back to get the tray of food. Panic set in — there was no food. Frantically searching, I realized I had never put it in the van. The dinner was still on my kitchen counter where I had left it while loading my Bible study materials. My heart sank as I headed up to the front door empty handed.

As I reflect on this most embarrassing event, God is teaching me an important life lesson. It is foolish to offer to take a meal to someone and show up at the door empty handed. It is even more foolish to charge into our days filled with spiritual battles and show up empty handed. Ephesians 6:10-12 says, *"Finally, be strong in the Lord, and the strength of His might. Put on the full armor of God, that you may be able to stand firm against the schemes of the devil. For our struggle is not against flesh and blood, but against the rulers, against the powers, against the world forces of this darkness, against the spiritual forces of wickedness in the heavenly places."* Verses 14-17 instruct us to *"Stand firm therefore, having girded your loins with truth, and having put on the breastplate of righteousness, and having shod your feet with the preparation of the gospel of peace; in addition to all, taking up the shield of faith with which you will be able to extinguish all the flaming missiles of the evil one. And take the helmet of salvation and the sword of the Spirit which is the word of God."* (NAS)

I want to make it my top priority to put on the full armor of God every day so that I can withstand the schemes of the devil. I'm tired of fighting the battle without being properly prepared. By the way, Kristyn and her family didn't go hungry. Another friend happened to bring her family dinner the same night. ♡

CHAPTER *Two*

They Are No Longer Two, But One

"A WIFE OF NOBLE CHARACTER WHO CAN FIND?"

PROVERBS 31:10

49

A Love That Lasts

SHARON JAYNES

I grew up in a home where my dad was a heavy drinker, and my parents fought, both verbally and physically, in my presence. Black eyes, broken furniture, yelling and fear were very much a part of my mental scrapbook. At fourteen, I became a Christian through the witness of a friend and her mother. In my late teens, I thought I would never marry. I made a vow to God that I would never be joined to a non-Christian and take a chance of having a marriage like the one in which I was raised. Also, most of the Christian guys that I did date were not any fun. (Remember, this was a teenage viewpoint.) I then reasoned in my mind that if I did marry, it would be to a Christian, and while I might like him OK, he'd probably be a dud. I didn't expect passion and it would most likely be a boring life. Oh well.

I'm sure God had a good laugh at my bleak picture of the future. But Ephesians 3:20 says that *"God is able to do exceedingly abundantly more than we could ever ask or think."* — and boy, did He!

At 22, I felt God calling me to return to school, to the University of North Carolina at Chapel Hill, to get my BS degree in Dental Hygiene. I left my much-loved job in Rocky Mount, N.C. and went back to the books for two more years. An old boyfriend of mine was also at UNC working on his MBA degree. He had a Bible study at his apartment and invited me to come. I walked into his apartment one night, and there Steve stood — this handsome dental student, with a tan face and strong angular lines, muscular arms, dark brown hair and sold out for the Lord. He reminded me of a Christian version on the Marlboro man. I thought, this guy is too good to be true.

After several weeks Steve asked me out on a date. My heart skipped a beat! But then he told me of his plans for the evening. He wanted me to go with him to hear H.P. Spee, a missionary from Jackson, Mississippi, talk about ministry opportunities.

OK God. I told You so. Handsome, Christian and no fun. Not that hearing a missionary isn't inspiring, but it was not my idea of romance.

When Steve came to pick me up on that first date, I wasn't quite ready.

Beach music played on the tape player and my roommate entertained him for a few minutes. When I finally emerged from primping, Steve asked, "Hey, do you like Beach music?"

"Yes. Heathen that I am. I confess I do," I replied.

"I do too," he said. "As a matter-of-fact, I have a Beach music collection." (For those of you non-Southerners, this is soul music from the 60's from groups like the Platters, Four Tops, and Barbara Lewis).

Then he asked, "Do you know how to shag?"

"I've shagged since the sixth grade," I answered. (The shag is a dance like the swing but with more of a shuffle.)

Then Steve grabbed my hand and we took a spin around the room. Could this be happening? Could it be that this guy was going to be......fun?

I could almost hear the outrageous laughter of my Heavenly Father as His angels watched two of His chosen ones begin a journey of a lifetime.

We did go to hear the missionary that night. But afterwards, we went to a place to dance the night away. On the third date, we knew that this was going to be more than friendship, and we prayed together, asking the Lord to stop the feelings that we had for each other if this was not what He desired for our lives. But the feelings grew stronger with each passing day. Ten and a half months later, I became Mrs. Steven Jaynes. That was over nineteen years ago.

How was a woman who grew up with such a poor example of what God intended for a marriage going to succeed in a culture where the divorce rate was 50% among Christians and non-Christians alike? Didn't all newly married couples "feel" this way about each other? What could possibly go wrong to cause something so wonderful to go awry? What are the keys to maintaining and growing a healthy marriage?

Because I did not know the answers to these questions, I decided to become an avid reader on the subject of marriage. I decided that words like "he doesn't meet my needs," and "we just grew apart" would never have the opportunity to cross my mind or pass by my lips. As the years passed, I collected nuggets of gold that have made me a wealthy woman. Wealthy in love.

In the eighties, there was not the plethora of books on marriage that there are today. One book that gave me an inspiring view of what a relationship could be was a biography written by Sheldon Vanauken about his incredible love story with his wife. There is one paragraph that I'd like to share with you as one of my nuggets of gold. You may want to read it out loud, but listen to it with your heart.

"Look we said, what is it that draws two people into closeness and love? Of course there's the mystery of physical attraction, but beyond that it's the things they share. We both love strawberries and ships and collies and poems and all beauty, and all those things bind us together. Those sharings just happened to be; but what we must do now is share everything. If one of us likes anything, there must be something to like in it — and the other one must find it. Every single thing that either of us likes. That way we shall create a thousand strands, great and small, that will link us together. Then we shall be so close that it would be impossible — unthinkable — for either of us to suppose that we could ever recreate such closeness with anyone else. And our trust in each other will not only be based on love and loyalty but on the fact of a thousand sharings — a thousand strands twisted into something unbreakable."

What we must do with our spouses in to create commonalties. It is like money in the bank. There is so much in the media today about how opposites attract. *Women are from Venus, Men are from Mars.* Yes, men and woman are different and praise the Lord for that. But our society has lost the understanding of what is means to "be one." I wonder if if has ever understood it.

Many know that in marriage, "the two shall become one." But they are just not sure which one! When many couples extinguish the two candles in the wedding ceremony to light the unity candle, they begin a journey of continuing to snuff each other out!

Part of our success in marriage has been cultivating the commonalties. First of all, we both had Jesus Christ at the center of our being and relationship. Jesus meets my needs, which lets Steve off the hook to some extent. Because our professions are the same, I understand his work. I worked with him to help build his practice. I understand the struggles of getting a PFM margin just right on #8. (You're not supposed to understand that. But we do. That's the point.) We speak the same language.

I know it is rare for spouses to share the same profession. But I encourage you to learn. Is your husband a stock broker? Take a class at a local community college and learn to read those little numbers in the Wall Street Journal. Is your husband a banker? Learn about IRA's, mutual funds, and compound interest. Is your husband a builder? Go to the building sites. Learn about sheet rock quality or why a 2 x 4 is really a $1\frac{1}{2}$ by $3\frac{1}{2}$. Is he

52

a salesman? Know his product. Show interest in what he does, not just the paycheck he brings home at the end of the week.

This applies to outside interests as well. What does a tight end do in football? Why is a birdie better than a bogey?

I hope you understand that this is more than a "tip." If we want to truly become one, we will want to share more than each others' interests. We will share their lives. There are no "His" and "Hers" towels at our house. It is simply one life being lived out in two bodies.

I want to leave you with this repeated thought from Sheldon Vanauken, "And our trust in each other will not only be based on love and loyalty but on the fact of a thousand sharings- a thousand strands twisted into something unbreakable." ♡

In-laws Or Out-laws?

SHARON JAYNES

*I*t was our first Christmas as Mr. and Mrs. Steven Jaynes. We had spent four months of absolute bliss in our tiny college apartment in Chapel Hill, NC. Christmas break would be the first time that we had ventured from our honeymoon town to spend some holiday time with our family. But the question was — which family?

Thus began our first experience with the tug-of-war on the tie that binds. My family thought, of course their only daughter would spend her first married Christmas with them. Steve's parents thought, of course we would come to *their* home for the holidays. Their twins had always returned to the nest for Christmas, and they weren't about to let that tradition end now.

Torn between two families, we visited my family first, ate Christmas Day breakfast with them, and then traveled four hours to have Christmas dinner with Steve's family. We tried to make everybody happy, but in the end, no one was satisfied — including the exhausted newlyweds.

On top of the stress of trying to make both families happy, the day after Christmas, Steve's grandmother passed away and his sister's 2-year-old daughter contracted meningitis. So his brother, sister and parents left Charlotte for three days to attend the funeral. My sister-in-law and I stayed behind to take care of Steve's sister's other two children while her husband stayed behind at the hospital with their 2 year old. This all sounds rather confusing, so let me make it simple. The Jaynes (the "real" Jaynes) left town. The in-laws (the "not-so-real" Jaynes) stayed behind.

And during the first crisis in my new husband's life, I was not able to comfort him or be by his side. I sat in the dark after putting the children to bed and I felt a tremendous void. I was torn because I wanted to be a help to the family, but at the same time felt that we were being torn apart by the family.

Among the most common problems in marriages today, three top the list: sex, money, and in-laws. And while we hear the words, "what God has joined together, let no man put asunder," sometimes it is a couple's very own families that seem to be the ones doing the "asundering."

54

There is certainly an ample supply of mother-in-law jokes floating around, but in-law problems are no laughing matter. As I've searched the Scriptures on the subject, I've found very little in how to handle the situation. However, one verse does resound, Genesis 2:24, *"For this cause, a man shall leave his father and mother and shall cleave to his wife; and they shall become one flesh."* (NAS)

Steve and I have always felt that the number one priority in family, is our family. Before we had children, it was our family of two. When Steven, Jr. was born, it became our family of three. This decision has made both sides of the extended family angry at times when we did not meet their expectations. However, it has kept us unified. After that first Christmas of being separated, we both decided that we would never again face a crisis apart. And we never have.

There are many common in-law problems that couples tend to face. How often do we visit? How long do we stay? How long do the in-laws stay when they come to visit us? Where do we spend Christmas or Thanksgiving? How much do we tell our in-laws about our personal finances? Our marital struggles? Our parenting decisions?

Questions like these can be very difficult to agree upon. But the most important point is this: come to an agreement before the problem is staring you in the face (or knocking on the door) and causing marital discord. Remember, the most important family unit that God has ordained is you and your spouse.

God does call us to honor our fathers and mothers. We are not to ignore them or their needs. But He also calls us to leave and cleave to the mate that He has chosen for us. Dr. James Dobson, in his book "Solid Answers" states that "If either the husband or wife has not been fully emancipated from the parents, it is best not to live near them. Autonomy is difficult for some mothers and fathers to grant, and close proximity is built for trouble."

If in-law problems are causing divisiveness between you and your spouse, God is not pleased. If there is a problem with the husband's family, the husband needs to support his wife and handle the problem for her. The wife needs to know that her husband loves her, is dedicated to her, and that he is her protector (Ephesians 5:25-30).

However, if it the problem is with the wife's family, she is the one who needs to do the confronting. Her husband needs to know that she honors him above all else, that she respects him, and that nothing will stand in the way of her total commitment to him and their relationship (Ephesians 5:22-24).

Here are some suggestions for handling in-law difficulties that may come your way.

1. When you're around in-laws for an extended period of time and feel yourself growing weary, go for a walk, go shopping alone or simply get away for a few hours.
2. Don't try to resolve family conflicts during the holidays. If you have a beef with someone, wait until after the holidays to air it. You might think better of it anyway when you are away from the situation for a few days.
3. Be unified. Commit to your partner that your relationship is the priority and that you will not let anyone come between you — not even Mom.
4. Try not to talk bad about the in-laws after a family gathering. Don't have a review session, pointing out each family member's faults.
5. Decide beforehand on an acceptable length of stay for visits that both you and your spouse are comfortable with, then stick to it!
6. Avoid an open door policy with in-laws unless both you and your spouse are comfortable with it.
7. If you are concerned about possible conflicts with an in-law's upcoming visit, spend extra time praying and reading the Scripture. Ask the Lord to give you a servant's heart.
8. When around the in-laws, hug and kiss your mate — a lot. Don't make him or her feel like they play second fiddle when the blood relatives arrive.
9. Borrowing from Paul's technique of repetition, be unified, and again I say be unified.

Are your extended family members in-laws whose goal is to help you build a godly home that lasts a lifetime? Or are they out-laws who are robbing you of the oneness that you committed to on your wedding day? Pray about it. Talk about it. And above all, enjoy the miracle of two becoming one. ♡

First Things First

SHARON JAYNES

"*First comes love; then comes marriage; then comes Susie with the baby carriage.*" When I was 6-years-old, this was a familiar chorus we used to chant when teasing a friend about a prospective beau. But no one ever mentioned what came after the baby.

In my 19 years of marriage, I've observed differing ways that relationships change after the children come. Some couples handle it well. Others do not. What seems to make the difference is how well the couple maintains their marriage unit as the primary focus of the family.

Family psychologist, Dr. John Roseman, noted that "Today's typical wife, as soon as she becomes a parent, begins to act as if she took a marriage vow that read, 'I take you to be my husband, until children do us part.'" (Charlotte Observer 2/10/98) I can remember a time not too long ago, when a wife who became a mother remained first and foremost a wife. The title for a woman who worked outside the home was a "working wife." The woman who worked in the home was referred to as a "housewife."

But all that's changed now. There has been a shift in that way of thinking, and today's language reflects that shift in society's values. Today's woman in the same circumstances is referred to as a "working mom" or a "stay-at-home mom." Some may think this is a change for the better. After all, who wants to be married to their house? But I see a grave problem. Our focus has shifted from a home that is centered around the marriage unit, to one centered around the children.

Rosemond goes on to say that, "this shift came about largely because as America shifted to a self-esteem-based, child-rearing philosophy, women became persuaded that the mother who paid the most attention to and did the most for her child was the best mom of them all." Unfortunately, many times this has occurred at the expense of the marriage. The wife becomes engrossed in the lives of her children, and the husband becomes more engrossed in his career. Twenty years later they look up from their cereal bowls and say, "Who are you?"

As a small child, there was nothing I wanted more than for my parents to love each other. When I was 5 years old, my aunt took me shopping to buy presents for my parents. I was so proud of my purchase for my mom: a very see-through, yellow negligee. This of course brought lots of laughter from the adults, but in reality, it was a child's feeble attempt to bring the two most important people in her life closer together.

Rob Parsons, author of the "60-Minute Marriage Builder" wrote, "I spend a fair amount of my work urging parents to spend time with their children, never-the-less, when one parent becomes obsessed with a child to the exclusion of the other parent, the marriage begins to operate as though there's an affair going on." Let's make sure that never happens in our marriages. Here are some ways to make sure that your husband remains a priority in your life.

1. Spend a few nights away by yourselves once or twice a year. Steve and I left Steven for a weekend for the first time, when he was 1 year old. I missed him terribly, but it did wonders for my husband to be the focus of all my attention for three days. And guess what? Steven lived through it! We've done this now for 15 years.

2. Create commonalities such as activities that just the two of you do together such as golf, ballroom dancing or jogging. Have a regular date night. This could be as simple as a cup of coffee at the local café. When there, ask your husband questions about himself and don't spend the whole time discussing the children.

3. Make sure your husband knows that he is the most important person in your life. Buy a special nightie, let the children spend the night with a friend or relative and send an invitation to the office inviting him to a romantic evening alone. (Make sure and write "personal" on this piece of mail!)

4. Stop and re-evaluate the relationships in your home. Ask your husband where he thinks he fits in and then make necessary adjustments.

I believe that the best mom of all is one who loves her husband and gives the children the security of living within the protection of a rock-solid marriage — a marriage that exemplifies and models for them what God intended. Listen to what Paul says in the Amplified Version of the Bible. "Husbands, love your wife as Christ loved the church and gave Himself up for her ... Let each man of you (without exception) love his wife as (being in a sense) his very own self and let the wife see that she respects and reverences her husband, that she notices him, regards him, honors and prefers him, venerates, and esteems him; and that she defers to him, praises him, and loves and admires him exceedingly." Ephesians 5:33. That says it all!

Now, back to the 6-year-old's little chant. *"First comes love; then comes marriage; then comes Susie with the baby carriage. Baby grows up; kids are all gone; mom and dad still in-love even though they're all alone."*

Be Your Husband's Biggest Fan

JULIE BERNARD

Great fans have been known as the sixth player on a basketball court. What a difference support and encouragement can make. Win, lose or tie, they are there, devoted and cheering. We all need fans, our husbands included! As wives we can work towards being our husbands' biggest fans.

In the same way a sports fan is focused on the game we can focus on our husbands. We do that every time we give them the precious gift of our undivided attention. When we tune into them and tune out the distractions around us, when we really concentrate on the feelings and thoughts behind their words, we encourage them.

Fair weather fans reject their hero when he doesn't perform up to expectations. Genuine fans remain devoted even when they face defeat and failure. When our husbands experience failure and discouragement, we have an opportunity to show how much we believe in them. Every time we talk positively about them or tell them privately that we have confidence in them, we encourage them to go out and try again.

Every team going into the playoffs hopes for the home court advantage. It is so much easier for them to face a crowd that is cheering for them than to face a crowd that is hurling insults and sending jeers their way. During the day our husbands may be out battling, suffering some hard blows, criticism and well-planned attacks, but home should be a place where they can put their guards down. When our husbands walk in the front door they should breathe a sigh of relief knowing they now have the home court advantage.

Athletes who compete have to believe down deep that they have the potential to win the big game. A true fan also believes in the dream. We can put a damper on our husband's dreams and aspirations or we can help them to become realities. We may have to choose to hold our tongues when logic says it can't be done. God may be wanting to do something big through our husbands.

From the sidelines we can pray for our husband and ask God to protect him, to lead him and to block Satan's attacks. What an encouragement to know that when he is out there playing the game of life he is wrapped up in prayer support. Not only can we be our husband's biggest, most devoted fan but we have the privilege of being on the same team with him. As we follow the game plan God has for us, we will be winners! ♡

And They Lived Happily Ever After

PAULA YEE

As a little girl, I believed in the happily-ever-afters found in Snow White, Cinderella and Beauty and the Beast. The heroines' problems always melted away as the couples galloped off to their new home. After the story ended, I often dreamed of what went on in Cinderella's castle. Images of Prince Charming picking his new bride flowers from the castle garden floated through my mind. I fantasized that the bridegroom rushed home after his battles with the Black Knight to be with his new bride. Of course, there were those countless evenings the couple spent dancing under the stars until midnight.

When I became a bride, I expected my husband to be something like that. It wasn't long before I discovered that he wasn't Prince Charming, and he soon found out that I was not Cinderella or Beauty — in fact, I probably resembled the Beast. Nevertheless, the vows had been said, so with chin thrust forward, I set out determined to bring forth some changes. With a little help from me, I was sure my young husband could still be Prince Charming.

Years passed. My husband didn't change. In fact, he resisted my efforts. I plodded on, disappointed, and painfully reminded that God hates divorce. Then, one day, as I pondered what I was doing wrong, the Lord spoke to me. "Are you ready to do things My way?" He asked. "Yes," I answered wearily. My list of how to turn my husband into the perfect man was exhausted. And so was I.

To my astonishment, the Lord set about changing me, not my husband. The first thing He called me to do was accept my mate the way God had accepted me: lovingly, unconditionally. Then, the Lord revealed to me what my girlish dreams really were: lies. They were lies from an enemy who prowls around seeking to destroy families and promote discontent. There are no Prince Charmings or Cinderellas in this world. We are all imperfect people, yet loved deeply by our Creator. As I read God's Word, I came to understand what love was. Love is patient, love is kind, love does not envy, it does not boast, it is not proud. Love is not rude, it is not self-seeking. Love is not easily angered, it keeps no record of wrongs (I Corinthians 13:4-5). Love is staying up all night with a sick spouse. Love is standing by his side when his business fails. Love overlooks when he forgets our anniversary. Love always protects, always hopes, always perseveres. I realized that when we cling to our mates, instead of our God, we do our spouses a great disservice. We also cheat ourselves from a deeper relationship with our Savior. God wants to be God in our lives. When we expect others to fulfill our every need, then they become our god, and that's idolatry.

Suddenly, I watched my husband with new eyes. He was Prince Charming when he worked late in order to provide for our family, took the children to the park, whisked us all off unexpectedly for a weekend getaway and laughed with me over a bag of popcorn as we watched a late night movie together. My husband had been my Prince Charming all along. I just hadn't realized it. I still dream. I often think of what heaven will be like. And I know that in that place, there will only be happily-ever-afters. ♡

Putting Your Marriage On The Right Path

LYSA TERKEURST

Every marriage will move in one of two directions. As the smiling couple exits the church they will either choose the path toward the oneness God intended or a path toward bitter isolation. Unfortunately, divorce has become such an accepted reality in our country that many times when a couple realizes they are headed in the wrong direction, instead of turning around, they simply give up. Turning around is not easy, but with God's help anything is possible. Trust me, I know. I have walked in the valley of a bad marriage and experienced the overwhelming pain. I also know that God can work miracles from shambles and set you back on the path headed toward the peak of oneness. The point at which my husband and I started to climb back up the ladder was a very low point but the most important thing is that we started! We knew when God promised us in Jeremiah 29:11 *"a future and a hope"* that He would be faithful and true to His word. Now we have the miracle to prove it.

Here are a few suggestions to help you start the journey toward the oneness God intended in your marriage:

1. Many times when a marriage starts to fail, one partner decides their spouse needs to be "fixed." The problem with fixing someone else is that it is an impossible task. All of my efforts to fix my husband, Art, just made him pull farther away. I learned that if things were going to get better I had to get my focus off of Art and let God change me. Pray and ask God to reveal some things you can start to change about yourself to help improve your marriage.

2. You are and forever will be a holy and dearly loved child of God ... and the same is true for your husband. Look at your husband through God's eyes and your whole perception will change. Yes, he has flaws, but who doesn't? Pray that God will give you a deeper understanding of your husband and a true desire to meet his needs.

3. Harboring resentment will never make your marriage better ... only bitter. Ask God to reveal things you need to forgive your husband for and then forgive him. Remember the beauty of forgiveness is that it releases you from the bondage of unforgiveness. There may be some things God needs to deal with in your husband, but leave those things to God and live in the freedom of being able to forgive as Christ forgives you.

4. If your husband is willing, find another Christian couple to whom you can be accountable, a couple you can really trust and pray with. If your husband is not willing, then find a woman you can do this with. Focus on praying for each other and your husbands.

May your marriage experience the true intimacy of oneness that only God can bring. ♡

Enabled Of God, For Good

COLLEEN ALLISON

"She will do him good and not evil all the days of her life."
PROVERBS 31:12 (KJV)

These 14 simple words are packed with meaning. The English translation is very close to the original Hebrew. The word "day" means "hot" or from "sunrise to sunset." So, when it says "day" here it literally means "daylight hours" or our "waking hours" — that time when we are actually up and doing! This verse gives me a sweet command to care for the man who took me for his bride 10 years ago. I am beginning to comprehend what a special and unique relationship I have with my husband. He is the only person in this world that I am charged by God to seek to "do good for all the days of my life." I am beginning to see the unique person I am to be in my husband's life each day!

Of course homemaking and mothering are an extension of what I "do" as a wife — yet as I go about the tasks of my daylight hours, I am now reminded who is to be my number-one priority: Sean, my husband. I can get so caught up with taking care of four children, nursing a baby, home schooling, cleaning the home and taking care of "my" needs, that I forget doing my husband good is the reason why I do all else! Doing good for him is to be my goal for each day. I want to be really transparent and confess that even though I am married to a Christ-like man, deep down there has been a fearful, selfish part of me that seeks to "protect" myself from being "used, abused, walked on or taken advantage of" by my husband. I know this fear is not of God, and not warranted by any behavior of my husband. I could take a few paragraphs to trace the origin and root of this fear, but suffice it to say, I have grown up in a generation of feminism and a culture that attacks the family, marriage and men. Simply reading Proverbs 31:10-27 makes me understand how much I need to grow as a Christian wife if I am to do my husband *good and not evil*! I know I am to be like Sarah, for *"Even as Sarah obeyed Abraham, calling him lord: whose daughters ye are, as long as ye do well, and are not afraid with any amazement."* (1 Peter 3:6 KJV) The Lord is freeing me from fear, enabling me to love my husband wholeheartedly, and seek to "do him good and not evil all the days of *my* life"!

The Lord has shown me three areas I need to work on.

• What I think about my husband

• What I say to/about my husband

• What I do for my husband daily

Reading the Bible and meditating on verses specific to husbands and wives will give me a right heart towards my marriage and husband. Once my heart is right, the things I speak and do will reflect that attitude of my heart. I know I personally have a long way to go before I will be the wife God desires me to be!

What does this verse speak to your heart? How do you apply this command to your everyday life with your husband? As you meditate upon this verse, do instances when you failed to do good come to your mind? If so, ask for forgiveness and pray for strength.

May God bless your marriage as He leads you into a deeper understanding of how you are to *"do good and not evil"* for your husband all the days of *your* life! ♡

What Seeds Are You Planting In Your Marriage?

SHARON JAYNES

When my husband and I first built our home, the lawn was a carpet of lush healthy fescue grass. The tender shoots just beckoned us to kick off our shoes and walk barefoot across the soft shock of green. However, the following spring, I noticed a few unwelcome strangers in my lovely yard: dandelions, crab grass, ground ivy and clover.

"Where did these weeds come from?" I asked Steve. "They came from seeds that blew in from other people's yards. They came from our neighbors," he explained. For a while I tried to pull the uninvited guests from the landscape but I was quickly losing the battle and the weeds were taking over. By the third spring, there were even more of these intruders, and we knew that if we didn't get a yard service to spray, we would be left with no grass at all but only a yard full of healthy weeds.

This made me think about the seeds we sow in our marriages. I think the most important things between a husband and wife are the words they speak to each other. During the dating stage and even in the first few months of marriage, we praise our men. "You're so handsome in that shirt." "It amazes me how you know so much about baseball." "How do you remember all those numbers at the office?" "I can't wait until you get home from work today." This is the healthy grass.

Then as many marriages progress, the praise starts to dwindle until encouraging words become endangered species. Many husbands are robbed of the adoration they felt from in the early days. Instead they may hear, "That tie definitely does not match your shirt." "All you ever do is watch baseball." "Your work is more important to you than I am." "Can't you do anything right?" These comments are weeds that creep in and choke out the very life of a healthy marriage. And if left unattended, they will take over until the marriage that was once a thing of beauty, admired by all who observe it, becomes merely a mass of crab grass, dandelions, ground ivy and clover.

There is a children's poem that reads:

> EVERY PLANT HAS LITTLE SEEDS
> THAT MAKE OTHERS OF ITS KIND.
> APPLE SEEDS MAKE APPLE SEEDS
> AND THEY'LL DO IT EVERY TIME.
>
> SEEDS MAKE FLOWERS, SHRUBS AND TREES.
> SEEDS MAKE FERNS, VINES, AND WEEDS.
> WHAT YOU PLANT IS WHAT YOU GROW,
> SO BE CAREFUL WHAT YOU SOW.

Here are several suggestions for weed control in your marriage:

Use a strong pre-emergent — Pray and meditate on God's Word to kill the weeds before they ever spring up. Spend time praying through scripture for your husband. Commit your marriage to the Lord and pray for it regularly. If you don't, who will?

Weed — Get rid of those negative thoughts by thinking before you speak. Proverbs 15:28 says, *"The heart of the righteous ponders how to answer, but the mouth of the wicked pours out evil things."* And Ephesians 4:29 says, *"Let no unwholesome word proceed from your mouth, but only such a word as is good for edification (building up) according to the need of the moment, that it may give grace (be a gift) to those who hear."* (NAS)

Water — Remember the qualities that attracted you to your husband and shower him with praise. Take time to hide verses in his lunch box, write him love letters, make a cassette of his favorite songs and plan special date nights each month.

Fertilize — Use Ephesians 5:33 as the fertilizer to keep your marriage healthy. *"Let the wife see that she respects and reverences her husband, that she notices him, regards him, honors him, prefers him, venerates and esteems him, and that she defers to him, praises him, and loves and admires him exceedingly."* (Amplified Version)

What kinds of seeds are you planting in your marriage? Why not try this weed control plan to insure a healthy marriage and a happy spouse? Remember: "What you plant is what you grow, so be careful what you sow." ♡

He Won't Go To Church

KEVIN WOODY

*W*hy won't my husband go to church?" "Why does he always expect me to lead in family prayers and Bible reading?" "How can I help him to know God or grow mature in his relationship with Jesus?" These are common questions of Christian wives today. Every Sunday, church meetings draw a large number of wives whose husbands "already had a commitment today."

What can a woman do to encourage her husband to love and serve the Lord? The most common effort is to get him to church. Gently and kindly, a wife may ask her husband to attend worship with the rest of the family. He may come or he may not, but often no great difference in his life develops. The pattern of a wife's invitation and a husband's refusal can become a painful problem in the life of a family. The longer the process continues, the more deeply resistant to church a husband becomes. Often the encouragement to attend church becomes counterproductive.

The apostle Peter recognized this same problem in the early churches. God inspired him to write guidelines for the wife longing to see her husband in Christ:

"Wives, in the same way be submissive to your husbands so that if any of them do not believe the word, they may be won over without words by the behavior of their wives, when they see the purity and reverence of your lives. Your beauty should not come from outward adornment ... Instead, it should be that of your inner self, the unfading beauty of a gentle and quiet spirit ..." (I Peter 3:1-4).

I think every church needs a W.O.W.W., or "won over without words," group — women encouraging each other in their ministry to their husbands. The challenge for the wife of the unbelieving or spiritually lazy husband is to make her life and actions stunningly beautiful. Her life becomes so much like Christ's, so full of grace, power, gentleness and service, that her husband wants to know more.

You know from experience that you can't control your husband. You have influence, but not control. What Peter challenges a wife to focus on, is what she can control — her own obedience to Christ.

Keep in mind that it is the wife's job to demonstrate the Gospel and her love for Christ by her behavior. The Holy Spirit, and He alone, has the ability to convict individuals of their sin and their need for Christ.

Leading a husband to Christ is hard work. Sometimes it is a long process. Give him the room he needs to think, question and discover, and commit yourself to making your life so beautiful that he will want to know who dressed you. ♡

Her Prayers Changed My Heart

CURT WHALEN

Many women today find that they are the ones in the home who get their family to church, initiate family devotions and desire a Christ-centered home while their husbands are resistant. You might be one of them. I know my wife Marybeth was. Many people might have assumed that her spouse was always as devoted to Christ as she was. Sadly, that wasn't true.

There was a time when God, the church and my spirituality weren't very important parts of my life. I was a church-goer (sometimes) and we had (she had!) Christian friends, but I wasn't interested in getting any closer to God than that. Prayer, Bible reading and intimate Christian fellowship wasn't part of my plan. My wife was the one always trying to get our family to church. She was the one scheduling our Christian activities. She was the one who reached out to others trying to be a servant for the Lord. As a matter of fact, I can remember times in our marriage when I poked fun at her for doing her daily devotionals, and communicated how uncomfortable I felt when she made me go to Christian functions.

Looking back, I can see the pain that I caused in her life. I can remember quite specifically looking into her eyes and seeing the hurt and the sadness I caused. And now as I'm striving to grow closer to the Lord, I wonder how many other women have these same feelings. How many have husbands who are so devoted to their job that they check out of any family life? How many have husbands who have left home to seek another relationship? How many have husbands who spend more time absorbed in their own lives than that of the family? I seem to run across many women who are working hard to build a strong Christian family, yet are being defeated by the person who is supposed to be their spiritual partner.

Obviously, something in my Christian walk and in our marriage changed. I've got a long way to go in developing my relationship with Christ and with my wife, but slowly, over time, I've felt the hardness that surrounded my heart melt away. You might be wondering how something like that could happen. You might think that it took something complex or some significant emotional event, which honestly, it did. But the change in my life began very simply. It began with a prayer.

71

In May 1996, my wife and I took our two kids to the beach for a week's vacation. She was pregnant, due in late July, and I was trying to give her that time to relax and enjoy herself before the baby came. While we were there, she was involved with a woman's devotional that led her to pray for three specific things:

- that my heart would turn towards the Lord
- that our family would become Christ-centered
- that God would break her heart with the things that break His.

God, in ways that only He can understand, answered all three.

July 29, 1996 changed me forever. It was supposed to be a day full of happiness. Marybeth and I were in the hospital about to deliver our third child. Like any expectant parents, we were both excited and scared. I couldn't wait to see this little person who had been growing inside my wife for the last nine months.

The staff induced Marybeth early in the morning, and by mid-afternoon she was in full labor. As they were getting the room ready for her delivery, our doctor realized that our child was coming and coming fast! I watched in amazement as he calmly talked Marybeth through delivery while the rest of the staff frantically got everything in place. It was all happening so quickly. And ten minutes later I watched my third child enter into this world.

Immediately, I was filled with joy and felt my eyes watering with the incredible happiness of birth. I remember beaming with pride as I told my wife that we had a new son. What struck me then as I looked upon her was the fear and concern on her face. She kept saying that something was wrong. Our doctor had the same expression. Within a split second the world I had known was torn apart. What had been incredible joy turned into indescribable sorrow as I realized that my newborn son couldn't breathe.

The respiratory team immediately tried to stabilize him and tried to let us hold him, a moment that is usually treasured. Instead, we felt only grief and fear watching him struggle so desperately for a breath. Then they rushed him to NICU (Neonatal Intensive Care Unit.) The rest of the day was a blur. We tried to listen as all the different doctors explained why they thought our son couldn't breathe, but the explanations just sort of ran together. One memory though will always be with me. I will never forget telling our son good night as he laid in NICU with all the different tubes and wires running into his tender body. I can still feel the longing I had inside to hold him and comfort him and make it all better.

The last two years have gone by so quickly and are filled with many memories, both happy and sad. Our hearts were broken as we talked with other parents and heard them describe the problems of their children. Some children made it, some didn't. We encountered people whose love of the Lord overwhelmed me. I remember one woman, whose 12-year-old son Joshua was dying of leukemia, praising Jesus for the time the two of them had together in this life. I remember weeping as she told of Joshua's desire to be with Jesus and getting to sit in His lap.

Marybeth and I also experienced the miracles of healing that took place with our son, Matthew. At 15 months he still couldn't eat anything by mouth and was mystifying the best feeding specialists in Charlotte. We then watched as specific answers to prayer concerning his feeding difficulties corrected the problem within a week.

I felt the changes within myself. The new desire I had to learn about the Lord burned within my soul. I hungered for Him. I began to reach out to the Lord and wanted to learn everything I could about Him. Being active in church and trying to walk with God suddenly became very important. It seems so obvious now, but I began to understand that nothing is more important in this life than my relationship with the Lord, my spouse, my children and my church.

I've come to realize that I must be the spiritual leader of our home, which is never an easy task. Many days I feel I take one step forward and two steps back. But let there be no mistake — God is calling men to lead. Today's family is under attack. I see a husband's role as not only a provider but a protector. He prays for his wife and his children and teaches them daily about God and Jesus Christ. He leads his family in worship. He is the spiritual point man.

"Wives, in the same way be submissive to your husbands so that, if any of them do not believe the word, they may be won over without words by the behavior of their wives, when they see the purity and reverence of your lives" (1 Peter 3:1,2).

Looking back at the life of my wife Marybeth, I can see how true this verse was in her everyday living. Nothing she could have said would have done more to change me than witnessing the love she had for Christ. Obviously, we didn't have a perfect marriage. None are. But she would consistently take things to the Lord and try to model her life after His.

I could feel how her love for Christ strengthened her love for me and helped her overcome the times in her life when I hurt her emotionally. Most importantly, she continued to pray for me during both the good and bad times.

It's almost funny to me now to realize how blind I was to what was going on in our marriage. Here we were husband and wife and I didn't even realize that she was praying for me, but I could feel my heart beginning to change from deep within. I became aware of a vast emptiness inside. I found myself longing to go to church and to worship together as a family and to become spiritually active. I found that I was looking forward to learning more from our pastor. I realized that the emptiness inside was one that only God could fill. Before our son Matthew was born, I thought I had the means to face any challenge by myself, but what I found was that I needed God and longed for Him. The Lord used that brokenness inside of me to humble me and to draw me to Him. Neither Marybeth nor I could ever have imagined the way that the Lord would answer her prayers.

To the wives that read this message and understand the pain that I discussed, please let this article be words of encouragement. God loves you deeply and understands the pain in your heart. He loves your husband. He loves him for who he is, regardless of past mistakes or past sins. He's the loving Father who everyday scans the horizon searching for the prodigal son to appear so that He can rush to him and embrace him and carry him home. I say these things to let you know that God will hear your prayers. He longs to chip away at your husband's heart, just like He's been chipping away at mine.

And to any men reading this, to those who have heard me describing a man lacking God's love in his life and recognizes himself, please know that it's never too late to turn to God. It's never too late to drop the barriers that we surround our hearts with. Let the barriers down and let Jesus Christ in. Let Jesus Christ inside and discover His immeasurable love. ♡

Appreciate Your Husband Biblically

MARCIA K. HORNOCK

As a woman, you probably have the ability to express yourself with words. Try your hand at writing a tribute to your husband, based on Proverbs 31:10-31. List your husband's strengths, pursuits and accomplishments. Decide where these characteristics fit the passage, then model your statements after the verses. It might look like this:

Proverbs 31 For My Husband

Who can find an excellent husband, for his worth exceeds wealth.

The heart of his wife safely trusts in him, so that she lacks no important thing.

He will place his family's needs above his own every day of his life.

He seeks tools and paint and works willingly with his hands.

He is like a mighty hunter, bringing his meat from afar.

He rises also while it is yet night and gives food to the animals and takes his children to school.

He considers a house and buys it. With the sweat of his brow he keeps it repaired.

He girds his loins with strength and runs marathons with endurance.

He perceives that his accomplishments are good. He is always available to those who call him.

He lays his hands to oil changes, and his hands do tedious yard work.

He extends his hands to the neighbors and his parents, and helps at the rescue mission.

He is not afraid of the future for his family, for he depends on his God.

He makes bookshelves and cuts firewood. His skills are both verbal and manual.

His wife is known as a fulfilled woman among her peers.

He makes interesting Bible lessons and delivers the truth in love to his congregation.

Respect and leadership come to him, and he wears them well.

He opens his mouth with wisdom and supports his ministry with a blameless lifestyle.

He provides for his family and does not idle himself watching TV.

His children rise up and call him happy. His wife also, and she praises him: "Many men are good husbands and fathers, but you excel them all."

Ego-rub is deceptive and macho image is vain, but a godly man will be praised.

Give him the secure family he has raised, and let them praise him for his integrity. ♡

Time In With Your Husband

MEG AVEY

*I*f you have to think hard about the last time you spent quality time with your husband, then it has been too long. Couples need to make time to be together, to reconnect and to keep the love growing. I hear you ... where are you going to squeeze a single second from your already hectic schedule? There are ways. Look at your day, make this top priority and be creative. Remember any effort on your part will be noticed and appreciated by your beloved.

- Schedule a date night – Weekly is best but once a month will work also. Get a sitter and go out. It does not have to be expensive: fast food and a walk, dollar movies, a drive around town. Remember, the main thing is to be together.

- Swap kids with a friend – Not forever, just for a night. Take turns taking care of each other's children. You can enjoy the quiet comfort of home or plan a romantic evening at a hotel. Splurge and order room service. You may be mistaken for newlyweds.

- Meet your husband for lunch out or pack a picnic and eat in his office.

- Feed the kids early, put on a long movie for them to watch and enjoy a romantic dinner.

- Do the dishes together. Not many children will bother you in the kitchen.

- Plan not to turn on the TV after the kids go to bed. Sit and talk about anything except the children. Remember your dating days, what first attracted you to each other or reasons why you fell in love. Ask him about his dreams and goals. Share some intimate thoughts with him.

- Plan to wake up a few minutes earlier to talk or cuddle. It's a great way to start the day. Beats a bowl of cereal any day!!

These are just a few ways to keep the flames burning in your marriage. Your husband is the most important man in your life. Isn't he worth taking time for? ♡

How To Pray For Your Husband

SANDY DAY

SUNDAY — That he would become a holy man, a man of prayer, mature in the Lord, growing in his knowledge of God and daily seeking Him with all his heart. (1 Thes. 5:23; Col. 4:12; Eph.1:18-19; Eph.3:16-19; Ps.119:1-2)

MONDAY — That he would learn to take every thought captive, to not be conformed to the world's thinking, but to think scripturally. (Rom. 12:2; 2 Cor. 10:5)

TUESDAY — That his self-image would be a reflection of the Lord's thoughts toward him. (Eph. 1:17-19; Rom. 12:3; Ps. 139)

WEDNESDAY — That he would become a called man, not driven, with well thought-through and prayed-through goals in life. (1 Cor. 9:24-27)

THURSDAY — That he would stand firm against the schemes of the devil and resist Satan in all circumstances. (Eph. 6:10-18; James 4:7)

FRIDAY — That the fruit of the spirit would be exhibited more and more in his life. That he would learn to love as God commanded. (Gal. 5:22-23; 1 Cor. 13:4-7; Rom. 12:8-10)

SATURDAY — That the Lord would protect him, guarding his course. That he would learn to manage his time well. (Prov. 2:8; Eph. 5:15) ♡

Do We Really Listen?

ANA M. GAMBOA

One morning, I was riding with my friend and neighbor, Pat, to work. She was really up in arms about her husband. "That Robert! Can you believe that man?" she said with exasperation. "The kids and I had breakfast this morning and when he came to the table he started complaining, 'You guys ate all the corn flakes and didn't leave me any!' So I said 'Here! Here's a brand new box!' He said, 'Yeah, but this one's NOT OPEN!' Can you believe that man?! He can't even open a box of corn flakes by himself!"

I looked at her and said softly, "Pat, you're not listening to what he's trying to tell you." "What do you mean?" she asked. "It's not about a box of corn flakes at all," I said. "Of course he can open the box by himself! What he's trying to tell you is, 'You guys didn't wait for me and had breakfast. I feel left out.' He just can't say it in those words because he was raised to believe that men have to be tough. It's not masculine to express those needs and hurt feelings, that's all."

It's been over 16 years, but the memory of that little flash of insight comes back to me every now and then, especially when someone I love gets all upset about something that appears totally unreasonable and ridiculous to me. If I stop and listen, truly listen, I always discover that it is not about the box of corn flakes at all. ♡

God Guides Us In Our Marriage

JENNIFER MCHUGH

A lot of times in our society, we give the impression, especially in the Christian realm, that our marriage is perfect; nothing wrong here! My friends are super at building their husbands up and being the wife of noble character. They are careful about not bashing their husbands. I think this is great, but I also think that we as wives need to be honest and realize that our marriages aren't perfect. Does that mean that there is something wrong with us? Are we not being Proverbs 31 wives?

I think many women feel that if their husband is not a Christian, they don't have a good marriage. They also think that if their husband were a Christian, everything would be okay. Well, I do believe that even if you and your husband are both Christians, it doesn't mean that marriage is heaven on earth. Mike and I have a really good marriage, but it is not perfect!!!

I really feel led to encourage you, wives, that ALL marriages go through struggles. None is perfect! Don't give up. When I feel like just losing it with Mike, I turn to Proverbs and look at those oh so convicting scriptures like *"a quarrelsome wife is like a constant dripping"* (Proverbs 19:13b), or *"better to live on a corner of the roof than share a house with a quarrelsome wife."* (Proverbs 25:24). We go through difficult times in our lives, be it with husbands, children, neighbors, in-laws, whomever. I am finding more and more that when I quit focusing on their faults and look to the Lord, I can recognize these problems as sin. Then I can look at how I can change myself, while looking past the sin to where the Lord would have me look: at my love for others made in His image.

Another thing I find extremely helpful is having a really good Christian friend with whom I can share my personal stuff. I know that she will encourage me to see the best in my husband. I also know she won't allow me to bash him, but will give me the freedom to share my struggles. There is almost nothing better than a good friend like this.

It is important for us to not speak unkindly about our husbands to others, but it is also important to be REAL. There may be someone who is watching you as a Christian homemaker (believe me, there is!) and they think, "Wow, she has it all together." I am learning that they need to see that we as Christians don't have it all together, we just know Who to turn to with our struggles.

I still have times when I get SO frustrated with my marriage, kids, etc., but now I realize that everybody goes through tough times. I need to be a little more humble, love a little bit more and realize that God is using these "sandpaper" times to make me smoother. Pledging my life to my husband and committing myself to my children did not come with a guarantee that it would be easy. But I know with the Lord's help, He will show me the grace and blessings that come to me through my family. ♡

Grace For A Father

NANCEE SKIPPER

I knew I had exaggerated the injustice perpetrated by my condemned brother. It was a not-so-clear case of aggravated assault. I did the aggravating and he the assaulting. At 12 years of age I was an expert in subterfuge. Mercifully I did have a conscience, albeit sluggish, but on this occasion I seared my conscience and let the gavel fall without telling the whole truth. My brother was guilty as charged and when the punishment was administered, nothing but the truth smothered me in guilt and I wept.

My father never knew of my private conspiracy. You see, even the best of fathers cannot be ever present and all knowing. No dad, no matter how discerning and involved, is going to do it all right. They will make mistakes; some painfully evident, some they will never know. As challenging as mothering can be, I wouldn't trade places with my husband for all the adult conversation, dry-cleaned suits and envied lunches out in the world. However, too often I neglect to encourage him in his role as father and yet fully expect him to applaud my sacrifices as Mommy. Were it not for the grace God extends to us and to our children, no spiritually rational, caring male would attempt to father children. The task is too immense and our sin nature too obvious, but because we have an all-knowing and ever-present Father we can, with confidence and humility, accept those blessings and challenges.

It behooves us as wives to be in constant prayer for our husbands as they face not only the challenges of fathering, but the world's stresses and those hard knocks we are being spared. As our wedding vows stated, may we strive "to make our home a haven from the cares of this world." God's grace is sufficient for both mighty tasks. Yes, they will make mistakes and so will we, but His love covers a multitude of sins and His grace is still greater. For when all is said and done, credit will be given where credit is due — at His feet.

Dear Lord, bless and keep all fathers. May we as wives be slow to chide and quick to bless. Grant them the strength to persevere and may they have the courage to confess their sins readily and know the gracious love and forgiveness of both God and their children. ♡

Takes A Licking And Keeps On Ticking

LYSA TerKEURST

*D*o you have just a minute? Let's have a little fun. If you happen to be part of the vast majority of people who faithfully strap a timepiece to your wrist everyday, you will enjoy this. Do not look at your watch ... not even a little peek. Let me ask you a few questions about your watch that you obviously should know if you check the time quite often. First question: Does your watch have numbers, Roman numerals, dashes, dots, or something else to designate the hours? Second question: What is at the 12 o'clock space, the 3 o'clock space, the 6 o'clock space and the 9 o'clock space? Do you have your answers? Now, check your watch. Examine it very carefully because I have one more question for you. Stop looking at your watch. Third question: What time is it?

If you didn't pass this quiz, you're not alone. I recently heard it on a Zig Zigler tape and failed it miserably. As I laughed at my mistaken answers, a thought struck me: my husband is a lot like my watch. Somewhere in all the details of life what used to be extraordinary has given way to commonplace. When I first got my watch I could have told you every detail. Now I can't even remember what kind of numbers it has. Very similarly, when I first met Art I could have talked about all his wonderful qualities for hours but time has a way of dulling our memories.

I have decided that I want to renew my passion for my husband and pay attention to all the things that make him so very special. That's right — passion. Yes, I want to put aside the fact that he sometimes forgets the trash, occasionally drives too fast, and has been known to ask the forbidden question of what I did all day. Too often I focus on these trivial mishaps and get all in a tizzy over things of little significance. I think the key to a renewed passion is going to be found in how well I can adjust my attitude. You see, I know that I can't choose the things that come my way each day, but I can choose how I react to them. Too often I am so critical that I can't see past my own negativism. The fact is that my husband is kind, loving, giving and very patient. I know he would lay down his life for me and I yell at him over trash?

Well, I'm going to write my husband a love letter that recaptures my true feelings for this wonderful, precious man of mine and within the lines of my prose will be lots of passion. If I run short on romantic words the Bible's Song of Solomon has some great suggestions. Take time to give your husband the gift of passion and rediscover your love. ♡

What A Marriage Is Not

JOE AND MARY ELLEN BIANCO

My husband and I attended a marriage seminar some time ago, given by our pastor. His insight into what many of us look for in a spouse helped us work through some of the rough spots early in our marriage. We wanted to share this wisdom with you.

1. A marriage is NOT a solution to all of your problems.
2. A marriage is NOT an escape from a bad home situation.
3. A marriage is NOT a way to feel good about yourself.
4. A marriage is NOT a ticket to happiness.
5. A marriage is NOT easy.
    It requires a lot of compromise.
    It requires saying "I'm sorry."
    It requires swallowing your pride.
6. A marriage is NOT a way to escape loneliness.
    Some of the loneliest people in the world are those who are married, but who were not called to marriage by God. Marriage does NOT insure that we will always have the companionship we desire.
7. A marriage is NOT a way to insure immortality.
    Some of the most bitter, disappointed people are those who are angry because their children do not remember them as they would like them to.
8. A marriage is NOT the right to exclusive jurisdiction over every moment of your spouse's life.
    A husband does NOT "own" his wife; a wife does NOT "own" her husband. Spouses do NOT have the right to demand every bit of the other's time or attention. Spouses need time apart, "space" and even separate friends. However, marriage DOES require absolute fidelity to your spouse.
9. A marriage is NOT a substitute for a good relationship with God.
    Only God will never fail us; every human relationship fails us in some way, at some time. A good marriage will lead both partners to a greater intimacy with God — each in ways that are appropriate to the conscience of the partner in marriage. ♡

A Creative Way To Say "I Love You"

TERESSA HIGDON

I wanted to share something that really seemed to bless my husband. We were at a marriage seminar last year, and one night we were instructed to go to our hotel room and read Song of Solomon to one another. I read it to myself, but I didn't understand why it was so romantic until someone explained it during the seminar. Guess what? That book came alive and real to me!

Months later I wondered what I could do to encourage and bless my husband. So, with the help of the Lord and His word, I wrote down the Song of Solomon verses that pertained to my husband each night for a week. I paraphrased some to make it more personally fitting to my husband and for it to make sense since it was taken out of context.

For example, I inserted my husband's name for "he" in the following passage:

He brought me to the banqueting house, and his banner over me was love. (2:4)

Maybe others could try this followed by a personal note to their husbands and they will be blessed, too! ♡

More Than 50 Ways To Love Your Lover

BONITA LILLIE

*D*o you remember the old '70's song that talked about ways to leave your lover? Looking at the divorce rate, I can see that a lot of folks must have taken that song literally. Well, if there are 50 ways to leave your lover then there must be more than 50 ways to renew your love and commitment to your mate. Don't let your marriage be another statistic. Do the little things that make it thrive.

1. Learn your mate's love language.

2. Never forget his love language and speak it often.

3. Read I Corinthians 13:4-8 and live it.

4. Treat your spouse to an old-fashioned foot washing.

5. Give him a body massage and, as you do, pray aloud for him.

6. Leave an intimate note on his pillow that lets him know he is a great lover.

7. Create an atmosphere of peace in the home, especially when he arrives home from work.

8. Pray for his life and success daily.

9. Do a chore that is supposed to be his responsibility.

10. Help him make and maintain male friendships by allowing him time away with the boys.

11. When he has had an especially hard day or on the day he pays the bills, romance him that evening.

12. Praise him in public.

13. Praise him to your parents and in-laws.

14. Save money in a jar and buy him something he really wants.

15. After the kids are in bed, slow dance by candlelight or firelight.

16. Build him up in the eyes of your children. Make him their greatest hero.

17. Handle small irritations for him such as junk mail and getting things fixed around the house.

18. When he asks you to do something, do it.

19. Support his life ambitions in both word and deed.

20. Don't complain.

21. Make sure he always has clean underwear (and clothes for that matter).

22. If he's agreeable, take up a new hobby or interest together or share those you already have.

23. Be quick to say I'm sorry and even quicker to forgive.

24. Be a woman he can trust. Don't share more than you should with others.

25. Don't depend on him to meet all your needs. Make friends with other women.

26. When he arrives home from work, allow him some quiet time and then discuss his day before you talk about yours.

27. Maintain your health and beauty. Don't be a sight for sore eyes.

28. Avoid jealousy. Trust him.

29. Make a cassette tape of inspiring words and thoughts (yours or those from another source) that he can play on the way to and from work.

30. Play a funny, but safe, practical joke on him to add humor to your life.

31. Pray for his weaknesses, praise his strengths.

32. Exercise together.

33. Keep the bedroom exciting.

34. Put your husband before your children and make sure he knows that he will always hold that place.

35. Plan regular date nights. Be creative and do different things.

36. Have a special treat sent to his workplace, such as a cookie that says "I love you."

37. Give him a nickname that only the two of you know.

38. Spend time talking about your dating days and what first attracted you to him. When you are tempted to think of him in a negative light, remind yourself of these things.

39. Always express thankfulness for all he does for your family whether it be big or small.

40. Use physical affection often — a hand on the shoulder, neck rub, stroke on the cheek, pat on the rear, etc..

41. The next time you are tempted to usurp his authority, don't.

42. Avoid pointing out his mistakes. No matter how many mistakes he has made in the past, believe for the best this time.

43. Surround yourself with friends who want to see your marriage last and listen to them. Stay clear of those who point out your husband's faults.

44. Speak kindly and watch the tone of your voice. Avoid being loud or whiny.

45. Be there in his hour of need.

46. Be content with what you have, not always demanding more.

47. Be slow to speak and quick to listen.

48. Drop an encouraging note or scripture in his lunch or briefcase.

49. Always celebrate your anniversary in some way.

50. On each anniversary remember old times and plan for the future.

51. Display your wedding pictures as well as any awards he may have won.

52. Keep the house reasonably tidy.

53. Accept his criticism and learn from it.

89

54. Treat him with respect and teach the children to do the same.

55. Keep your promises.

56. Let him sleep in occasionally and serve him his favorite breakfast in bed.

57. Begin each day with a hug. End each night with a kiss.

58. On your anniversary or on Valentine's Day send him a love note via the classifieds in the paper.

59. Be thankful for your husband. Many people don't have what you have so never take him for granted.

60. Add to this list continually. ♡

CHAPTER *Three*

Children Are A Gift

"SHE SPEAKS WITH WISDOM,

AND FAITHFUL INSTRUCTION IS ON HER TONGUE."

PROVERBS 31:26

While You Were Sleeping

SHARON JAYNES

ow did this happen? My child was always such a sweet girl. She grew up in the church and became a Christian at age 6. We even sent her to Christian school. How could she have gotten involved in such a terrible situation?" Unfortunately this is a common saga heard among Christian parents of teens. The familiar question, "How could this have happened?" continues to ring out through the ages.

In the infancy to toddler years, our children are always right by our side. We control everything they eat, see, smell, touch, and taste. As preschool comes along, they are first exposed to the value systems of someone besides their parents. Even though many children do not experience pre-school, the inevitable comes as little Johnnie and Susie skip off to kinder-garten. Just as he or she is exposed to many germs from putting hands, pencils, crayons and other children's food in their mouths, so are they exposed to new "bad words" and other delightful horrors from children whose family values do not match your own.

However, in most elementary schools, the moms are never very far away. They are room moms, center moms, drivers on class field trips, servers for food at holiday parties, and moms always ready with scissors and glue to help the teacher with the many art projects. Then comes mid-dle school. The first thing I noticed in the hallowed halls of my son's mid-dle school was the drastic reduction in the number of visible mothers. They were few and far between, and the ones that were present had better have a good reason for being there — like a death in the family.

The less-visible-mother syndrome is a natural course in a child's grow-ing up and teen years. But that does not mean that it is time for us to take a breather from parenting. Many times parents say, "O.K., I've trained him up and he knows the principles. No more Valentine parties. No more field trips. I can relax a little now." And off we go to do our own thing. Then BANG, something happens to bring us back to reality and to let us know the job is not finished yet!

This reminds me of a parable in Matthew 13:24-28. It tells of a farmer who sowed good seed in his field. *"But while men were sleeping, his*

enemy came and sowed tares also among the wheat and went away." No one knew the enemy had even been to the field, because he came <u>while they were sleeping</u>. It wasn't until the wheat sprang up and bore grain that the tares became evident also. The slaves who planted the wheat came to the landowner with the same question that many parents ask themselves when something goes wrong. *"Sir, did you not sow good seed in your field? How then does it have tares?"* In other words, "I've sown good seed: Bible memory, church, family devotions, youth group. How did this happen?" And the answer for us is the same as it was for the workers in Matthew: *"An enemy has done this — while you were sleeping."*

Even though we moms cannot be the ever-present force in middle and upper school as we were during those elementary years, may we never sleep. We must forever stand watch over our children with prayer. We must ask them good questions to find out what's going on in their lives. I Peter 5:8 says that our adversary *"the devil prowls about like a roaring lion, seeking someone to devour."* And what meat is more tender than the calves or baby lambs of youth? Ephesians 6 also says, *"Our struggle is not against flesh and blood but against the rulers, against the powers, against world forces of this darkness, against spiritual forces of wicked-ness in the heavenly places."* Prayer is our defense against such an enemy. Pray that your child will:

- Know Christ as Savior early in life. (Psalm 63:1, II Timothy 3:15)

- Have a hatred for sin. (Psalm 97:10)

- Be caught when guilty. (Psalm 119:71)

- Be protected from the evil one in each area of their lives: spiritual, emotional, and physical. (John 17:15)

- Have a responsible attitude in all their interpersonal relationships. (Daniel 6:3)

- Respect those in authority over them. (Romans 13:1)

- Desire the right kind of friends and be protected from the wrong friends. (Proverbs 1:10-11)

- Be kept from the wrong mate and saved for the right one. (II Cor. 6:14-17)

- Be kept pure until marriage (as well as the one they marry). (I Cor. 6:18-20)

- Learn to totally submit to God and actively resist Satan in all things. (James 4:7)

- Be single hearted, willing to be sold out to Jesus Christ. (Romans 12:1-2)

- Be hedged in so they cannot find their way to wrong people or wrong places and that the wrong people cannot find their way to them. (Hosea 2:6)

Let's not be caught sleeping during those adolescent and teen years but instead pray without ceasing for their spiritual growth and protection. ♡

Raising Your Children Unto The Lord

CAROLE K. ARDIZZONE, M.ED.

The integrity of our society is dependent on the course of the next generation — whether it is a bonded generation with a well-developed conscience and a clear set of absolute values or the detached product of the latch-key culture, with an underdeveloped conscience and a cultural system of relative "whatever-works-for-you" values. The humanists understand this premise and the need to control the minds of children. God however, has prepared a way. A way that preserved the Jews as a people for 4,000 years — a way that will preserve the disciples of Christ!

Now we know the reason for taking God's gentlest admonitions seriously. He told us to "bring up a child in the way he should go" because He Himself made the child's brain malleable and moldable for the first eight to 10 years of life. It was He who set the stages of conscience development with the newborn at his mother's breast and He who arranged the intermittent windows of learning during the primary years of development. What an incredible God!

Look at how specific the meaning of His words are in Deuteronomy 6:4-10. After giving the Ten Commandments, He has Moses telling His people in Israel to be careful to OBEY so that it would go well with them and they would increase greatly. Then He reinforces the first commandment, telling them to *"Love the Lord your God with all your heart and with all your soul and with all your strength"* and to keep the commandments *"upon your hearts."* It is clear that raising a godly child begins with US. We are the most effective teachers by the way we live out our love for God and the Word planted in our hearts. If a mom doesn't love the Lord with all her heart, it will be difficult for her to pass on the concept of that behavior or the behavior of that concept to her progeny.

Then Moses says, "IMPRESS them on your children." Don't take for granted that they will have faith because you have faith (the process of osmosis). IMPRESS is a heavy word; it means "to produce a marked effect upon." Moses tells us how to do it; TALK about the commandments of God (the principle of faith) when you SIT at home and when you WALK along the road, when you LIE down and when you GET UP. This is not only a description of how you are to impress, but also a description of *how the child will learn.* I recently attended a conference where neurological researchers shared cutting-edge information about the brain, noting how intricately intertwined the motor system is with the thinking and speaking part of the brain. Motor activity (getting up and sitting down, walking and resting) actually helps the brain to learn, to remember, to understand, to read, and to speak! (They even suggested children learn math tables while running up and down stairs.) We need to take Moses seriously here. In all ACTIVITY we need to recall the Lord, speak of His wonders, thank Him, praise Him and ponder His greatness.

Next Moses reminds the Israelites to put symbols on their hands and on their foreheads, and write them on the door frames and the gates. While TALK engages the AUDITORY/VERBAL channels of the brain, the symbols appeal to the VISUAL/SPATIAL/MOTOR EXPRESSIVE areas. WRITE them, he says, then you will also be reminded to READ them. What a multi-modal God! He leaves no area of good teaching unused.

How does all this translate to you, the mom, on a daily basis? Here are a few suggestions:

1. First, develop a love relationship with our Savior. Feed your spirit daily (quiet time, Bible study, prayer, etc.). Allow the Lord to constantly be about changing you.

2. Share your faith, gratitude and praise with your family. Point out God's involvement in the little things of life *as they occur daily.*

3. Pray with your children when they lie down, when they get up, when they go out and when they return, before meals and when they have a concern. Develop a God language in your child's "neurological computer" that will last a lifetime.

4. Read to your children: Bible stories, stories with moral values, historical truths and those that perpetuate the spiritual and cultural traditions you wish to pass on.

5. Begin traditions in your family (little rituals that focus on the spiritual aspects of an event). Do this for the holidays, birthdays, and other events pertinent to your family. Include special prayer times and a weekly family evening of Bible study, food and fun activity, etc.

6. Teach your children about their spiritual heritage — the faith history of your family, including the testimonies of salvation.

7. Teach your children how to walk through difficulties — how to pray about specific problems, how to forgive and ask for forgiveness by walking with them, modeling and dialoguing as they struggle with friends and school situations.

8. Memorize scripture as a family game. This will exercise their memory in general as well as instill scripture in their hearts.

9. Attend church regularly and participate in the life of the body of Christ with your children.

10. Watch allowable movies and television with your children so that you can interpret what they see and experience from a godly perspective. Remember, teens especially need reinterpretation by someone other than their peers.

11. Teach your children to love their neighbors and friends with *agapé* love by modeling kindness and helpfulness to others. Reach out to those in need with time and assistance.

12. Speak positively of others, purging words of bigotry or blasphemy from your vocabulary. Help your children identify and avoid words of judgment (this does not refer to discernment of right and wrong).

13. Teach your children manners. Respect for elders, teachers, people in authority and places as well as the etiquette of meals, introductions and other social graces. This will help them stand out in a less-friendly society and find favor as they pursue God's call in their lives. It also imparts consideration to others.

14. In all of the above, live these principles JOYOUSLY — never demanding or associating godly principles with force, anger or negative judgment. If you have to force any of the above, go back and spend time on the first suggestion.

God bless you as you train up your children in Him!

Carole is a specialist in Learning Disabilities/Attention Deficit Dysfunction (LD/ADD) and the attendant concerns of neurological development. Carole has prepared a booklet that explores the topic of parenting and child development from a Christian perspective. For more information, please contact the Proverbs 31 ministry at (704) 849-2270. ♡

Train Up A Child

SUSAN GARDNER

*F*amily worship is extremely important, not only for the most obvious reason of glorifying God, but also because it teaches our children the importance of having Christ live in the home. A mother should lay the groundwork in her child's infancy for a pattern that the child can carry through the rest of his or her life. If an adult's quiet time can be established, the child sees that, and it becomes a way of life. When that child goes off to college, he has 18 years under his belt of mom's helping him with his relationship with the Lord.

In The Morning

When a baby is born, read Scripture to him or her in the morning and/or at night. Give the baby a Bible to hold.

When your children are old enough to sit in a high chair, pray with them over meals. Before they can talk, you pray for them. Develop this pattern at a young age by folding their hands for them. In the mornings when they are eating, have a devotional with them. There is material available for children even at this tender age.

Many families have a morning devotional at the breakfast table. Some dads use that time to read scripture to their children. This is also a good time to have prayer requests.

Another suggestion is to have a quiet time in the morning with your children. Before they can write, have them draw a picture about God or what God has made. For example: "God made the sun. Can you draw a picture of the sun?"

Once they can read, let them begin the day by kneeling by their bed and having their own quiet time. Again, the pattern is formed early for them to pray and read a Bible book or an easy-to-read Bible. Encourage them to keep a journal. Before they can write, have them keep a picture journal. After breakfast they can share what they learned in their quiet time that morning.

Older children can share on a more in-depth level. One suggestion is to have them share three things they can apply to their life from the morning's quiet time.

In the Evening

There are many different things you can do at dinner time. Of course, this depends on the spiritual atmosphere of the home.

You can get placemats that have different Bible activities on them. On a special occasion, each person can have a different activity to share around the table. If dad is spiritual, have him ask how the Lord has worked in everyone's life that day. Help them to see how the Lord works. Ask, "Did you witness to anyone today?" Look for mighty moments — moments throughout the day when we are aware of God working in our lives. This establishes the pattern of looking for God throughout the day.

Some fathers read about biblical characters. You can also use animals and nature to show God's creation. Older children can bring out godly principles (e.g., the owl can represent wisdom).

Mom can read to the children while they eat. When they are focused in on a story, eating goes much better. Biographies of great Christians are appropriate for older children, and fun God-related stories are good for the younger ones.

Before Bed

For young children, stand over the crib and read a couple of sentences from a Bible story. They may not understand, but once again you are establishing a pattern in their lives. Even a 2-year-old can sit for a couple of minutes to listen. There are many good resources available for this time.

Bedtime is also a good time to work on Scripture memory. "A Box of Precious Promises" and "Our Daily Bread" are two good resources. These are daily scriptures printed on little cards. You can put a Scripture for the week on a wipe-off board on the refrigerator and award the children a sticker or piece of candy when they can recite the verse by heart.

Sundays

Remember to keep Sundays holy. Show the children it is a special day. Our family plays Bible trivia or a simple Bible game on this day. This is a good day to share a special meal together.

Find what works for your family, and don't become overwhelmed. Know that God will lead you in what will be best for your family. ♡

Heavenly Insight

HEATHER RICHMOND

oday I realized how important "time" is. As I lay down next to my 4-year-old, dressed up like a ballerina, I found I didn't want to get up. As I saw her sleep peacefully, I wanted to keep her just like my beautiful "little" princess forever; so pure and sweet. But then, I thought, she will always be my princess, but right now I can take the time to pray for her purity and for her life. I held her close and prayed for my dear Kelsey. Tears flowed as I began to understand my job and role in her life. God gives us these moments to cherish. These times help us to endure all the strong wills, attitudes and sacrifices. There are always "hard" days but little glimpses from heaven here on earth sure keep me going. *Thank you, God, for your faithfulness in making my life intimate with my children.* As a homemaker I am able to share each precious memory with my most valuable gems, my children. I help them "sparkle." ♡

Hidden In Their Hearts

JANE STANFORD

"The Lord is my shepherd," Ben began, "I have everything I need." He took a deep breath, clasped his chubby hands next to his left ear, and bowed his head sideways. "He gives me rest in green pastures ... ."

The year before, a kind lady suggested I try teaching my kids, ages 3 and 5, whole chapters instead of individual verses. "You'll be surprised how quickly their young minds will absorb the words," she explained.

Psalm 23, written in a children's translation, seemed perfect. After I read the chapter to them twice a day for a week, both children began reciting the verses on their own. Then Ben invented hand and body motions to illustrate the concepts. We all imitated his movements, covering our faces as we went through the "very dark valley."

As my children grew older, I'd hear them muttering Bible chapters while in the bathroom or when lying awake in bed.

Sometimes we'd slack off reviewing chapters already learned. When my kids were unable to finish reciting a passage, we'd review it and soon their memories took over.

I'm praying that the words now hidden in my children's hearts will be acted out not only in simple hand motions, but also in daily situations with others. ♡

What Children Need

NANCY AGUILAR

CHILDREN NEED MORE
THAN CLOTHES ON THEIR BACKS,
A ROOF O'ER THEIR HEADS
AND LUNCH IN THEIR SACKS.

CHILDREN NEED MORE
THAN CABLE T.V.,
THE LATEST NINTENDO,
AND VIDEOS TO SEE.

CHILDREN NEED MORE
THAN A BEAUTIFUL HOME,
A ROOM FULL OF TOYS
AND THEIR OWN TELEPHONE.

CHILDREN NEED MORE
THAN FAR-OFF VACATIONS,
AMUSEMENT PARK RIDES
AND GRAND CELEBRATIONS.

THOUGH TREASURES WE BUY
BRING THEM SMILES — IT IS TRUE;
OUR CHILDREN NEED LESS
THAN WE MIGHT THINK THEY DO.

CHILDREN NEED TIME
TO TALK AND TO SHARE,
FOR GROWING IS PAINFUL
AND NOT ALWAYS FAIR.

CHILDREN NEED SOMEONE
WITH LISTENING EARS
TO HEAR HOW THEIR DAY WENT
AND HELP CALM THEIR FEARS.

CHILDREN NEED SPACE
A HOME WHERE THERE'S REST,
A PLACE WHERE THEY'RE NEEDED
AND TOLD, "YOU'RE THE BEST!"

CHILDREN NEED HANDS
TO HOLD WHEN THEY'RE SCARED;
CHILDREN NEED ARMS
TO HUG THEM AND CARE.

YES, CHILDREN NEED LESS
THAN WE MIGHT THINK THEY DO;
CHILDREN NEED LOVE —
YOUR CHILDREN NEED YOU. ♡

None Of The Piggies Stayed Home

LYSA TERKEURST

*F*amily snuggle time has become a daily tradition in the TerKeurst home. Every morning our two daughters, Hope and Ashley, sleepily make their way downstairs to crawl in bed with Mommy and Daddy to start their day with some good old-fashioned snuggling. There are plenty of good morning kisses and giggles to go around.

On one such morning, Hope, my oldest, decided to play the piggy game with her little sister's toes. We've played this game many times but that day her rhyme caught me by surprise. "This little piggy goes to aerobics, and this little piggy goes to a meeting. This little piggy goes to the grocery store and this little piggy goes to swim lessons." I was quite tickled by her rendition of the familiar rhyme; however, the thought struck me that none of her piggies stayed at home.

I decided it was time to rethink how I was spending my most precious commodity ... my time. It's important to take time to nurture and teach my children in the ways of the Lord. Time to sit and read. Time to play hide-and-go-seek, beauty shop, and cowboys and Indians. Time to share secrets. Time to kiss scraped knees and tear-stained faces. Time for imaginations and childhood dreams. Time for discussions about tadpoles and frogs, caterpillars and butterflies. Time for listening about first loves and comforting broken hearts. Time to cheer my children on to victory in all of life's races.

There is a time for everything, and a season for every activity under heaven.

Now don't get me wrong — I'm not saying that going to aerobics, the grocery store and meetings are bad things — except when they start to crowd out time with our children. Life needs to be kept in balance and then all things run smoother. Ecclesiastes chapter 3 says, *"There is a time for everything, and a season for every activity under heaven."* I have to remind myself of this every day as I keep the demands of running this ministry in balance with my first priorities: God and my family. I've learned to use my husband as a gauge and if something gets out of balance he holds me accountable.

Don't miss out on the precious time you have with your children today because they are only children for a season. A child is a lot like a garden; it takes a lot of hard work before you ever see the fruits of your labor. It takes time to fertilize, water, prune and weed but even in the work there are tremendous blessings.

One day, I hope to hear Hope's new version go something like this: "This little piggy played hide-and-seek and this one read stories. This one ran errands and this one fixed dinner. But this one exclaimed 'yea' as we all headed home." ♡

The Responsibility of Discipline

JENNIFER SCHROEDER

*I*magine yourself staring into the eyes of your precious little one. You have just instructed him not to touch something. He stares right back at you and proceeds to do the very thing that you have forbidden! You probably don't have to imagine the scenario — you have lived it. You may be able to remember the first time that your child willfully disobeyed you. I know I do. When my son entered this stage, I began to struggle with the issue of discipline. I knew the Bible commanded me to *"train up a child in the way that he should go ..."* (Proverbs 22:6), but how was I to train him up? What did the Lord expect of me as a parent?

Ephesians 6:4 says, *"And fathers, do not provoke your children to anger, but bring them up in the nurture and admonition of the Lord."* I was surprised to find that the word **nurture** translated from the Hebrew word *paideia,* which means to discipline, correct and chasten. This was so different from the idea that I had of nurturing. This same word is used in Proverbs 3:11-12a: *"My son, do not despise the Lord's <u>discipline</u> (paideia) and do not resent his rebuke, because the Lord <u>disciplines</u> those He loves."* God gives us a perfect example to follow as a parent — He disciplines us because He loves us.

The second area we are to bring our children up in is the **admonition** of the Lord. This word is taken from the Hebrew word *nouthesia* from *nous* which means understanding, and *theo* which is to settle or to sink down. Notice the order of these words: nurture (discipline) first and then admonition (settling an issue in the mind) second. This is so different from what the world teaches — that we can reason with our children. God is showing us that we must use discipline when teaching our children right from wrong.

The Lord has shown me that it is my responsibility to discipline my children and to bring them to an understanding of His word. At times I am overwhelmed by this awesome responsibility, but I know that God's grace is sufficient for me (II Cor 12:9). I pray every day that He will guide and direct me as I strive to bring up my children in the nurture and admonition of the Lord. ♡

When Your Child Is Sick

M. JEAN SOYKE, M.D.

One of the inevitable hardships that comes to any family is illness. If you find that you have a child who must be confined to bed for an extended period of time, you may find the following ideas helpful in relieving boredom and creating a *"merry heart (that) doeth good like a medicine"* (Proverbs 17:22).

1. Make a "Sunshine Box" for each child. Throughout the year, be on the lookout for good, inexpensive toys for bedridden children, such as coloring or puzzle books, stencils, stickers, paper dolls, small toys (such as farm animals or cowboys), simple wooden puzzles, easy crafts (such as embroidery or plastic lanyard), kaleidoscopes or Colorforms. Wrap the toys in colorful wrapping paper and store in the "Sunshine Box." When a child becomes ill, allow him to unwrap one or two toys per day and play with the new surprises. (Note: An old shower curtain or tablecloth can be spread over the child's bed when he is eating or using small toys; the sheet can be picked up and removed so that nothing is left on the bed.)

2. If you have some time to sit with your child, look through family photo albums or your high school yearbooks. Your child will particularly enjoy the stories that go with the pictures.

3. Involve the child's siblings in home care. Younger siblings may enjoy donning a paper nurse's hat or toy stethoscope and help care for the "patient" by bringing drinks or toys. Older siblings can use their creative talents to entertain the child with a puppet show, skit or fashion show.

4. Make food more appetizing by allowing your child some creativity in its presentation. Let your child use a table knife to cut sandwiches or toast into interesting shapes. Encourage him or her to find words in alphabet soup or pasta. (You can even tease, "Oh, no! You're eating a D-O-G!") Mix two small packages (or one large package) of flavored gelatin with 1-1/4 cups of hot water and cool the mixture in small cake pans. When the gelatin is hard, take a pan to your child and let him use cookie cutters or a table knife to cut it into interesting shapes.

5. Origami is a wonderful craft for bedridden children to learn. You can get instructional books from the library; origami paper is sold in craft stores, or you can cut regular paper into squares.

6. Children who are on the mend may want to participate in more active games. Wads of newspaper can be tossed from the bed into a box or trash can; rolled-up socks can be tossed into a drawer. Scrap paper can be folded and decorated to create paper airplanes. Strings can be attached to plastic darts or rings (for a ring-toss game); the child can then pull them back to play again without leaving the bed.

Illness can be stressful for a family, but with a little creativity, cooperation and prayer, it is a time that can be endured — maybe even enjoyed. ♡

Aliens, Hondas And A God Named Howard

SHARON JAYNES

What image comes into your mind when you read, "*Do not mistreat an alien*" (Exodus 22:21)? If you are a 4-year-old, you might have visions of little green men from Mars. And if you are a 10-year-old boy and read " ... *they lifted up their voices in one accord*" (Acts 4:24), you might have visions of a shiny four-door Honda sedan.

We have been reading the Bible together as a family since my son Steven was about 2 years old. It didn't take long for me to realize that what I heard from scripture and what Steven heard were sometimes totally different. One night my husband was reading about the prophet Nehemiah returning to the land of his forefathers when my 4-year-old son stopped him and exclaimed, "Wait a minute. How does somebody have four fathers?!" Since that time, we have made it a point to be very "interruptible" during family devotions.

It is important for us to remember that many words adults know from exposure to spiritual things may still be foreign to a young mind. For example, as a young child, a friend of mine thought God's name was "Howard" because he understood The Lord's Prayer to say, "Our Father Who art in heaven, Howard be your name." "Hallowed" was not a word in his vocabulary.

So during Bible reading time with young children, encourage questions and interruptions, ask them to summarize or tell you in their own words what they have just heard and try to think like a child to spot those words which could be easily misinterpreted. You may find family devotions full of many delightful surprises and very teachable moments! ♡

Train Him Up

PATRICIA POWELL TRIPP

I was standing outside on a beautiful spring day, watering the flowers. Our 14-year-old son came out the front door and plopped down on the step. His facial expression showed he was perplexed. "How's the homework going?" I questioned. "I can't seem to get started," he replied. "This paper is going to count as a test grade. I know if I can just get past the first paragraph I'll do fine." "Come on, I'll help," I said with encouragement.

After turning the water off, we went inside to tackle the project. I was his sounding board. While writing, he talked, causing a wellspring of ideas to come forth. He turned on the computer, concentration visible on his face. As we brainstormed, his imagination accelerated. His own concepts emerged. Writer's block was quickly defeated.

"If you don't need me anymore, I'll start dinner," I said as I got up off the floor. He replied emphatically, "I'm not hungry yet," which translated into, "I'm not ready for you to leave." He continued spouting thoughts requiring responses from me. At 14, he is ready to seize control of his life — yet something holds him back. Adult or child? Alive within him is a little of both.

Sitting on the floor, I watched him search the thesaurus for the perfect word. As the evening shadows crossed over his face, my eyes played tricks on me. In a moment, time flashed forward. College! How did we get here? Only a short time ago he was a baby! At the speed of light, I was back in the present. In three short years, a university dorm will be his home! Next summer, driver's ed.! Tears welled up in my eyes.

Blessed with this child/man growing up with us, we have busied ourselves preparing him for life. Now in his own metamorphosis, spirit, body and soul are changing simultaneously. The joy of a child one second, the mood swings of a teenager the next. What do we do with him? Let him be free as the wind? Or be as a kite in the flurry, controlled with twine that gives the illusion of freedom? If out of reach, a quick tug would reel him to safety. How do we know when to let go, and how much? Is this a man in a child's body or a child waiting to bloom into a man's body? Sitting at the kitchen table, he grumbles under his breath with displeasure.

The next instant he imparts a smile and tells about his day at school.

The Bible says to train them up in the way they should go and when they get old they will not turn from it. What happens between train and old? Pray he'll be blessed with a good wife, a healthy family and a prosperous future. Most of all pray that Jesus remains the center of his life. ♡

The Wonder Of You
To Steven: From Mom

SHARON JAYNES

I crept into your room today as the sun was peeking over the horizon. A single ray of light reaches through the blinds and illuminates your angelic face like a lone actor on a stage. Two tiny fists frame your olive face as you snuggle peacefully under your yellow blanket.

A small head, capped with black bushy hair. Long Bambi-like eye lashes. Perfectly formed cherub lips. A red forceps mark on your forehead. Knees curled and tucked under your tummy. A mound of love that just three days before kicked my ribs and moved inside my tummy, now sleeps in a crib and moves my heart.

Yellow gingham bumper pads frame this picture of sweetness, tranquility and love. I drink in the scent of baby powder, fresh wipes and lotion. A Noah's Ark soft, sculpted toy with 10 bulging pockets carry animals two-by-two. A bunny-shaped rattle. A tinkling music box. Stuffed animals with bright satin bows huddled in a corner. A beckoning white wicker rocker.

I stroked your head and watched you breathe, finding my chest in sync with yours. Three days old. My precious gift from God. What journeys await our family of three?

I crept into your room today and thanked God for the wonder of you.

I crept into your room today before my little man awoke. In just a few minutes you'd be calling out in your 2-year-old voice for mommy and daddy to get you out of your now too-small crib for a little snuggle time before dad is off to work.

The black hair has been replaced with golden corn silk capping your precious head. Long thick eye lashes now dubbed as "angel wings," rest on chubby cheeks.

The yellow blanket that once kept you warm now keeps you secure as you clutch it tightly to your side.

Somehow your thumb has found its way to your mouth and I hear the sound of gentle sucking.

Big Bird and Ernie wait patiently for their little friend to stir. A train parked in the corner. A stick horse tethered to the doorknob. Rubber balls and wooden blocks in a basket. Pop-up books, Richard Scarry's "Lowly Worm", "Busy People", "Things That Go" — all familiar friends crowded on the bookshelf.

Wooden puzzles, plastic trucks, card board tubes for jousting. A well-worn wicker rocker that has become my favorite spot in the house.

I stroked your blond head and watched your gentle breathing, still amazed that so much love could be found in one small package.

I crept into your room today and thanked God for the wonder of you.

I crept into your room today on this your first day of school. In Superman pajamas, hugging a well-worn Teddy bear, you dreamed of new friends and adventure.

A new shiny red lunch box sits on the dresser. Stiff new jeans and a crisp striped knit shirt laid out on the floor. A blue back pack stuffed with fresh crayons, markers and wide-ruled notebook paper, hangs from the door knob.

Plastic swords, playmobile Indians, Nerf balls, a sheriff's badge, cowboy boots. All would be motionless this day.

A T-Ball trophy on the dresser. A team picture of 12 miniature athletes smiling back at me from a red frame on the wall.

I stroked your sandy blond head and tears streamed down my cheeks. In just a few minutes, I'd be walking you down a sidewalk and entrusting my most valued possession into the hands of another woman.

Would your teacher know that you were the most creative child that God has ever fashioned?

Would she know that you already knew your ABC's and could count to 100?

Would she know that you had already asked Jesus to come into your heart and could recite the Lord's Prayer and Twenty-third Psalm?

Would she know that you needed lots of hugs?

Would she know that this was one of the hardest days of my life?

Oh how I'm going to miss my little man today.

I crept into your room today and thanked God for the wonder of you.

I crept into your room today before the sun made its way into the morning sky. You, my little soldier, lay tangled in the sheets with Beary, the white polar bear, tucked under your arm and staring admiringly into his charges tranquil face.

The cars and trucks wall paper has been replaced by plaids and coat-of-arms.

Baseballs hats hang from the corners of your four-poster bed. Soccer pictures line the walls. A Boy Scout handbook. Well-worn matchbox cars parked in a slotted carrying case. Stray Legos peek from under the bed. G. I. Joe's back from their latest mission share a shelf with hard-to-part-with stuffed animals. A flash light rests on "The Chronicles of Narnia."

I stroked your head and wondered if you had any idea how much I have loved being your mom for these past 10 years.

I crept into your room today and thanked God for the wonder of you.

I crept into your room today before the day was new. Breaking all the new rules of privacy and personal space, I gazed at my 12-year-old young man with a sense of awe. A knowing Michael Jordan smiled at me from a poster taped on the closet door.

Muddy baseball pants hang over a chair. Inverted tube socks wadded up and tossed in a corner. A CD player, headphones and magazines. Deodorant, boxers, and fuzzy legs.

Five feet 9 inches of muscle and bone — a man child metamorphosing before my very eyes.

A school yearbook open to page 87 where Rosemary's smiling face had been the last thing on your mind. A new era was on the horizon.

I whispered a prayer over your sleeping form as I rubbed your sandy head. A prayer of protection, purity and purpose.

I crept into your room today and thanked God for the wonder of you.

I crept into your room today before the alarm signaled the dawn of a new day. Your 6-foot frame lays angled across the mattress. A man's hairy leg peeks out from under the tangled sheet. Your face needs a shave. A muscular arm hugs a willing pillow.

The chubby cheeks and pug nose have been replaced with handsome, sharp, angular lines. A strong jawbone. A determined nose. A thick shock of unruly hair.

A geometry book leans against the dresser. Ribbons and plaques from races won proudly hang from the floor lamp arm. A rack of neck ties and khakis mingle with T-shirts and jeans. A track team warm up suit slung over a chair. A basketball letter and pin lean against the mirror. An electric guitar, amplifier, distorter and Christian punk CD's.

A TARHEELS license plate rests on an easel, pointing to future dreams.

My little boy has become a man — in the twinkling of an eye, in the flash of a moonbeam, in the time it takes a shooting star to traverse the night sky.

I smooth your thick hair and watch your chest rise and fall. What a gift you have been to me. How will I ever let you go?

Today I drive you to the Department of Motor Vehicles to pick up your license to new freedoms. I go as a driver, but return as a passenger.

A tear escapes my eye and trickles down my chin as I am reminded once again that this chapter of my life is coming closer to an end.

I crept into your room today and thanked God for the wonder of you. ♡

The McDonald's Of Money

RENEE SWOPE

ave you ever thought about a child's perspective of money? Most of them know that it doesn't grow on trees, but if I were a child, I'd wonder whether they serve it at McDonald's. Now that's pretty silly you might say, but when was the last time you pulled up to the "drive-thru" money window, pressed a few buttons and rode away with cash? To a child, getting money is as easy as ordering fries and a milkshake.

As parents, it's vital that we teach our children the proper perspective of money. In order for our children to understand why we can't afford everything their hearts' desire, they need to see where our money comes from and where it goes. When our children are old enough to understand, my husband and I plan to bring home his paycheck in cash and then divide it out according to our budget categories. This way our children can participate in paying the bills and planning for extra purchases. We may even use cash envelopes for each category and when the cash is gone, nothing else can be purchased until the envelope is filled again.

It's also important that we teach our children to be faithful stewards. A great idea I've heard is to make a bank with three sections: giving, saving and spending. When your child earns money, teach them early on to automatically give back 10% to God, save 10% and use the rest for spending.

I believe the Lord also wants our children to see the value of a giving spirit. We should be the best example they see by giving food to the needy and encouraging them to give some of their toys to less fortunate children. Remember Jesus' words in Luke 6:40, *"Everyone, after he is fully trained, will be like his teacher."* ♡

Reading Aloud To Your Children

JULIE REIMER

*A*s a part-time reading and language arts teacher in a public secondary school, I constantly strive to provide positive reading materials for my students. I read aloud each day in class and always offer suggestions for reading when the classes visit the media center. But I believe the message of moral choices in the things our children read begins in the home, and thus I have started educating parents on the importance of selecting good books for their children. In the school setting, I encourage parents to read aloud to their children and offer tips and suggestions for selections. In the Christian setting, I offer a few sessions each year to adults in the congregation about the importance of reading out loud to the children in their lives.

I rely heavily on the research and materials presented in "The Read Aloud Handbook" (1995, Penguin Books) by author Jim Trelease. In it are strong cases for reading aloud, the how-tos of starting out, some dos and don'ts, and comparisons between the influence of television versus the influence of reading on children's imaginations, reading abilities and tendencies toward negative behaviors.

In my sessions I stress that the single most important indicator of school success is reading ability and a love of reading. This begins as soon as children are exposed to books and reading aloud, and should ideally start when children are very young.

Reading proponents recommend that children get at least 15 minutes each day of read-aloud time. In our home, we read aloud 30 minutes before nap and bed times, and the children also pick up books on their own several times during the day and "read" them silently. If these numbers seem like a lot, compare them to television watching. An average child will watch approximately 1,300 hours of television (including videos) this year alone! That breaks down to about two hours each day!

Here are the most frequent questions I am asked, along with my replies:

How do I choose age-appropriate materials? Generally, materials can be judged on their length and illustrations when choosing books that are age appropriate. For instance, "Pat the Bunny" with its interactive style and short text is great for the youngest of readers. Younger readers also love board books which they can handle and not seriously damage.

119

But if children are read to from an early age and develop longer attention spans as their love of reading increases, those factors may not be so important. Age appropriateness is important, but so are a child's interests.

When, where and how should I read aloud? Read aloud DAILY! For younger children, it might be best to read aloud first thing in the morning when everything is fresh and attention is high. Or you may choose to relax with books at nap or bedtimes as our family does.

As long as young children will allow it, I recommend cuddling a child on your lap as you read aloud. That physical bond adds to the love of being read to. You might also choose to read aloud on your child's bed each night or while lying on the floor. Just make sure there are no other distractions.

If you are uncomfortable about reading aloud, remember that the listener does not have the ability or the confidence to do what you are doing. Simply read to the children as you would speak. When you feel confident and enthusiastic, add voices and sound effects. But always read so that the kids can see the pictures. If you're really daring, teach yourself to read upside down!

My recommendation is to let the child choose the book in most cases. Children often choose the same book each day or choose books on the same topic (e.g., dinosaurs, trains, animals). Although it may get monotonous for the reader, kids love repetition.

The exception in letting kids choose the books comes later on, I believe. When they are young, I choose what books come into my home and get no complaints from my children. However, even when they are older, I believe it is my duty as a parent to be aware of what my children read. As a teacher, I read young adult books so that I can be a credible source for my students, and they never once complain when I restrict horror novels (like the popular *Goosebumps* series). Parents need to be aware of what their children are reading and make the decision about whether it falls in line with their values and morals.

How do I get all of these books? The most logical free choice, of course, is the public library system. Children love the importance associated with having their own library card and being able to select books that THEY want to bring home. Low-cost options for book purchases are garage sales and second-hand book stores, and school book clubs have a number of good books at relatively low prices. Another way to bring books into the home is to suggest them as gifts and to give them to others. ♡

Preserving Family Memories

SHARON JAYNES

There are times we enjoy our families so much that we wish we could make time stand still. Even though that is an impossibility, below are some creative ways to preserve those memories that will last long after our children are grown.

- Make a birthday memory book. Each year, include a picture of the child and a description of the celebration. Also include a typical day, events and headlines of the year and goals for the following year.
- Save school work from each year that portrays the child's personality and interests. Store each year in a separate, labeled accordion file folder. It's also fun to save some lower grades so they have them to share with their children.
- Write a letter to your child on her first day of kindergarten and give it to her the day she graduates from high school.
- If your child becomes a Christian at an early age, have him give his testimony on tape. This way they'll never doubt when they made the most important decision in their life.
- Mark children's growth with dates on a select door frame in your house.
- Make a Christmas memory book with a family photo and a letter recounting important events from each year. Store the book with the Christmas ornaments and read each letter from the previous year before decorating the tree.
- Make Christmas ornaments from children's school pictures each year.
- Make imprints of their hands in plaster purchased from your local craft store.
- Save calendars as keepsakes of those many family activities.
- Take pictures of first events such as first steps, first ball game and first date.
- Tape record your child telling their own created stories. You can also transcribe those stories as a keepsake to read to them later.
- Send announcements of special awards or achievements to your local newspaper. Your child will enjoy the recognition and you will have the clipping.
- Videotape the everyday events at home such as dad wrestling with the kids, mom baking cookies, the family washing the car, etc. These times can be some of the most meaningful to look back on. ♡

121

It's Time For A Change

STEVE PERDUE

My precious husband, Steve, wrote this article for the Sooner On Guard newspaper of which he is the editor. He is the principal of a junior high school and a wonderful husband and father. His sense of humor and ability to communicate keep me going on difficult days. His arms are always open and he's always willing to love me. I thank God for giving me Steve Perdue. This article just tickled me pink the first time I read it and still tickles me today!
— Donna Perdue

Many who know me know that my wife and I just had our second child. She did most of the work, of course, but I like to think that I did my part. Something else that many of you won't believe ... I don't change diapers. It's not that I am not willing, it's just that my wife prefers that I not, and since none of the diapers use diaper pins anymore, I'm not sure just why she prefers this.

It happened just before church one week. My wife had 15 things going at once, we were running late and the baby needed changing. It was not just a routine change, but one of those "number two" doozies. I thought I could really earn some points and possibly keep my preferred husband status if I volunteered to change that didy.

Of course, there's nothing to changing didys. I've watched her do it many times. She always starts out by cooing and pressing her face close to the baby and talking to him. "Ohhh, it's okay. Momma's got you. Let's just lie here and get you all cleaned up." (You know how that baby talk goes.) Well, she lays the kid down, and in one continuous motion, takes the old didy off, cleans the posterior, powders, lotions, creams, conditions, kisses and puts the clean diaper on. Its simplicity is almost a work of art. With the advent of Velcro, even a kid could change one.

I knew what to do. "Come here, baby," I cooed. "Let's lay down here and Daddy will get you all cleaned up." By the time I figured out how to get down to the didy, the baby already suspected that I was a rookie.

Snaps are a simple thing of course, but finding them was not. I managed to get the dirty didy undone but was not quite prepared for the RLMs (Rapid Leg Movements) which followed. Baby only has two feet, but it seemed like more as I tried to keep them out of the chocolate-colored mess he had made. Now, try to remember, I told myself: How did she hold these legs and clean the baby at the same time? Oh, man, there goes a stream of "number one" all over the place. I'll clean that up later. And why is this baby screaming like I'm hurting him? What would be wrong with taking him to the kitchen sink and using that sprayer to rinse him off? I thought about calling for help many times, but was not ready to admit defeat. So, several minutes and a half a box of wipes later, I presented the child to his mother, all clean and almost calmed down, hoping that Mom would realize just how nice I was to help out.

This experience reminded me of a few nuggets of wisdom which are worth repeating. (Hey, there is a moral to all of this.)

a.   Things worth doing are worth doing poorly until you can do them well.
b.   All things are difficult before they are easy.
c.   Practice makes perfect.
d.   Nothing takes the place of on-the-job training.
e.   Behind every flawless Olympic performance are hours of practice.
f.   If something stinks, change it. ♡

Travel With Baby

ELIZABETH SEWING

With the birth of our first child, my husband and I thought that one of our favorite pastimes, traveling, would be over for a while. However, after a week's vacation with our 6-month-old, we were pleasantly surprised by how enjoyable and relaxing the trip turned out. Here are some helpful ideas:

1. Have realistic expectations. Instead of the usual sightseeing marathon, aim for a slower-paced schedule that works around your baby's nap times, which will minimize fussing while you are out. After a morning of touring and lunch, return to your lodgings so Baby can take a nap while you relax, read or take a nap yourself.

2. Besides hotels, consider a bed-and-breakfast, guest house or cabin. Check with the chamber of commerce for family accommodations. We rented a small attic apartment in a guest house for a reasonable rate, with kitchenette and a sitting room which was ideal for the baby's equipment.

3. Compact baby equipment, like an umbrella stroller and "Pack-N-Play" playpen/portable crib, works great. Add a few toys, floor gym and bouncing seat, which packs well when disassembled. At the last minute we even added the swing (disassembled) and got everything into our little Nissan Sentra.

4. When driving to your destination, shopping malls are excellent places to stop for a meal. The ladies' lounge in department stores usually has nice facilities for nursing and changing diapers.

5. Baby will enjoy activities such as walking tours which are suited for strollers.

6. Take turns with your spouse watching the baby while the other goes to an exhibit, shopping, etc.

7. Take a basket of treats like favorite teas or coffee, chocolates, bubble bath and scented candles. After baby goes to bed, order room service or takeout and have a romantic evening with your spouse. ♡

Making Car Time Fun

SHARON JAYNES

"If a mom's place is in the home, why am I always in the car?" Moms today spend so much time in the car and those times can be awful or awesome. Here are some creative ways to make car time fun.

FOR SMALL CHILDREN

Snacks — Pack something for the road such as goldfish crackers, Cheerios and juice.

Toys — Keep a special box just for the car. Pass toys back one at a time.

Stories/books on tape — "Adventures in Odyssey" audio cassettes from "Focus on the Family" are a favorite. Each story is about 25 minutes long and they are good for children of all ages. Set up a lending system with other families. For books on tape, check out your public library's selection.

Music — Listen to classical or praise music and ask the children what pictures or stories come into their minds as they listen to the melody. As the melody or the tempo changes, ask what they think is happening now. Ask if they can pick out different instruments such as the violin or drum.

Sunglasses — Have a pair handy for each child. Some children can get very fussy or even contract headaches when the sun is constantly in their eyes.

Planning/calling ahead — Make lists of errands in advance to prevent back-tracking. Call to verify that something is ready before leaving the house.

Create teachable moments — If your preschooler is learning shapes, ask him or her to point out circles, squares and triangles on traffic signs, billboards or anything you see along the way.

FOR ELEMENTARY-AGE CHILDREN

Seating plan — Prevent arguing over who gets to sit where by creating seating assignments and changing them monthly. Separate kids who don't get along well.

Traffic Bingo — Cut a 6 x 8 inch rectangle and draw a grid with five spaces across and five down. In each square put signs or things commonly seen in traffic. The center square is the free space. Draw the signs or cut them out from a Department of Motor Vehicles book. When all the pictures are in place, cover the card with clear contact paper. Use erasable markers or small dot stickers to play.

Verbal Math Games — Use speed limit signs. For example, a 35 miles-per-hour sign might prompt the question, "What's 3 x 5 (or 3 + 5)?"

"Who Am I?" — Someone in the car picks a person they pretend to be. Others take turns asking "yes" and "no" questions until they figure out who the person is. The only rule is the person must be someone everyone in the car has heard of.

Word search books and maze books — Find them in your local bookstore or toy store.

Mad Libs — These are booklets of short stories that have key words left out. The writer asks the other travelers in the car for nouns, verbs, adverbs or adjectives to fill in the blanks. After completing it, the scribe reads the story with the new words filled in. The results are usually hilarious.

Animal counting — Count them all or specify a certain kind, such as black cows.

Storytelling — One person makes up the first line. Then go around the car, each person adding the next.

Alphabet game — Start with the letter "A" and look for all the letters of the alphabet in order. Look on signs, billboards — anything with words.

Brainteasers — Like riddles but usually a little bit harder, these are available in both book and board game forms.

Scrapbook — Buy each child a scrapbook and let him or her draw a picture or describe what they saw each day. They may want to include postcards, maps or small souvenirs in the book.

License plate game — Look for plates from other states. If you are traveling long distances, keep a U.S. map in the car and mark each state as you spot it. This also helps kids learn their U.S. geography. ♡

Children's Corner

MARY ELLEN BIANCO

ave some fun with your little children. This is a recipe they can help make and then enjoy. It's sure to keep them busy for a few minutes. Kids love play dough and this recipe is not as messy as the store-bought kind.

Play Dough
1 c. flour
1/2 c. salt
1 T. oil
2 tsp. cream of tartar
1 c. water

Cook in microwave or on the stove until no longer sticky; knead to smooth. For extra fun, add food color while cooking. Store in Tupperware or zip bags, but NOT IN A TIN CONTAINER. ♡

A Queen's Visit

MARY BETH SPRY
MELISSA CVETOVICH BOOTHE

Our mother was always creative when we were growing up, giving us many memories to cherish. We know in the future more will follow. As adults, we've already repeated some of them with our three small children (all under 2-1/2 years of age). One of our favorites was the way Mom taught us table manners.

When we were around 7 and 9, our mother decided it was time to teach us proper table manners. All along she had been showing us how to hold our utensils and telling us not to use our "pusher" finger to assist stray peas onto our fork. Finally, the time came to put our knowledge to a test.

Dad was away on a business trip, so our table of four now had an empty chair. Mother told us when we sat down to eat that the Queen had come to dinner. The Queen was sitting in the empty chair and we were instructed to be on our best behavior and eat properly. Of course Mom did the same. That evening was a huge success! Mother told us after the meal how good we were and how proud she was of us. We were beaming and couldn't stop talking about the Queen. Needless to say the Queen returned the next night.

During those meals, our mother showed us how to set the table properly. We had to pass everything around the table before we could eat and we had to sample all the food. It just wasn't polite to not take the potatoes if the Queen had made them. We learned to put butter on our plate and then pass it on. We learned where to set the knife after using it and the all important technique of using bread or our knife to push those peas onto the fork. Those meals were lessons right out of Emily Post. We didn't even know we were learning. Our mother always said afterwards that she felt comfortable taking us to friends' houses for dinner or out to eat. Now that we are parents, we know she had a few anxious moments, but she never let on.

The Queen's visit still exists. To this day if a table "faux pas" occurs, we all say, "I don't think the Queen would approve," then we laugh. We tried the Queen's visit when our dad was at home, but it just wasn't the same. There was something special about playing with Mom. Thanks, Mom, for always going the special mile to teach us. ♡

Responding To Children With Disabilities

TERESA SCISM

Many parents struggle with teaching their children how to respond to children with disabilities. It is heartbreaking for adults and sometimes scary for children when they see a child with a disability. Because of that, we often respond in ways that can be embarrassing or hurtful for the special child.

My son, Drew, is 12 years old and has Muscular Dystrophy. He has been unable to walk for several years. He uses a motorized wheelchair. When Drew was in first grade, he began to use a manual chair for long distances. After talking with the teacher and Drew, we brought the chair to school. I explained Muscular Dystrophy in a very simple way and answered his classmates' questions. Each child got to ride in the chair or push it. It really helped the children to experience the chair first-hand and ask questions.

Drew's friends have always been very encouraging and supportive. They have made sacrifices to be with him and include him. His friends don't focus on the disability, just their friend. Drew is very active and involved at our church and in Boy Scouts where he enjoys being with his friends and participating in the activities. It also helps the children to see people with disabilities included in all possible activities. They realize that he's just like them except for the physical limitations. I encourage parents of children with disabilities to help their child be involved with their peers. Church, scouts, school activities and parties are all great opportunities. It will require a tremendous amount of time and energy, but the rewards for the child are priceless.

Parents might want to begin teaching their children how to respond by reminding them that God created and loves all children. As Joni Erickson Tada once said, "Red and yellow, black and white; standing, sitting, blind and with sight; Jesus loves all the children of the world." Encourage them to reach out and get to know the child with special needs. They will learn this best by your example.

Look for ways you can include the child in your activities. One of Drew's friends chose to have his birthday party at a local bowling alley that has a special ramp for bowlers with disabilities. When Drew is invited to the movies, we meet the child and his parents at the theater. The children in the neighborhood have always adapted the rules to games so he can participate. When someone new doesn't follow along, the children quickly set them straight.

Finally, remind your child not to stare or ask questions that might make the special child uncomfortable. Drew doesn't mind questions about his chair and how it works, but he's not always comfortable talking about why he has to use the chair.

When Drew was a toddler, we prayed for special friends; at that time, we didn't know he had Muscular Dystrophy. God answered our prayer. His friends and his younger brother, David, are truly gifts from our heavenly Father. God is using them to teach us His great command, *"Love one another."* ♡

From Diaper Cream To Acne Cream

SHARON JAYNES

*W*ait a minute here! Yesterday it was diaper cream and today it's acne cream. How did that happen? Well, I guess it wasn't yesterday, but it surely does feel like it.

The year that my son turned 12 held many traumatic changes (for his mother, that is). He started middle school, which meant changing classes, but I didn't realize that so many other things would change as well. His voice dropped an octave, the smell of the laundry took a definite turn for the worse and his 5'7" passed my 5'5". For the first time since kindergarten, Steven told me that it really wasn't necessary for me to drive on one of his class field trips. That translates, "I'd rather you not go, Mom." I was crushed, but it was my job as a good parent not to make him feel guilty about his growing need for independence.

Then there was the swing set. When Steven was 3 years old, my husband built this awesome wooden swing set with two swings, a trapeze bar, a slide and a two-story fort. For several years, I would squeeze through the door of the upper level of the fort where Steven and I ate many a lunch. Of course, we never ate in the lower level, because that was the jail and "nobody wants to eat in a jail."

At age 12 Steven brought to my attention that the swing set hadn't seen much action in the past year and that he could barely fit through the fort doors. Of course, I thought that was ridiculous because I could still fit through the doors. But then he reminded me that he was bigger than I was. He and my husband wanted to take the swing set down and put up something else in its place. We took a family vote and I lost two to one. The shrine to Steven's childhood came down and a gazebo was erected.

A final blow came at breakfast one morning when Steven looked up and sheepishly told me that Monday was the birthday of a particular girl in his class. I could tell that this was not meant to be small talk. Knowing that there was to be more to this story, I said, "And?" He went on to say, "And, I'd like to get her a little something. I'll use my own money." This was hard to take, knowing that I was now not the only girl in Steven's life. But without flinching, I took him to a gift shop and helped him pick out "a little something."

Independence from parents and dependence on the Lord. That's what I have prayed as the ultimate for my child as he enters into adulthood. But cutting those apron strings can be hard, even at 12. However, I know that if I don't keep those scissors sharp, and clip them gradually when it's time, they'll be ripped out and torn apart later.

As I prayed about all these changes that seemed to be coming too fast and too soon, the Holy Spirit brought to my mind another mother who faced many changes as her Son turned 12. She and her husband had taken their 12-year-old Son on His first journey to Jerusalem to celebrate the Passover. On their way back home, they noticed that their Son was missing. They frantically searched the caravan, only to come up empty handed. Finally, three days later, they found Him back in the Jerusalem temple, listening and asking questions of the teachers.

I think that Jesus' 12th year was probably a traumatic time for Mary as well. And if we had been there, and if Mary had worn an apron, we probably could have heard a snip. What a privilege Mary had to be the earthly mother of Jesus, even though it was only for a short time. And what a privilege I have had to be the mother of a precious son, also knowing that he is God's gift to me for a short season. Mothers through the ages have had to learn the awesome lesson of letting go of their children. But when we realize that they are merely going from our arms to the Father's, the transition can be sweet and the apron strings a little easier to snip.

This and additional inspirational stories by Sharon Jaynes can be found in her book "At Home With God — Stories Of Life, Love and Laughter," published by Honor Books. Release date: Fall 2000. Used in this work with permission from the publisher. ♡

CHAPTER *Four*

Practicing Servanthood

"SHE OPENS HER ARMS TO THE POOR AND

EXTENDS HER HANDS TO THE NEEDY"

PROVERBS 31:20

The Importance Of Mentoring

JULIE LAWING

Kathy Murray knows the importance of mentoring. At one time, this wife and mother of four was working 50 hours a week while trying to homeschool her children, ages 15 to 3. She shared her struggles with me. "I thought I could be Super Christian Mom, but every night I would fall into bed and cry. It was really a farce. My Christianity was riding the fence, I was not a good witness, our children were suffering and there was no peace in our home," she recalls.

Then the Lord directed an unexpected friend into Kathy's life, a Christian woman who began sharing the Titus 2 scriptures with her. The woman voiced her beliefs that Christian women should be discrete, chaste, keepers of their home and holy before Him. Soon after their introduction, Kathy was fired from her job as the result of an injury. She began spending time with her new friend each week. In addition to providing spiritual guidance, her mentor taught Kathy how to bake bread, sew and care for her household. Raised without the guidance of a mother, Kathy had long yearned for such instruction in the art of homemaking. Kathy thought, "Why haven't other women shared their wisdom and experience?"

> *As Kathy began to implement the godly things she was learning, she noticed the atmosphere in her home changed drastically — for the better.*

As Kathy began to implement the godly things she was learning, she noticed the atmosphere in her home changed drastically — for the better. As she learned how to love her husband and accept his authority in the house, she noticed changes manifesting in him as well. "He speaks to me in a gentler voice and is more at peace with himself because his house is more peaceful. He can relax and make decisions without me second-guessing him. Lately, we've had more peace than we've ever experienced in our 13 years of marriage," she notes.

Mentoring has also made Kathy more accountable to her actions and attitude. "Now I have a 24-hour watch in effect on what I say and do. There's more of a check in my spirit. I still mess up, but I'm more often aware of whether I am pleasing to the Lord or not," she observes.

"We need to be careful that we don't make mentoring a career or something that takes away from our family, but we do need to be willing to share our convictions more boldly," cautions Kathy. "If my friend hadn't shared with me, I probably would be in the same ugly situation I was in." She sees her primary assignment as mentoring her daughters, teaching them what He expects them to be. "I wish there were more Christian women who would share their convictions about being a godly woman and talk more about the calling the Lord has given them. There are many young women struggling as I was. The older women should step in and teach them." ♡

From The Mentor

RUTH ANN WILSON

WANTED: OLDER WOMEN TO MENTOR YOUNGER WOMEN. Do you qualify? If you saw a new mother struggling to change a diaper and you had successfully changed thousands (or so it seemed), could you give an encouraging and helpful hint or two? If you heard a new bride lamenting the task of trying to get dinner on the table every night (with all the food cooked and served warm), could you give a few favorite quick and easy recipes?

I don't want to turn anyone off before you have a chance to read beyond "mentor." What an intimidating word! I wonder if that is why so many older women don't want to mentor younger women. Or could it be the word "older" that makes them decline? I don't think of myself as a mentor, just a friend. I certainly did not (and still don't) have all the answers; however, I do know the One who does. I am willing to share what has and has not worked for me.

On some occasions in the past, mothers have called me or asked to meet with me. Sometimes these initial contacts developed into weekly visits. I began to see a need for friendships where women just spent time together talking. Years ago, extended families lived closer together and visited more often. Questions that arose about housekeeping, children and motherhood would be answered quickly over a cup of coffee or during many other family gatherings.

Have you ever had a day when everything goes wrong, you wake up late, the car won't start, the roast is raw, and you have company coming? Have you ever felt like the title of Barbara Johnson's book, "Where Does A Mother Go To Resign?" Well, I have. In fact, just yesterday was one of those days. Even though my children are older, it is not any different for me. As a mentor, I share various incidents — the good, the bad, the ugly - and I am reminded of God's faithfulness to bring us through these times (Ecclesiastes 4:9-10)

If we saw someone stumbling, we wouldn't hesitate to reach out and keep her from injury. Mentoring is the same thing, so why do we stay silent and stand back when we know how to help another woman? We so easily get caught up in how we feel about ourselves. If you dare to reach out in this area, you may discover the satisfaction and fulfillment you were lacking and looking for elsewhere. Some of God's most precious blessings are realized when we trust and obey.

WANTED: EXPERIENCED WOMEN TO MENTOR INEXPERIENCED WOMEN. Do you qualify? ♡

A Tisket, A Tasket, Put Some Love In A Basket

LYSA TERKEURST

*H*as the Lord ever put someone on your heart who may need an act of kindness? It may be a friend in crisis or just someone in need of a little encouragement. The Bible tells us in Romans 12:9-13 *"Love must be sincere. Hate what is evil; cling to what is good. Be devoted to one another in brotherly love. Honor one another above yourselves. Never be lacking in zeal, but keep your spiritual fervor, serving the Lord. Be joyful in hope, patient in affliction, faithful in prayer. Share with God's people who are in need. Practice hospitality."*

When my daughter Ashley was 12 months old, she had to have emergency surgery. I can't tell you how much it meant to have our friends reach out to us by making dinner, running errands, keeping our older daughter and bringing us encouraging cards. One friend put together a gift basket with a beautiful tin filled with cookies and a small Christian book. These acts of love not only touched our hearts, but it was also a great witness for the other people in the hospital to see what it's like to be involved with people who love the Lord. I've decided to make it one of my goals to practice hospitality and heed to the Lord's calling when He puts people on my heart. Here are some ideas to help you get started:

- Once a week during your quiet time ask the Lord to bring to mind people in need of an encouraging word. Then write to that person and let them know they were lifted up in prayer that day.

- When grocery shopping, plan to pick up a few extra goodies to put together a "love basket" for anyone who may be in need of a smile.

- Call a friend and offer to watch her children while she plans a romantic surprise for her husband.

- Pick wildflowers with your children to give to a neighbor and attach the verse from Romans.

- Host a summer recipe swap where everyone brings one dish, along with copies of their favorite recipes to share. Encourage all who attend to cook dinner for a working mom they know.

- Pass along your copy of the *Proverbs 31 Ministry* newsletter to a friend in need of a little encouragement. ♡

Six Ways To Welcome
A New Neighbor

GINGER McGRATH

I remember my neighbor Katrina. The day we arrived at our new house, Katrina greeted us with a plate of cookies and a friendly hello. It wasn't long before I trusted her with a spare house key. I also trusted her with my children. In a pinch, if I couldn't be home when the kids got out of school, I could call her and she'd be there for me. During our vacation she'd water my house plants and flower beds and bring in the mail. She'd join me for a trip to the store or a cup of tea. Katrina was a good neighbor.

A good neighbor is special. In order to have a good neighbor we must first be a good neighbor. Sometimes we get so carried along in life's rushing river we overlook the occasional tributary that joins our path. In this case that tributary is a new neighbor in need of a friend.

Here are six practical ways for welcoming a new neighbor:

1. Introduce yourself. Chances are you will run into your new neighbor outside. If so, be friendly, go right up and introduce yourself. If not, a thoughtful gesture is to initiate a visit with a loaf of friendship bread or plate of cookies. She may be shy.

2. Offer helpful information. Practical things like the best supermarket, closest hospital and a good doctor are invaluable. If she has children she'll want to know about the school system, parks and recreation and city programs. Take her for a tour of the city or a trip through the mall. She may be restless. Be a Welcome Wagon for Jesus — the family may be new in town.

3. Invite them to church. It's the perfect opportunity. If you and the lady of the house are both home during the day, you could also invite her to your ladies' Bible study or a social function.

4. Acquaint your new neighbor with your other friends. For instance, if she is a young mother of preschoolers and your children are teens, introduce her to another young mother you know. Perhaps have them both over for a cup of coffee. She may be lonely.

141

5. Be sensitive to their needs. If your new neighbor is without a car during the day, offer to pick up groceries on your next trip to the market; better yet, take her along. If you plan an outing with the kids to the park and your new neighbor has kids, invite them to join in the fun. The kids may be lonely, too.

6. Share your faith. As your relationship builds into a trusting friend-ship and she's not a believer, you'll have occasions to share your faith. If she already knows our Lord, you'll be blessed by the sweet fellowship of another sister. Reach out in Jesus' name! She may be ripe for the harvest. ♡

Going Fishing

BONITA LILLIE

According to I John 5:3, to love God is to obey His commands. I thought I was really loving God and walking closely with Him until I examined my life one day. I lived with my Christian family, went to my Christian church, visited my Christian friends, went to Christian Bible studies and returned to my Christian home. Although this was a very comfortable, cozy lifestyle, I was neglecting what was most dear to the heart of God: the lost and perishing world for which He sent His son to die. In the gospel of Mark, Jesus begins and ends his ministry on the same note, winning the lost. Obviously, this is important to God. I reasoned in my heart that if it was so important to God then it had better become important to me.

I knew that I would need to become more sensitive to the needs of those around me and accept opportunities to minister as they came my way daily, but I also wanted to set aside time specifically for evangelizing. Hence, the idea came for a "fishing day."

On my first fishing day I prayed and allowed God to make my agenda and then set out keeping my eyes, ears and heart open for opportunities He would bring my way. It was a fairly typical day. In the morning the children and I did the grocery shopping, then contractors came to replace the windows in our house and in the afternoon I attended a book fair alone. Although I met a lot of new people and was able to serve others in some new ways, I questioned the Lord when I arrived home. After all, this was a fishing day and I hadn't caught a fish. Then I received a phone call from a non-Christian friend I hadn't seen or spoken with in 15 years. As we conversed the topic turned to God and for a solid hour I explained to her what it meant to be a Christian and have a personal relationship with Jesus. What a great ending to my fishing day.

I'm determined to make fishing days a regular part of my schedule. As homemakers we're incredibly busy. It's so easy to get caught up in our smug little worlds and forget everyone else out there, but God will always have a heart for the lost and so must we. ♡

Fishing Day

BONITA LILLIE

GRAB YOUR ROD,

PUT SOME BAIT ON THE LINE

FOR I HEAR THE FISH

ARE BITING MIGHTY FINE.

IF YOU DON'T KNOW WHAT TO DO

JUST GET YOUR FEET WET,

OBEY THE WORD OF GOD

AND LET DOWN YOUR NET.

YIELD YOUR HEART TO JESUS

FOR HE WILL LEAD THE WAY

AND YOU'LL COME HOME REJOICING

WITH THE CATCH OF THE DAY! ♡

The Order Of Friendships

JENNIFER SCHROEDER

A beautiful story of friendship is found in Luke 1. Mary and Elizabeth experienced the mighty hand of God working in their lives. The Lord allowed them to share their experiences and to encourage one another. What a blessing they were to each other! As I read about their friendship, I asked the Lord why He had not blessed me with an Elizabeth — a true friend who knew and understood me. Over a year had passed since the Lord led us to move to a city far from our friends and family. Although I was involved in many areas of our church and community, I had not developed a deep and special friendship.

I asked the Lord why Mary was given the privilege of bearing the Christ child. What qualities made her "highly favored" in His sight? In His ever-gentle way, the Lord began to reveal what He saw in Mary. She knew how to praise and exalt the Lord (Luke 1:46). She knew the scriptures and the promises they contained. Proverbs 31:26 described her, *"She speaks with wisdom and faithful instruction is on her tongue."* She was entrusted with teaching and nurturing the Son of God! Mary *"treasured up all these things and pondered them in her heart"* (Luke 2:19). She was not the type to gossip or be undisciplined in her chatter or emotions. She knew what it meant to be *"quick to hear, slow to speak"* (James 1:19). She was a woman adorned with the *"imperishable jewel of a gentle and quiet spirit, which in God's sight is very precious"* (I Peter 3:4). She was secure in her relationship with God, not only His servant but also His friend. Psalm 25:14 was real to her: *"The Lord confides in those who fear (revere and worship) Him, He makes His covenant known to them."*

I realized I was seeking friendships with others while the Lord desired to be my dearest and closest friend.

145

As the Lord showed me the beautiful qualities Mary possessed and how she sought God above everything else in her life and knew Him intimately, I realized I was seeking friendships with others while the Lord desired to be my dearest and closest friend. He wants me to look to Him when I need comfort, encouragement, companionship and fellowship. He told me He would confide in me and make His promises known to me.

Mary did not desire popularity, a busy social calendar or an answering machine full of messages. She sought *"first His kingdom and His right-eousness, and all these things were given to her as well"* (Matt. 6:33). This is not to say that God did not create women with a need to fellowship with other women. Mary and Elizabeth's relationship was truly a blessing from the Lord. God desires to bless us with our Elizabeth and give us the desires of our heart (Psalm 20:4). But first and foremost, He calls us to be like Mary — to have an intimate relationship with Him.

Homemaker, if you are struggling with loneliness and wondering why God has not blessed you with an Elizabeth, ask Him to show you His plans for you. Allow Him to fill that need for companionship and fellowship in your life. If the Lord *has* given you an Elizabeth, remember to thank Him for His blessing. ♡

Blessing Your Neighborhood Through Love And Prayer

PART I

MARY LANCE V. SISK

*"But seek first His kingdom and His righteousness,
and all these things will be given to you as well."* Matthew 6:33

This is the friendliest neighborhood we've ever lived in!" ...

"Every time I enter your neighborhood I feel peace." ...

"I need your prayers." ...

"Next week my daughter will celebrate her first anniversary of being born again!" ...

"My daughter has become religious like you." ...

"I've lent the Christian book you gave me to five people this year. May I have another one?" ...

"I don't know what's happened to me, but I weep so easily at church these days." ... and so it goes. These snips of conversation with several neighbors of mine over time bear powerful witness to God working in my neighborhood. Want to know the secret? The blessings were given as God's people were obedient to the Royal Law of Love as given to us by Jesus and repeated in James 2:8: *"If you really keep the royal law, found in the Scripture, 'Love your neighbor as yourself,' you are doing right."*

The Christians in my neighborhood simply began to reach out in love to the neighbors around them through prayer and acts of kindness. The beauty of this tactic is in its utter simplicity. Anyone, anywhere can do it! Let me share with you how it all began.

I have lived all my life in Charlotte, North Carolina with the exception of a few years spent in Chapel Hill, North Carolina. In the last year of my stay in Chapel Hill, the Lord led my husband, Bob, and I to return to the place of our birth. We began to pray for God to put us in the house and neighborhood of His choosing. Interestingly, the Charlotte house we sold when we moved to Chapel Hill was again listed for sale, but we were certain it was not God's choice for us. He had taken us on a journey in those five years — not just away from Charlotte — but away from our old life and standard of living. Our new life and home would be quite different. Foremost among our needs was a quiet place where we could pray and invite others to join us in prayer. Bob is the one who actually found our house but surely it was God who led him there. As we walked up to the front door of the house on that peaceful street, we sensed that the Lord wanted this to be a house of prayer for all nations. We walked through the front door, went into the family room, knelt before the fireplace and gave our new home to God then and there.

I began praying for my neighbors immediately, even before we moved in. After settling in, I began to walk the five streets of my small neighborhood, praying for every home I passed. I prayed that God would put a Christian neighbor on every street so that we could cover our neighborhood with prayer. If I walked by an empty lot or a house that was for sale, I prayed, "Lord, please bring your person to this house, either a Christian or someone who will want to know you." It became an adventure then to watch and wait to discover who God placed on the street and my heart. On days when I could not go out, I let my fingers do the walking through my neighborhood directory. It contained a map of my neighborhood and a list of all my neighbors with names, addresses, phone numbers and even the names and ages of their children. The neighborhood directory continues to be a powerful prayer tool as my thoughts and prayers deliberately travel the streets on those pages — in season and out!

Later, I joined a friend in an adjoining neighborhood and we alternately walked the streets of hers and then mine, praying together as we went. I wish there was space here to list and encourage you with extraordinary answers to prayer that God gave as we united our hearts and prayers for our neighbors.

In March of 1992, a March for Jesus (a joyous parade of praise and prayer through the streets of a city) was planned for Charlotte for the first time. I coordinated the prayer for that event. Borrowing from the Billy Graham Crusade prayer strategy, I divided my city into 10 districts and asked 10 prayer warriors I knew to serve as district coordinators. In turn, they invited others in the district to be area and neighborhood coordinators. Now we had Christians in place all over the city who were seeking hundreds of others to pray for their neighbors. But we had a problem. We discovered that people did not know their neighbors! It was at this point that we realized that none of us could readily identify the fellow Christians in our neighborhoods.

In July, I invited the district coordinators to my home to thank them and to share experiences. A woman from a neighborhood not far from mine stayed after every one else had gone. As we continued to talk through the problem of not knowing our Christian neighbors, the Lord seemed to be leading us to "gather the troops." We organized an area-wide neighborhood prayer meeting to which we planned to invite as many of our Christian neighbors as we could find. As we made our calls, we were encouraged to find that each one knew of another so our prayer group began to grow.

In August 1992, we all gathered and began to pray in one accord for the salvation of our neighbors and for God's blessing on our neighborhoods. To my delight, I discovered that many had been taking prayer walks just as I had! Not only did we pray for our neighbors, but also for the churches, schools, parks and shopping areas around us.

After the initial meeting, we met monthly to praise God and pray. Soon, those attending were leaving the monthly meeting feeling so encouraged and blessed that they began telling others who then started neighborhood prayer groups in their own neighborhoods! We found ourselves watching God bless a plan that was clearly His own.

God's Word is so clear on this point: we are to love our neighbors as ourselves. To obey need not be complicated but it is necessary if we are to please Him. To neglect reaching out to our neighbors with love through prayer and acts of kindness is to disobey and miss the blessings that God wants to share with us! Let me encourage you to begin right now, right where you are by covenanting with God to pray regularly for your neighborhood.

For information on ordering Mary Lance Sisk's complete works on ministering to your neighbors, please contact the Proverbs 31 office at (704) 849-2270. ♡

Blessing Your Neighborhood Through Love and Prayer

PART II

MARY LANCE V. SISK

In this article I would like to share some of the particulars of what God has taught me and I have prayed for my neighbors. Because capturing and nourishing God's vision for your neighborhood is vital before you can bless your neighbors through love and prayer, I want to use this article to impart to you the powerful vision that God gave me to share.

The first thing you must do is get a vision for your neighborhood as each one is different. Begin by asking God to show you what He desires for it. When I asked, God impressed upon me Habakkuk 2:14: *"For the earth will be filled with the knowledge of the glory of the Lord as the waters cover the sea."* (NAS) He enabled me to "see" my neighborhood being filled with the presence of the King of Glory (note Psalm 24). I could almost see God opening up the heavens, pushing back the darkness over my streets, and pouring out His glory over my neighborhood. To this day, many of my friends say that when they get to the entrance to my neighborhood, they sense the peace of God. This is God's presence given in response to fervent prayer.

My neighborhood is a place that has been prepared for the Lord and He is welcome there in the same way that He was welcomed in the little village of Bethany so long ago. Bethany was an earthly refuge for our Lord; a place where He was comforted, where He could rest and be nourished. In fact, the distinguishing mark of Bethany was that the Lord was there! Mary of Bethany didn't have to go to Jerusalem or anywhere else for a miracle — she stayed right where she was, saw her brother raised from the dead and saw hundreds come to Christ (note Luke 10:38-42, John 11:1-45, and John 12:1-8). Like Mary, you and I can stay right in our own neighborhoods and experience that mighty, life-giving power of God sweep down the streets we know and love so well.

In Acts 17, Luke records a period of time that Paul spent in Athens as he waited to reunite with Silas and Timothy. What Paul said in verses 26-

31 became the light of heaven to me: *"and He made from one, every nation of mankind to live on all the face of the earth, having determined their appointed times, and the boundaries of their habitation."* (v.26 NAS) I suddenly realized that God appointed not only the time I was to live, but also the place. Where you and I live is no accident! God could have put you in any nation of the world in any time period He chose, but He chose to send you to your neighborhood now. If you don't go, who will?

Keep reading through verse 27 to grasp the grand purpose: *"that they should seek God, if perhaps they might grope for Him and find Him, though He is not far from each one of us."* If you aren't seeking God for the elderly and the sick and the problems up and down your street, who is? This is a wake-up call! You bear the mark of God and that makes you a member of the most distinguished people on the face of the earth. You bear His likeness and His glory and you are appointed to take it to your neighborhood. The authority is yours. It is your feet that must do the walking, your lips that must utter the prayers, and God will give you the land (Joshua 1:3).

Are you ready to begin? What will you say; what will you do? Look at verse 30: *"therefore having overlooked the times of ignorance, God is now declaring to men that all everywhere should repent."* Repentance means now just what it meant then: it is living God's way and not your way. God has placed you in your neighborhood to bring the message of repentance to your neighbors. He wants you to show them what heaven on earth looks like in the person of a human being. The very way you live your life is a declaration of repentance. Let them see the light of Christ reflected through your life!

I feel a divine urgency because of a day that is coming. The urgency is stated clearly in verse 31: *"because He has fixed a day when He will judge the world in righteousness through a Man whom He has appointed, having furnished proof to all men by raising Him from the dead."* God exhorts us to deliver our neighbors who are being *"taken away to death"* (Proverbs 24:11-12). The very salvation of my entire neighborhood could be waiting upon my prayers and willingness to reach out in love to those around me! We are the gracious messengers of repentance and our message is urgent.

When I saw these great truths in Acts 17, I had to repent for not loving my neighbors as myself. God has appointed you and me to live at this very time in history and in this very nation, city and neighborhood. He has given us a reason for living — to seek His face; a message —

repentance; and an urgency stirring in our hearts. I love the way that Eugene Peterson renders John 1:14 in his translation, *The Message*: "And the Word became flesh and blood and moved into the neighborhood." Will you "be Jesus" to your neighbors?

Perhaps this is a good time to state the obvious. God knows that we are weak, somewhat fearful and don't know where to begin. He knows that we don't want to reach out to our neighbors and that we don't even like some of them. The good news is that God will go with us to do the work Himself. What He is asking us to do is make ourselves available. I give you this promise: once you get started, He will go with you and you will see God work miracles! Remember what He said to Moses, "Certainly I will be with you, ... I AM WHO I AM." His presence is your credentials and it is all you need! (note Exodus 3:11-14).

I sincerely hope that this article helps you to grasp and nourish the "heavenly vision" that God has given me (Acts 26:14-20).

For information on ordering Mary Lance Sisk's complete works on ministering to your neighbors, please contact the Proverbs 31 office at (704) 849-2270. ♡

Don't Just Think It, Do It

KIM DOEBLER

*B*orn givers cannot be outgiven. They are not competitive, but simply sensitive to others and always go the extra mile. I am not wired this way. If you are like me, don't give up; there still is hope for us to learn to be more like our generous peers. Logic is my greatest obstacle to giving more freely. Givers tend to respond to their emotions while I am guided by reason. Instead of picking up a little something to say I was thinking of you, I would probably put it out of mind assuming, "She will think this is silly," or "If I am going to give a gift, it should be nicer than this." A giver would pick up the memento no matter how trivial or strange. Longfellow summed it up well: "Give what you have. To someone it may be better than you dare think."

My husband and I experienced the truth of this a few years ago when we were going through a tough time. Dear friends left a care package on our door step. The goodies inside were simple and fun: bubble gum, a stapler, note paper and similar things. Included was a short note saying they remembered how much a care package meant when they were in college and wanted to share that joy with us. It worked! If our actions begin with taking note of a person's special needs or interests, then our gifts can be tailor-made, too. Other thoughtful things I have received include: cute, modest pajamas given to me after our daughter was born (they helped me feel pretty which isn't easy to do right after having a baby); a May Day basket made from a cup; and a love note written in the grime on my windshield. Once a couple brought my husband and I a pint of our favorite ice cream and waffle cones. Another friend remembered I like flavoring in my coffee and bought me some. The unusual or unexpected is what made these acts of kindness memorable.

*A*cts of kindness DO
make a difference.

The power of a heart-felt note should not be minimized. Words of encouragement are powerful. They don't have to be fancy or many, they just need to be sent, and a note can be reread. The sender is likely to forget the note long before the recipient ever will. I once jotted a word of thanks to our pastor for an exceptionally applicable sermon. Months later, he expressed how grateful he was for the card. This reminded me that little acts of kindness DO make a difference. They don't have to require a lot of money or time — just listening and responding to other's needs and interests. Doing so gives life-brightening gifts that speak from our heart. Even if giving doesn't come naturally, we can start being do-ers and not just thinkers by attaching action to our good wishes. ♡

Hospitality With Heart

MARY KAY McCRACKEN

*H*elga Henry, wife of theologian Carl Henry, forcefully expresses this point: "Christian hospitality is NOT A CHOICE; it is not a matter of money, age, social standing, sex or personality. However, it is a matter of obedience to God."

It is a loving response to the Lord as He exhorts us in Romans 12:13 to "practice hospitality." We, as Christians, have somehow confused biblical hospitality with social entertaining. In contrast, our focus should be outward, not inward. Not on ourselves or how well we do things or the status of our worldly belongings. Rather, it's simply loving other people with the gifts and provisions God has given us, anytime, any place and to anyone He calls us to serve. And, the most natural place to start would be our home. Because, you see, everybody has one, whether it be a one-room apartment or a 100-room mansion.

During your quiet time, ask the Lord to show you specific ways to love your family, friends, neighbors and workmates ... anyone you might encounter during your day. You'll be amazed as to who He'll bring across your path to be encouraged with a cup of coffee, a simple meal, a hug or just a listening ear. And then, as you become more relaxed and confident, organize a plan to invite guests into your home on a regular basis.

Remember our "castles" are a blessing from the Lord to be shared. As we open our hearts and our homes and take seriously the PRACTICE OF HOSPITALITY, the world will truly be a better place.

*W*orking smart and keeping it simple takes the hassle out of practicing hospitality on a moment's notice. One way to accomplish this is to develop a toolbox of helps or basic items you can build on as time and money permit.

For instance, a hospitality toolbox might include such things as the following: adequate and efficient cooking utensils, dinnerware, table coverings, candles and a simple centerpiece. "Pantry perks" are frozen or prepared baked goods and cookie doughs you can pop in the oven the minute the doorbell rings. Also, for that unexpected drop-in neighbor or friend, keep a supply of flavored coffees and teas on hand in the winter and cold drinks and juices in the summer. For quick delivery to shut-ins or patients just home from the hospital, stock ingredients for simple, easy meals including frozen casseroles and boxed dessert mixes. Other practical and fun additions might be a variety of books on party planning, etiquette, creative napkin folding, tips for organizing your home, favorite recipes, greeting cards and gift wrapping supplies.

As we're called to practice hospitality and love people right where they are, the opportunities go far beyond a home cooked meal and a room for the night. For you see, in a hospitality toolbox there are many items that are intangible as well. A smile, a hug, good listening skills, and encouraging phone calls or a note of thanks ... not to mention TIME, precious time to develop and nurture loving and caring relationships where the gospel can be shared openly and honestly. As a matter of fact, the practice of hospitality is a wonderful tool for evangelism. In closing, I leave you with this challenge ... ponder it, pray about it, seek it with a passion ... and execute it in love. ♡

CHAPTER

"SHE IS CLOTHED WITH STRENGTH AND DIGNITY;

SHE CAN LAUGH AT THE DAYS TO COME."

PROVERBS 31:25

One Piece At A Time

LYSA TERKEURST

ave you ever heard someone question God in the wake of a tragedy? Where was God when all those people were killed in the Oklahoma City bombing, or when my friend lost her only child to SIDS, or when another child was kidnapped and brutally murdered? Have you ever questioned Him during a dark time in your life? I have.

Last month my family should have celebrated my sister Haley's 11th birthday. However, this occasion didn't take place around a table full of smiles, giggles, presents and birthday candles but rather a small flower-adorned grave site. She was taken from us when she was 16 months old after battling through a liver transplant. I will never forget her beautiful blue eyes, black curly hair and angelic smile. I will also never forget how angry, hurt and confused I was, thinking that a loving God could take my precious baby sister.

I guess you could say I have been on a quest for understanding since losing Haley. Other tragedies have come and gone, but through them all I have tried to glean nuggets of truth and wisdom. This is not to say that I have arrived and consider myself wise. No, it's just to say that I have prayed for understanding and God has been faithful to answer my prayers.

First, we must accept the fact that God is God and that the human mind will never fully comprehend His thoughts or His ways. In Isaiah 55:8-9, the Lord declares, *"For my thoughts are not your thoughts, neither are your ways my ways. As the heavens are higher than the earth, so are my ways higher than your ways and my thoughts than your thoughts."* If you compared life to putting together pieces of a puzzle, only God can see the picture on the box. We see life one piece at a time and must wait for God's timing before we can catch glimpses of the pieces coming together.

Second, we must love God for who He is and not what He does. Each time I've faced hardships, I've learned new names for Him. God is my Savior, my Comforter, my Healer and my Father who loves me more than I love my own children. He loves me with an everlasting, pure and unconditional love. I am accepted in the beloved! (Ephesians 1:6)

Let me encourage you to look back in your life and make a list of the many names you have come to know for God. Let your heart be touched by the love of the Father and fall in love with Him for who He is. Then, the next time you can't understand what He is doing, you'll be able to trust His heart.

Lastly, our heart's cry must be to have more of God in our lives. Even if my husband or my children were to be suddenly taken from me — yes, my heart would break — but even in my brokenness I would still cry, "More of you, God, more of you!" As I have grown closer to God I've realized that if my foundation is rooted solely in Him, then no matter what happens in my life, I may be shaken but I will never fall. ♡

> *We must love God for who He is and not what he does.*

The Best Kind Of Help

MARYBETH WHALEN

When my son Matthew was born with eating and airway problems, I suddenly found myself needing a lot of help from my family and friends. We needed meals, baby-sitting, and emotional support. What should have been a happy time became a time of struggle and upheaval as we found ourselves in the hospital and our family separated. Though my son has many obstacles to overcome in the future, the immediate crisis is over. Looking back at our ordeal, I'd like to offer some insight on being on the receiving end of a crisis.

Don't ask, just do

I found that many people asked me what they could do, but it became apparent that they only offered out of courtesy and obligation, not a sincere desire to help. The people who gave me the most assistance were those who sprang into action without my even asking. One person took the reigns and organized all the child care for our two older children and another made calls so I didn't have to constantly be on the phone giving updates. Someone coordinated meals for every night and simply handed me a schedule. People who took the initiative and organized my needs to make things easier did me the biggest favor of all.

To give is to live

I have always known that giving gifts brings joy to the giver. I never realized how truly appreciative you can be as the receiver. One of the most helpful gifts we received was money. People were very generous to our family, especially church groups who took collections for Matthew's medical bills. We also received several anonymous checks from some very wonderful donors. Anyone who has been through an extended hospital stay knows that even with insurance, the bills can pile up. We also received lots of cards and letters and small gifts at the hospital. It meant so much to know we were in people's thoughts and made the hospital a less lonely and sad place. We also received several month's worth of meals, which made life easier and also saved on our food bill.

Give advice cautiously

Many of our visitors would try to say comforting things, but totally missed the mark. Having never stood in my shoes, they had no idea how I felt. Their words of advice began to wear thin on me. I grew tired of hearing that God knew to give a special needs child to me because I am strong or that I needed only to believe and my son would be healed. The truth is, I didn't know I was strong until I had to be and that despite my strong faith, my son was not healed. The best words of comfort you can speak are not blanket statements about strength and faith, but the simple phrase, "I have no idea what you are going through, but I want you to know I'm here for you."

Pray

Whenever someone asked what they could do, I would say, "Pray for Matthew." I can't tell you what power I felt in knowing so many prayers were being lifted up for my son. The Bible says that when two or more people gather to pray, that the Lord will hear their prayers and answer them. It was astounding and reassuring to know that people all over the country were remembering Matthew in their church services and private prayers. It gave me the strength to go on.

Whatever you do, know that any effort is going to be appreciated by a friend in need. I have saved every card and letter we received, so that Matthew can see the outpouring of love and concern that was expressed for him. He is a very special little boy and I am blessed to have him. I am also blessed to have friends who cared enough to comfort me in my time of need. ♡

The Drought

BONNIE COMPTON HANSON

NINETY-NINE IN THE SHADE THE THERMOMETER STAYED

THREE WEEKS, SIX WEEKS, EVEN MORE.

TOO DISCOURAGED TO PRAY, ALL I THOUGHT OF EACH DAY.

WAS THE DROUGHT THAT LAY OUTSIDE OUR DOOR.

OUR TOMATOES AND CORN NOW LAY LIMP AND FORLORN;

OUR PASTURE TURNED BITTERLY BROWN.

THE COWS AND THE POND HAD GONE DRY. AND BEYOND,

THE SUN BEAT RELENTLESSLY DOWN.

BARREN AND PARCHED NOW THE FIELDS THAT ONCE ARCHED

SO JOYOUSLY GREEN AND ALIVE,

COMPLETELY UNDONE BY THAT BLISTERING SUN.

DIDN'T GOD CARE WE MIGHT NOT SURVIVE?

THEN ANDY, AGED FOUR, WANDERED IN THROUGH THE DOOR,

SAYING, "MOMMY, I'M TIRED OF THIS HOT.

GOD CAN GIVE US SOME RAIN." BEFORE I COULD EXPLAIN,

HE STARTED TO PRAY ON THE SPOT.

DEAR GOD, COULD YOU PLEASE MAKE IT RAIN? AND WITH THESE

SIMPLE WORDS, HE RAN BACK OUT TO PLAY.

NOW HOW COULD I TELL HIM WHAT I KNEW SO WELL?

NO WAY WOULD WE GET RAIN TODAY!

SIGHING, I ROSE TO GO HANG UP MY CLOTHES.

A BREEZE! WELL, AT LEAST THEY'D GET DRY.

WHY, A CLOUD I COULD SEE! THEN ANOTHER — NO, THREE!

SUDDENLY THERE IN THE SKY!

THE CLOUDS SOON TURNED GRAY IN A MENACING WAY,

WHILE MY CLOTHES WILDLY JERKED ON THE LINE.

"SEE, MOMMY," ANDY SAID, GRABBING BUTTER AND BREAD,

"GOD'S ANSWERING THAT RAIN PRAYER OF MINE."

I STARTED TO WINCE. JUST COINCIDENCE!

BUT AS DROPS SPLATTERED LOUD ON THE PANE,

THE DROUGHT IN MY SOUL GOD LIKEWISE MADE WHILE,

THROUGH A PRAYER THAT HE ANSWERED FOR RAIN. ♡

Turn To Others In Times Of Need

ANONYMOUS

The company my husband worked for was sold two weeks before the birth of our second child. He and the other managers, all excellent employees, lost their jobs. Baby is now 20 months old and Daddy is still looking for a new job. I'm not writing this to say "you may be in the same boat, so let me show you how beautifully God answered *our* prayers." I'm saying to you that hard times can and do fall on good people and often there are no easy answers.

We are believers and have been very active church members and leaders during our 16 years of marriage. We knew all the "right answers" and comforting responses for our friends and family members who were going through hard times. Yet I never would have predicted the marital difficulties and depression that have resulted from my husband's unemployment.

After our initial shock and my husband's anger at losing the job, we counted our blessings. Financially and spiritually we were fine. Sure, there were low days as my husband networked and interviewed as much as possible. Overall things were fine as my husband stayed in the Word and read encouraging Christian books — until mid-December when our hard times became *overwhelming* times.

My husband became severely depressed, turning inward and avoiding family and friends as much as possible. Thankfully he made a wise decision to see a Christian psychologist, which is something many Christians would be averse to doing. However, even after godly counsel, being a born-again believer and knowing the truth of the Word, my husband left our family two weeks after our 15th anniversary.

I cannot find words to express how I felt when he left. Like many other Christian couples, when we married we said "divorce is not even in our vocabulary — this is for life." A few days after my husband left, he came by to explain why he had done it. I was stunned and felt as I had been verbally beaten when every reason turned out to be my fault! My husband had become someone I didn't know, and truthfully, didn't want to know.

I knew I didn't want to lose my family, so the day he left I immediately called a few trusted friends to ask for emergency prayer. You see, I knew this was spiritual warfare that I could not fight with words. I called strong prayer warriors because I knew I could not fight this battle alone. There have been many times when my emotional and physical exhaustion and occasional depression would prevent me from praying. I have *felt* the prayers of my friends and I know I could not have made it this far without the intercession of others.

During our separation, God allowed many special things to happen. I did not discuss our marital difficulties with my Christian family or in-laws. I knew when the challenges were behind us it would be easier for me to forgive than it ever could be for relatives. God also made sure that I practiced tough love. When my husband called or came by, I simply told him that I loved him and he was welcome to come back when he was ready. I didn't beg and plead, and I thank God for the many wonderful books I read which encouraged me. As much as I wanted my husband to change, the Lord made me understand that I could only change myself. Fortunately, my husband was already seeing changes in me.

Another thing that God allowed for me during this time was the unconditional love and support of several special women. They never said a word of criticism toward my husband. With a wise word of caution, my friends helped me avoid making mistakes. Their prayer and support helped the most. I also found encouragement in some new, interesting and fun things to do in ministry for other women. He continued to give me the love of my two pre-school children and a daily routine that helped me keep it together.

My husband did return after an 18-day separation. We continue to seek godly counsel from time to time. My husband is still hoping for the same position in a very specialized field, which he loves. Meanwhile he is looking at other jobs, struggling mightily over whatever God might be teaching him through this. He is still depressed, although he knows that neither of us is to blame. We are both committed to our marriage, our children and each other. We know we love each other, although there are times of anger and resentment. I admit that I have been depressed recently; I try to be honest about it and not become pessimistic.

Christian couples experience depression, anger, resentment, contempt and even feelings of hatred toward each other. Perhaps the *only* reason I have learned to be honest about our problems is because our private lives became public during our brief separation. Yet in most families, marital problems remain carefully hidden. As Christians we *must* learn to allow our brothers and sisters to be honest in hard times. By being totally supportive, unconditionally loving and encouraging during hard times, we help our friends seek the guidance they need from us or from a professional.

A spiritual and wise woman I know was going through a difficult time several months ago. She said to me, "My prayer is that I will learn everything God wants to teach me through this because I don't want to learn this lesson over again." You better believe that's my prayer, too! If things are going relatively smoothly for you right now, thank God for that, then take a close look at the women you know. Let God lead you to someone who is in need. Let her know that you are available and ask what specific thing you can do for her. Offer to watch her children, take her to lunch or just talk over coffee. Most importantly, ask if you can pray for her. She may be hesitant to reveal the depth of her pain and her needs right away. Be patient, loving and confidential in your relationship with her.

Women who are dealing with difficult circumstances often feel trapped and very quickly become completely overwhelmed. Moms can't "drop out" or "escape" because they have to continue doing hundreds of small tasks daily to keep their children and home going. If you are experiencing hard times right now, acknowledge your true feelings (even those un-Christian feelings) to yourself and those who may be going through this storm with you. Then, when God leads someone to minister to you, allow them to help you. If someone isn't there just when you really need emotional support, material help or vital prayer support, pick up the phone and call a trusted friend or counselor. Don't let pride cause you to suffer alone when you desperately need godly support. ♡

The School Of Trials

LINDA DESSOLEE ROTH

Can't you all picture the Lord at the admissions counter of a school, saying, "Okay, you will be taking the Job Loss class. Go to Room 204 and you'll get your assignment there. Don't be scared. You'll learn a lot, and I'll be there with you.

"And you, young lady, you are going to be taking Mess Unlimited. Sometimes my students call it, 'More Than I Can Handle.' In addition to your text book, you'll need a sick baby, a dirty house and company coming. You go to Room 101, and I'll teach you how my grace can be sufficient for you. You say your hair's a mess and your laundry is piling up? That's even better. I'll show you how to give that to me, I'll organize it all for you, and give you a loving, thankful spirit.

"Next — ah, you already have your hands full in that marriage. That's fine. I also teach a class on 'Putting Christ First in Marriage.' You'll be surprised at the blessings you're going to get in this class. Take your burden to Room 208, and I'll show you how to handle it. Having a non-supportive husband is a benefit in getting all that you can out of the class. You and I are going to really enjoy each other in the days ahead. Don't worry about your husband. I have some things for him to learn as well."

All of us are taking classes in the Lord's school. Sometimes He assigns us more classes than we think we can handle. But the Master Teacher knows his students and the material.

I'm thankful He is my teacher. ♡

Infertility: What's A Friend To Do?

SHARON JAYNES

Infertility, the inability to conceive a child after one year of trying, is a condition that affects 15-20% of the couples in this country. Secondary infertility, infertility after the birth of one child, affects 25%. Unless one has experienced the sadness of childlessness, the emotions of infertility can be difficult to understand. The question arises for the friends of couples going through this experience as to how they can best support them without exacerbating the problem.

The following was not written for couples experiencing infertility. It was written for the friends of these couples. My prayer is that this will give the reader a better understanding of the emotional struggles of the problem and guide them in how to be a better support system.

One of the most confusing aspects of infertility is the unanswered questions. In 15-20% of all affected couples, no apparent reason for the condition can be found. Many questions arise in the couple's minds concerning the strength of their faith, possible punishment from God, possible unconfessed sin, whether or not they are worthy of children or whether or not they understand God's will for their lives. The amazing thing is, no matter how many questions the person struggling with infertility may have, there always seems to be someone who has a ready answer. The all-time favorite advice is: RELAX ... forget about it.

One can imagine the confusion all this advice brings. However, with the confusion, one thing becomes perfectly clear. The woman feels that the infertility is because of something she is not doing right. Not only that, but the helpful friend knows how to correct her error! This only makes her feel more inadequate and, after the suggestion doesn't work, more confused. Many friends feel the "need" to give spiritual advice because, after all, it is God who opens and closes the womb, so the infertility must be a spiritual problem. During infertility, spiritual self-evaluation is at a peak, with questions and confusion. The pain becomes very deep when the person's relationship with God is challenged.

So, what's a friend to do? The first thing you do is listen. James 1:19 says, *"Be quick to hear and slow to speak."* (NAS) Listening is a discipline that is well worth developing and one that is rare. Nothing shows more love than a listening ear and it is a discipline that is well worth developing. And when you listen, don't feel that you must offer some solution.

Secondly, Romans 12:15 states, *"Rejoice with those who rejoice and weep with those who weep."* (NAS) Each month the infertile friend may go through a miniature grieving process. Let her grieve for a few days and simply be sad with her. When she is depressed because the test came back negative or her cycle began, mourn with her until she feels better. It is best not to try to encourage her or pull her back up on the down days. Chances are, in a few days she will be "up" and ready to hope again. When that happens, you be right there with her, cheering her on!

Another suggestion is to avoid encouraging the friend by quoting familiar scripture to her that you know she knows. The Holy Spirit will quicken certain verses to her that will serve as a lifeline. At times, hearing easily spoken, familiar verses and Christian rhetoric may only serve to discourage the friend by reinforcing her perception of her own spiritual failure to live victoriously in all circumstances.

Let the person experiencing infertility bring up the subject. Don't let your need to know how the friend is faring override her need to not talk about it on any given day.

Finally, tell the friend that you have no answers (what relief that will bring)! Promise that you will commit to pray for her until the situation is resolved. What better friend could a person have?

Infertility can be a draining, confusing and painful time in a woman's life. Many times she does not know what she needs. But one thing she does need is a listening ear, a compassionate heart, a patient companion and a committed prayer partner. ♡

Infertility: A Test Of Faith

MEG AVEY

I remember that Friday in early December beginning as usual. I was rushing to get to my daily appointment at the infertility clinic before going to work. By mid-morning my day became anything but routine as a simple phone call culminated five years of infertility struggles for my husband Scott and me. We had been going to the center for 12 months, and the monthly phone call at this point in my treatment cycle meant that once again my hormone levels showed no pregnancy and my period would soon begin. But this time, praise God, our infertility nurse Libby was happily telling me that I was showing some signs of being pregnant! (I guess one can be a little pregnant.) I would have be wait until Monday to be re-tested to give my hormones time to rise.

Scott and I spent the longest weekend on record praying and reflecting on the incredible journey God had already taken us through. Pregnancy was always something we took for granted. I always said I wanted a large family with at least 10 kids. My mom would laugh and say, "Wait until the first one and then see how many will follow." Infertility was the furthest thing from our minds when we decided to start our family. As months turned into years we began to question why the Lord was not blessing us with a family. We both loved children, having served for years in the children's ministry at church. As time went on it became more difficult to share in the happiness of others when their babies were born. So often our hearts were broken when stories of abused or neglected children reached the news. Why would the Lord allow this to happen? It is only through the prayers and support of family, friends and church members that we were able to handle those tough times.

The treatment was so difficult and time consuming that Scott and I needed to rely totally on the strength that comes only from the Lord. The routine included two daily shots in my thighs and one in my hip. My first attempt to give myself a shot took the length of an entire Sandy Patti album, but I soon became an expert. Even two weeks without power after Hurricane Hugo did not slow me down — I simply used candlelight to mix the shots. My arms, thighs and hips soon sported large bruises, making me look as if I had been in an accident. Daily blood samples caused my veins to roll, which made drawing blood a difficult and painful procedure.

I had so many internal exams and ultrasounds that "shy" was no longer a word in my vocabulary. At times there was the chance of multiple births, so Scott and I were preparing for from one to four babies. Perhaps the most difficult and yet comical aspect of the infertility treatments was the scheduled love making. The center would call and tell me to be "with Scott" by 3:15 that day. I would then contact Scott and he would rearrange his schedule to come home. Another problem was that Scott traveled, and although the phone company could reach out and touch you, they were not that good. I would be put on hold with drugs until Scott came home, which put me in a highly uncomfortable state.

We went through the monthly process until that Monday morning in December finally came. I went to the center to be re-tested and everyone was so optimistic and upbeat. This time the midmorning call was greeted with screams that rocked the office. My hormone levels were off the chart! On September 18, 1990, Steven Avey came into this world, a much anticipated and loved baby.

We prayed for the Lord to bless our family again with a child, but after five years of trying and waiting we felt the Lord wanted us to adopt. We began the proceedings but an upcoming move to Kentucky put things on hold. I didn't want to worry about a new baby, selling our house again and settling into a new area. Well, once again the Lord decided for us. On the Friday after thanksgiving, the couple who was told they could never have children without treatment found out they were pregnant. We were able to conceive naturally and baby Avey is due in mid-July. Praise God from whom all blessings flow. This is a miracle and we are humbled by the power of the eternal God who cares for all our needs and answers the prayers of the faithful. ♡

In The Light Of
His Glory And Grace

LYSA TERKEURST

ears streamed down my face as I watched the intensive care doctor wheel my 7-week-old infant into ICU for emergency surgery. Why God? Why Ashley? Why my family, again? This was not a new pain for me. Six years ago my family had experienced an emotional roller coaster when someone we loved suddenly became very ill. That journey ended when Haley, my youngest sister, went to be with Jesus. In some strange way I felt that Haley's death was my insurance policy against any other tragedy happening to my family. So why would God let death knock on my door again? As my husband held me, he whispered, "Give her to God, Lysa. He blessed us with Ashley, but remember she is His first."

In the weeks to follow, Ashley was diagnosed with a rare auto-immune disorder. After two surgeries to put in central line feeding tubes, I.V. lines in her hand and foot, a blood transfusion through her head, oxygen tubes in her nose, heart monitors, a urine catheter and many, many painful visits to the treatment room, one would think this child's parents would have been on the brink of insanity. However, the Lord was with us. Philippians 4:6-7 promises us: *"Be anxious for nothing but in everything by prayer and supplication, with thanksgiving, let your requests be made known to God and the peace of God which surpasses all comprehension, shall guard your hearts and your minds in Christ Jesus."*

People rallied around us, bringing food and taking care of our oldest daughter Hope. Some did research to find specialists, many came to visit and most importantly they prayed for us. Because of these prayers Art and I found the peace the Lord promises. There were times when our faith wavered and we wished with all our might we could take Ashley's pain away. I remember feeling helpless at times that I had to entrust the life of my child to strangers, but through it all God's grace was sufficient.

Today, as I hold Ashley, I am captivated by the smile of this little miracle. We took her before the elders of our church to have her prayed over and anointed with oil. Since then she has not had any flair-ups and she's been off all medications. We praise God daily for healing Ashley and see-ing our family through this hard time. I know God has a great plan for Ashley. Her life, as with all of our children, is like a beautiful flower that will bud, slowly open, and finally reveal God's creation in full glory.

Let me encourage you, that no matter what your hardship may be, God will help you overcome. One of my favorite hymns says so clearly what my heart wishes for you to cling to during tough times ...

> Turn your eyes upon Jesus,
> look full in his wonderful face,
> and the things of earth will grow
> strangely dim in the light of His
> glory and grace. (1922 Helen H. Lemmel) ♡

God's Healing Touch

JULIE A JESSEN

This is a true story of what I consider a small miracle that renewed my faith. I wanted to share it with you in hopes that it might encourage others who are struggling with their faith or feel that the Lord is out of their reach. He is a loving God who truly cares for us!

This year started with difficulty for my family. One by one, we all caught a flu virus, starting with my husband on New Year's Eve, then my two daughters, ages 4 and 6 months, and lastly, myself. We all suffered high fevers, chills, body aches, runny noses, coughs and ear infections. It took three weeks and several visits to the doctor to run its vicious course.

I, however, was hit the hardest as both of my ears became badly infected and full of fluid. The pressure was very painful and so great, it burst both of my eardrums. As a result, I lost most of my hearing. The doctor said it would take two to three weeks to drain and heal. Let me say how difficult and frustrating it is to function normally when the only thing you can hear is your own voice. I couldn't hear my children. I couldn't understand conversations. I couldn't watch TV or listen to the radio. I was isolated, living in my own silent world. It could drive a person crazy!

After about 10 days, I became impatient. I began to lose hope of ever hearing again. I grew angry and bitter towards the Lord. Where was He? Why wouldn't He heal me? I felt as if He had left me. I couldn't reach Him. My prayers felt empty. Then, on one Sunday, something miraculous happened. No, I wasn't instantly healed. That would be too obvious. Instead, I was standing and singing during worship when a friend suddenly walked across the room and came to stand next to me. I felt a gentle tap on my right shoulder and turned. My friend then put her arms around me and said, "The Lord told me to come over here and encourage you." That's nice, I thought.

Later in the service, our pastor explained my condition and there was a laying on of hands and prayer for me. After church, my friend walked up to me again and explained that when she had approached me earlier, she had no idea what had happened to me. She was surprised to hear about my illness and loss of hearing. Without understanding why, she simply did what the Lord had told her to do. I then realized that I was not alone! It was He that stood next to me. Those were His loving arms around me. The Lord had used her to reach out and touch me.

Maybe my ears couldn't hear, but my heart listened, and my broken spirit was healed. Joshua 1:5 says that He will *"never leave you nor forsake you."* I believe that promise today. Do you?♡

God's Saving Grace

PAULA BORRELLI

"You have done great things, O God, who is like You?
You, who have shown me great and severe troubles,
shall revive me again, and bring me up from the depths of the earth.
You shall increase my greatness [character],
and comfort me on every side."
PSALM 71:19-21 (NKJV)

ugust 9, 1997 will stand forever chiseled in my memory as the day I personally saw the Lord in His infinite mercy and love bring our family out of great and severe troubles and allow us to witness firsthand an awesome miracle.

At 10:45 a.m., I climbed in my van with my 6- and 3-year-old, headed to a friend's house to exercise. I looked up to see my husband, Paul, carrying our 16-month-old daughter in the garage, and I quickly turned around to put my son in his seat belt. I started to back up and felt a thud as if I had hit something. I wondered what it was and knew instantly from the look on my husband's face as he came running out of the garage that it was serious. He proceeded to lift our little girl up into his arms and my heart sank. The rush of agony I felt at that moment can never be put into words. I began to scream and sob and place all the blame on myself. It was an unbearable weight that I felt, so much so that it knocked me to the ground physically. Paul pleaded with me to calm down, but I couldn't, I was so devastated.

Within minutes, we were on the way to the emergency room. We had determined that I had run over her pelvis and thighs. There were tire marks covering those areas, and she hadn't responded to my husband's squeezes, so he was thinking there was possibly some paralysis. I was panicked over the possibility of internal injuries. We prayed in the car and when we arrived at the ER I knew that we had to ask as many of our friends as possible to pray for us, so I called our pastor and asked him to please get others to pray. He prayed with me right there on the phone and by the time I walked through the ER doors they had already assessed she was not in shock. The nurse assured me that this greatly decreased her risk of internal injuries, which was the first sign of God's hand at work.

Within five minutes one of our dear friends and prayer warriors from our church was standing at the desk of the ER, and we prayed with her. A few minutes later our daughter went from being still and white to full color returning to her face and she began to point at the animals on her gown and talk about them. At this point, I knew that I had just witnessed a miracle and that God in His infinite mercy and love had chosen to spare our family a mountain of pain and grief. Another sign of God's handiwork was our daughter's disposition. She did not cry at all until the x-rays were taken and as we waited for the news, she was happy and talking to everyone who walked by. The x-rays came back with NO sign of any broken bones! The doctor was so baffled that he had other specialists check them and the specialists ordered more x-rays which only confirmed the first results.

Four hours after arriving at the ER, we joyously carried our sleeping 16-month-old daughter home. We were told by the nurses to expect bad to severe bruising, and she did experience some soreness — in fact, enough to hinder her walking and to cause me to doubt her complete recovery. Unbelievably, after all I had witnessed God do, I still struggled with the fact that she was completely okay. So on Tuesday we took her to an orthopedic specialist. He questioned us as to whether she was truly run over, and my husband confirmed that he had personally witnessed her rolling out from under the tire. The doctor examined her and said, "She is perfect." She not only has no broken bones but she also has full range of motion in her joints, and minimal bruising. We asked him to give an explanation and I quote his exact words, "Are you all religious?" What an awesome confirmation for me that the Lord had spoken, and yes, it was totally an act of God that had spared our little girl much harm, even her life.

God taught me much through this very difficult experience. First of all, our children are His on loan to us. In our humanness we can make some grave mistakes with them, but He never makes mistakes, and He cares for and loves them far more than we do. Secondly, prayer is a vital part of seeing God's handiwork. I do believe the prayers of all those we called on to pray made a huge difference in this incident. In closing, I learned how abundantly God provides for all of our needs when we are going through a major crisis by sending others to care for and nurture us as we go through the aftermath. Truly God did send all those special people to comfort me on every side. For all of this I am eternally grateful, and as I sit and watch our little girl run and laugh and play I am constantly reminded of what a great and mighty God we serve. ♡

Supporting Someone Who Has Miscarried

DONNA ELYEA

My husband and I recently lost a baby at 12&1/2 weeks of pregnancy. Once again, I experienced the great comfort of friends in the midst of a very painful time. There have been several times in my life when the prayers, visits, notes and phone calls from caring friends have meant so much. I remember with such gratitude how our close friends prayed that we might be able to have a child. I was infertile after two previous miscarriages and at the point where I had given the Lord my desire for children, but could petition Him no more myself. As I have reflected on what truly brought comfort to me following our recent loss, I see that there are a number of very meaningful ways we can comfort a friend at a painful time, such as:

- Letting our friend know that we have "walked the walk". Having a kindred spirit to talk with is so valuable. Being able to share honestly with someone who can truly understand your experience validates your feelings and that brings such comfort.

- Sending a note or making a phone call to a friend. Making a call or writing a note is a demonstration of love as it shows our friend that we have taken time away from our "agenda" to focus on her. Notes may also become encouraging keepsakes for the receiver. Often we are reluctant to call and "disturb" a hurting friend, but a phone call may be a balm to that friend.

- Delivering food to a friend who has experienced a loss is such a blessing. It is wonderful to be able to focus on healing rather than daily demands in the midst of a painful time. This act expresses sacrificial love and care.

- Praying for and/or with a friend who is suffering is one of the most powerful gifts we can give. Knowing you are being prayed for provides hope, strength and peace.

- Allowing a friend to talk about her pain, even after it appears that she has recovered. Often we do not know the hearts of our friends unless we give them permission or an invitation to share the burdens of their hearts. Doing so may help bring about complete healing and may deepen a friendship.

As we comfort our friends in these and other ways, it is helpful to see that we are serving as God's ears when we listen, God's arms when we hug, God's messenger when we send an encouraging note, God's voice when we pray and God's hands when we provide in physical ways for others. What an opportunity to witness to unbelievers and what an encouragement to other believers as we demonstrate both God's love and our own for our friends. ♡

Letter From The Lord

KAREN WIGG

*D*ear Father,

Where are you? Am I alone here? I need to know that you are with me.

Your Daughter

Dear Daughter,

I am wherever you are, and wherever you need me to be. I know sometimes you feel alone, but know that it was I who named you in your mother's womb, and I have been with you ever since. I've sent angels to walk with you and to guard your heart. You are protected my child. I will never leave or forget you. This is a promise. I have called you by name and you are mine! Don't let the enemy frighten or confuse you. You have nothing to fear, because although you may not feel my presence, I have been carrying you for miles and miles. I am forever with you.

How alone did Joseph feel at the bottom of that cold, dark well? The people he trusted the most, his own brothers, disregarding him as if he were trash; but was he alone? How did Job feel as he looked to see everything he cared for stolen from him by the enemy? However, when Job cried out for me, did I not hear him? I not only heard his cries, but I redeemed him, giving him double for his trouble. I never left these two very faithful men. Do I not care for you the same? Believe this, not one hair has left your head that I do not know about, and not one tear has fallen from your eyes that I did not catch.

One day soon you will be with me and you will see me face to face. And on that day I will smile and call you by name. But until that day comes, walk with confidence. Do not be afraid. Know that I am yours, you are mine and I am God.

Your Father ♡

The Bird Feeder That Fed My Soul

PATTI ANDERSON

When the crisp days of autumn start to turn chilly, I set up the bird feeding station. Right outside my kitchen window are two large bird feeders that the kids and I fill each year. It has become a family tradition. It started one fall when our family finances were pretty scary. On an evening when the future seemed pretty bleak, I read Matthew 6:25-27. *"Therefore I tell you, do not be anxious about your life, what you shall eat or what you shall drink, nor about your body, what you shall put on. Is not life more than food, and the body more than clothing? Look at the birds of the air; they neither sow nor reap nor gather into barns, and yet your heavenly Father feeds them. Are you not of more value than they? And which of you by being anxious can add one cubit to his span of life?"* (RSV)

The next morning, I set up the bird feeder for the first time. Each time I started to worry, I would watch the little sparrows dancing among the seeds. My cares would disappear as they reminded me of God's promises. This summer, a different problem entered our family's life when I had complications from surgery. I ended up at the Mayo Clinic looking for answers. One warm afternoon, my husband, my son and I went to the Quarry Hill Nature Center in Rochester, Minnesota. It was a wonderful break from medical tests! I discovered a beautiful poem there. The center guides were kind enough to give me a copy. I took it home and framed it in a birdhouse-shaped frame and hung it near my kitchen window. I have no idea who wrote this poem but would like to share it with you.

That simple bird feeder that I set up so many years ago has been a real reminder of God's love. It doesn't look very holy but it has been a real lesson of faith. Set up a feeder for your family to enjoy and let it feed your soul! ♡

The Bird Feeder

AUTHOR UNKNOWN

SPARROWS COME TO MY FEEDER
LIKE BROWN LEAVES OVER THE SNOW.
GREEDY AND DRAB LITTLE CREATURES,
HERE'S SOMETHING THAT YOU DON'T KNOW.

I'D HOPED FOR BIRDS WITH MORE COLOR,
SOME THAT WERE BRIGHT AND GAY.
LIKE THE BRILLIANT RED OF THE CARDINAL
OR THE CHEERFUL BLUE OF THE JAY.

I'D HOPED FOR THE FLASH OF THE ORIOLE.
BUT A DIFFERENT THOUGHT COMES IN VIEW.
BIRDS ARE SO LIKE PEOPLE,
WE'RE MOSTLY QUITE COMMON TOO.

WE DON'T ALL HAVE BEAUTIFUL FEATURES.
WE HAVE MEAGER TALENTS TO GIVE.
PEOPLE ARE MOSTLY LIKE SPARROWS
IN THE WAYS THAT WE LOOK AND WE LIVE.

WE'RE MOST OF US, PLAIN AND SELFISH
AND LOVED BY ONLY A FEW.
STAY, GOD'S DRAB LITTLE CREATURES,
FOR I AM A SPARROW TOO. ♡

182

Miracle Of Our Own

MARY BETH SPRY

I am no super prayer warrior. I can't boast of any great spiritual works or righteous deeds. I have never even been a Bible study leader. Most of the time I'm not humble enough to give God the credit and glory for the things that happen in my life. At least not until after those things happen. I can honestly say I didn't really believe God would reach out and perform a miracle in my or my family's life. How could He when I wasn't any of the above?

That perspective changed May 23, 1997. My husband's family was visiting and the 11 of us were playing and talking in the front yard of our new home. Having moved in just two weeks before, a few projects remained, one of which was to build a fence around the pool in the backyard. Other things had seemed more important, and besides, with a 2-1/2-year-old son and a 1-year-old daughter, we didn't let the kids play outside without adult supervision anyway. God used this imperfection in our prioritizing to perform a miracle in our lives.

I can account for all but about 10 to 15 minutes of that fateful Friday. But somewhere in that unaccounted time our daughter, Rebecca, wandered off to the backyard without anyone's knowledge. When we realized she was missing, we raced around to the back of the house. No Rebecca. All of a sudden my husband, Jim, leaped into the pool. Two seconds later he lay our blue-faced daughter on the concrete deck. Rebecca had been floating motionless, face down in the pool. Jim immediately cleared her passageway and began CPR. I wish I could say I did something heroic, but all I did was fall to my knees and pray to Jesus. I kept pleading and repeating, "Please, Lord Jesus, save my baby!"

On the third series of breath and compressions, Rebecca began to gurgle, cry and whimper. The EMS truck arrived and Jim rode in the back with Rebecca. Not once did she open her eyes or respond to Jim's voice. He held her still while an IV was started. Rebecca's breathing continued to be difficult and labored. Occasionally she would let out a short cry or scream. Once we were at the hospital, I thought, we need to have others praying for our daughter. I called some of our Sunday School friends. They immediately prayed and called the head pastor. During this time,

Jim drove his dad home — 45 minutes of time to reflect. He kept coming back to the verse, *"The fervent prayers of a righteous man availeth much."* When he got home, he called the two most righteous men he knew. I later realized that those prayers were heard rather clearly by God, for He healed my daughter in a way that can only be described as miraculous.

Eventually, Rebecca recovered and gained full consciousness. She acted so completely normal on Saturday that we expected to leave that evening, but the doctor on call wouldn't let her go that soon. He said the first week to one year after a near-drowning is the most critical, as the possibilities of pneumonia are prevalent. Rebecca, however, did not show any signs of slowing down and Sunday afternoon we were discharged. I made a follow-up appointment with our regular pediatrician for Tuesday.

I'll never forget our pediatrician's words during that Tuesday afternoon checkup. After checking her he said, "You could take her today to any doctor in this town, and unless they open her chart they will not be able to tell she was in a near-drowning accident." She was perfectly healthy. Rebecca has no recollection of her traumatic experience. In fact, within 10 minutes of being home, she headed around the corner of the house. This brings me to the real miracles of this event. First, Rebecca is too young to remember, so she has no emotional impact from the incident. Secondly, she did not suffer the possible intellectual damage. Since she was under-water for such a medically "short" period of time — probably around three minutes — and was so responsive afterwards, there are NO threats to intellectual damage and she has NO physical problems.

Praise be to God for His miracles and His mercy in our life. I'll never be able to say, "Sure, God performs big miracles, but they only happen in other people's lives." My daughter is a living miracle. Two sayings from friends that following week remain very dear to me: "How special it must be for Jim to know he gave his daughter life twice," and "Who knows? Maybe God will use this to bring Rebecca to salvation — her third and eternal life." God certainly uses everything for His good. ♡

CHAPTER

"SHE WATCHES OVER THE AFFAIRS OF HER HOUSEHOLD ..."

PROVERBS 31:27

Thank You Lord, For My Dirty Floor

SHARON JAYNES

*D*o you sometimes get tired of the endless hours of housework? The washing ... the ironing ... the cooking ... the washing again. I'll admit that sometimes this Proverbs 31 homemaker finds herself complaining when it comes to keeping the castle clean. Some days I think, "Why am I doing all this? Does anyone even notice all my hard work?" Then I come across that Bible verse that so many of us parents like to quote to our children, Philippians 2:14: *"Do all things without grumbling or disputing."* (NAS) Boy, that's convicting. Certainly Paul did not mean that "no grumbling" included housework, too!

One day mopping the kitchen floor had me in a less-than-cheerful mood. Then I had a thought. Suppose I was blind and I couldn't see the beautiful patterns on the linoleum floor or the spilt juice by the refrigerator or the crumbs under the baby's chair. If I were deaf, I couldn't hear the soothing sound of the soap bubbles dissolving in my scrub bucket. I couldn't hear the rhythmic sound of the mop being pushed back and forth across the floor's hard surface. Suppose I was in a wheel chair and I wasn't strong enough to stand upright and grasp the wooden handle to erase the muddy foot prints and make the floor shiny and clean again. Suppose I didn't have a home or a family to clean up after.

Each day let's think about the bountiful blessings the Lord has given us. The blessings of family, friends, freedom and faith.

When I thought about all these things, my grumblings turned into a prayer of thanksgiving. "Thank you Lord for the privilege of mopping this dirty floor. Thank you for the health and the strength to hold this mop, for the ability to wrap my agile fingers around its handle and feel the wood in my hands. Thank you for the sight to see the crumbs and the dirt, for the sense of smell to enjoy the clean scent of the soap in my bucket. Thank you for the many precious feet that will walk through this room and dirty it up again. Those feet are the reason I do this job. And Lord, thank you for the privilege of having a floor to clean."

Each day let's think about the bountiful blessings the Lord has given us. The blessings of family, friends, freedom and faith. May we look at life from His perspective and see Him in the seemingly insignificant happenings of our everyday life.

This and additional inspirational stories by Sharon Jaynes can be found in her book "At Home With God — Stories Of Life, Love and Laughter," published by Honor Books. Release date: Fall 2000. Used in this work with permission from the publisher. ♡

Taking The Chaos Out Of Our Lives

KELLEY REEP

Diligent hands will rule, but laziness ends in slave labor.
(PROVERBS 12:24)

How many of us, instead of ruling our children or managing our homes, are enslaved by them? Are we slaves to our children's whining? Are we slaves to picking up their toys or rushing around to fix dinner before our husband gets home? The key to our freedom, the Bible says, is <u>diligence</u>. The reason I am enslaved is because I am <u>not</u> diligent — I'm <u>lazy</u>! It takes diligence to teach my children daily that they are expected to take me at my word the first time. It takes diligence to teach them to pick up their own toys, when it's much easier to do it myself. It also takes diligence to find a schedule and stick to it.

Chaos reigns where there is no schedule. I am always amazed by mothers who allow their children to choose their bedtime, or whether they will take a nap. I'm startled by those who never expect their children to obey the first, or even second time ("Okay, Mommy's going to count to one hundred ...") and then complain that their lives are chaotic. Believe me, I am far from perfect. However, I do feel that the Lord has helped me find a schedule that keeps chaos from reigning in our home. The following will go a long way toward setting you free:

Set a regular schedule for children's naps and bedtime. If your child sleeps with you, first move him into his own bed and work from there. If your child is under three, he is not too old for a nap. If your child is over three, a minimum of one hour of quiet time should be required. Give him books and make him stay in bed until you say he may get up.

Set a regular time for your child to play alone. The best time to start is when your child is an infant. Put her in the playpen with a few toys for 15 minutes a day, working up to 30 minutes once or twice a day. If your child is older, it will take more work, but it will be worth it. Put her in her room, with the door open, for 15 minutes a day. A gate may be helpful for those under three. Do not allow her to come out, within reason.

Schedule regular time for housework. I try to do one load of clothes (wash, dry, put away) and a chore like vacuuming or dusting each day.

Some days it works, others ... well, let's just say it's getting better.

Plan a regular time for the family. If your weekly schedule does not allow for one or two evenings to just be home, then you are too busy. This also applies to women like me who run errands every single day, dragging exhausted children around who are maniacs by the time we get home. Then I rant and rave at them because they are "fussy." Find regular time to play with your children and do what they want to do. Remember the "stay at home part" of being a stay-at-home Mom.

Schedule regular time alone with your spouse. Some call this a date night — it doesn't have to be weekly, but it should be consistent. Take time to be a man and wife, not just Mommy and Daddy.

Commit to regular time with the Lord. Of course, this should really be first, shouldn't it? But how many of us place Him at the bottom of our list? You should see how early I tumble out of bed to hit the yard sales, but (yawn!) I just can't seem to get up to be with the Creator of the Universe and Lord of my life.

"A sluggard does not plow in season; so at harvest time he looks but finds nothing" (Proverbs 20:4). Now is our season to sow good habits into our children's lives. I long for my children to grow to be sincere, joyful Christians, but if I am not diligent now I will never see the fruit. Take courage! God made you the parent. Even though you are not perfect, have confidence that the Lord wants you to rule. ♡

My Hunk Of Burning Love

LYSA TERKEURST

One weekend, my husband and I had some friends over for a cookout and Bible study. While I was inside frantically trying to prepare the food, tidy up the house, put my child to bed, and greet my guests with a smile, my husband was outside firing up the grill. We were running a little tight on time, so my husband decided to quicken the process. He went to the garage in search of something to help speed up the fire. He found ... gasoline.

Things definitely sped up, so much so that our garage door wound up on fire. Luckily the dog's water dish was handy to remedy the situation.

Looking back on that day makes me chuckle, but also reminds me of an important lesson learned. How many times do we hurry through things because of a lack of proper planning, causing a crisis? Some days I seem to do all right, but more times than not I'm running late, rushing through activities, and dropping at the end of a day spent catching up. There has to be a better way!

Where do we end this cycle? The Bible offers many good suggestions. In Genesis 41:28-36, Joseph interprets Pharaoh's dream to be a survival plan for the next 14 years. They had to plan and properly manage in order to save their nation from famine. Granted, we aren't in danger of a famine, but when we properly plan ahead, it can help alleviate worry. Matthew 6:34 says, *"Planning for tomorrow is time well spent; worrying about tomorrow is time wasted."* (TLB) The worrier lets his plans interfere with his relationship with God. Don't let worries about tomorrow affect your relationship with God today. Our families need to see us as "warriors" for God, not "worriers". Here are a few tips to get you started:

Plan your day. Divide your activities into "must do" and "want to do" activities. Realistically assign time slots for your "must do's" and then fill in your "want to do's" accordingly. Be practical. With small children involved, the schedule has to be flexible.

Plan your errands. Use a map to figure out the most efficient routes. Call ahead to make sure the store you are going to carries what you need.

Plan your housework. Assign yourself certain chores for each day of the week to avoid getting overloaded.

Maybe you expert planners can give me more great tips. In the meantime, my "hunk of burning love" and I have a date to paint the garage door. ♡

Adjusting My Attitude Towards Organization

LYSA TERKEURST

*L*ast winter I received a major attitude adjustment. It all started when my husband and I were getting ready to go on a vacation. Art asked me if I knew where our ski gear was located, and I had no idea. I started to cop an attitude. I felt like saying, "Look, I am a servant of our Lord and Savior Jesus Christ; I am responsible for two very active toddlers; I keep up with laundry, soap scum, menus, social schedules, pest control, and doctor and dentist appointments. So what if I can't find the ski gear?!" Then Proverbs 31:27 started to creep in: *"She watches over the affairs of her household."* Another thought really knocked my attitude for a loop. If Jesus Christ, the Son of God, could labor in a carpenter's shop, how dare I complain about watching over the affairs of my household! We left for vacation with most of what we needed for our trip and nine long hours of driving time for my husband to encourage me to take on a new attitude toward keeping our home in order.

Now, if you were to ask my friends who frequently pop in to see me, they would tell you my house appears pretty tidy. But there are some trouble areas that really need attention. So I tackled the first of those projects when we returned from vacation: my closet. Ecclesiastes 3:6 tells us, *"there is a time to keep and a time to throw away."* I walked into my closet with a new passion for order and walked out with 10 garbage bags full of give-away, throw-away, and put-elsewhere items. It was so freeing!

Terry Willits, in her book, *Creating A Sensational Home*, writes, "Beauty replenishes while disorder drains. Disorder causes confusion and clutters the mind; it distracts your eyes from enjoying that which is beautiful." Amazingly, when I took out the clothes I never wore and made room for my favorites to hang in an orderly fashion, I felt I had more to wear than ever! Since this attitude adjustment began that winter, I am happy to report I have since tackled several other trouble spots in my home and I am that much closer to saying, "I am organized!"

The more organized my home becomes, the more beautiful it feels and the more I enjoy being there. The most important thing about this whole process has been my attitude. With a good and joyful attitude, we can complete even the most overwhelming jobs and maybe even have fun along the way.

Why not begin your projects now? As Ben Franklin wrote, "Well done is better than well said."

Here are a few ideas to get you started:

• Make a list of projects to be tackled.

• Schedule time each week to work on them.

• Divide larger projects into smaller jobs that can be accomplished in a day.

• Play upbeat praise music while you work.

• Reward yourself for a job well done with a bubble bath after the kids go to bed.

• Choose a place to donate items or gather them for a garage sale. Set a date for donating/selling and work to organize all your trouble areas before that date. (Donate all unsold items to a charity — don't save them for another garage sale!)

• Develop a plan to maintain the organization you have achieved. ♡

Activity Addict Or Cleaver Believer?

DOTSIE CORWIN

I munched on a sandwich as I chatted with a co-worker about family life. When I mentioned I cooked dinner every night for my family and that we ate together, she about choked on her tea and eyed me like I was from another planet. Then she looked at me seriously and remarked, "Your children will look back and cherish those times around the table and the meals you cooked."

We went on to talk about our childhood memories. Our recollections were similar: Mom always at home; the family eating dinner together; spending time at home playing rather than staying on the go; Mom sewing for us or darning our socks ...

My friend's eyes grew wistful as she tried to express herself. "I hate the way we live today. I wish ... I wish we could have a family life like ... like ..." she said.

"Leave it to Beaver?" I quipped.

"Yes! That's it! Like a 'Leave it to Beaver family'"! She then became serious. "What's happened to our society?"

As I've struggled with the busyness of our home, I've thought a good deal about our modern lifestyle. My mother frequently informs me of her amazement at all we cram into our lives. As we talk, I'm reminded that she literally stayed home each day and worked on making a home for us. We had one car, and one day a week she had it to do her errands and to take us to piano lessons. I remember the security I felt in knowing that our mother was always there for us. Our school was nearby and we came home for lunch each day. We walked to church activities and uptown if we wanted to shop. But most of the time we entertained ourselves at home playing with neighborhood friends, reading or listening to music. We chose not to have a television.

What has caused such a change in our American families? Why are we constantly rushing here and there? Are we frantically trying to keep up with other people? Are we afraid that our kids might be inferior if they aren't taking ballet, art classes or involved in a sport each season? Deep inside, do we worry that if our kids miss out on such activities their childhood resumés might be inferior to other's?

The media constantly bombards us with things. Possibly the lifestyles promoted on TV subconsciously create a need in us for something similar. Maybe if we turned off our TVs and opted for simpler lifestyles, Mom wouldn't have to work outside the home and we'd be satisfied with simpler things and less entertainment. Life seems to be a vicious cycle. Needs or desires are created and the tension of meeting those demands evolves, resulting in families existing on the edge of a stressed-out, ragged ruin. I frequently hear friends complain about their too-active lives. I'm concerned that children today are going to grow up remembering how busy their families were and how little time there was for simple times of enjoying just being together.

There are many quiet pleasures in life, but we may miss out on them if we continue rushing through each day. I hope my children's memories will be as enduring as the ones I cherish. This hope challenges the importance of all those things I rush around doing. It's a constant struggle, but I believe it is possible to beat the activity addiction and bring our families back home again. ♡

Ideas For A Stress-Free Family

COMPILED BY NEWSLETTER TEAM

Plan to do errands all at once. Write out menus and grocery lists for one or two weeks, shop for needed items and then determine not to run to the store for things forgotten.

Don't bombard yourself with media all the time. Spend more time listening to soft music, the sounds around you and the Holy Spirit!

Determine to eat together as a family every night, even if it causes some inconvenience or juggling of the dinner-hour.

Take a 10-minute nap each day and a long walk, both for exercise and to enjoy God's world.

Carefully choose your children's activities. Consider only one or two outside activities. Car pool as much as possible.

Think about scaling down Christmas and making it more home-centered. Skip some of your normal outside activities, decorate well and then take pleasure in spending time with family and reflecting on the Christ child.

List your top five priorities on a small card and carry it with you as Ben Franklin did to reduce stress. Look at it frequently as a measure for your involvements.

Learn to say no even if the event or task sounds appealing. A healthy balance includes plenty of at home time.

Take time to worship and reflect on the Lord in your quiet time and pray about all your activities, making sure each one is His priority for your life. ♡

Just What Did You Do Today?

AUTHOR UNKNOWN

TODAY I LEFT SOME
DISHES DIRTY,
THE BED GOT MADE AROUND 3:30.
THE DIAPERS SOAKED A LITTLE LONGER;
THE ODOR GREW A LITTLE STRONGER.
THE CRUMBS I SPILLED THE DAY BEFORE
ARE STARING AT ME FROM THE FLOOR.
THE FINGERPRINTS THERE ON THE WALL
WILL LIKELY STILL BE THERE NEXT FALL.
THE DIRTY STREAKS ON THOSE WINDOW PANES
WILL STILL BE THERE NEXT TIME IT RAINS.
"SHAME ON YOU," YOU SIT AND SAY,
"JUST WHAT DID YOU DO TODAY?"

I NURSED A BABY TILL HE SLEPT,
I HELD A TODDLER WHILE HE WEPT,
I PLAYED A GAME OF HIDE AND SEEK,
I SQUEEZED A TOY SO IT WOULD SQUEAK.
I PULLED A WAGON, SANG A SONG,
TAUGHT A CHILD RIGHT FROM WRONG.
WHAT DID I DO THIS WHOLE DAY THROUGH?
NOT MUCH THAT SHOWS,
I GUESS IT'S TRUE.
UNLESS YOU THINK THAT WHAT I'VE DONE
MIGHT BE IMPORTANT TO SOMEONE,
WITH BRIGHT BROWN EYES AND SOFT BROWN HAIR.
IF THAT IS TRUE ... I'VE DONE MY SHARE. ♡

197

When Is A Woman Like A Ship?

MARCIA HORNOCK

One hot August day, the girls and I picked and canned 15 pints of sweet pickles, six pints of dilled beans and cut up eight quarts of cucumbers to soak in lime. Then my oldest son juiced 14 quarts of tomato juice from the garden, while I made barbecue sauce from four more quarts. During this heavy canning day, I reminded myself that Proverbs 31:14 says the virtuous woman is like *"merchant ships; bringing her food from afar."* If I go to great lengths to provide healthy food for my family, I am following in Lady Virtue's steps and should be pleased with myself. I admit, I needed this self-directed pep talk to stave off "is-it-worth-it?" thoughts.

At dinner that night, I asked the children what Proverbs 31:14 means when it says the virtuous woman is like merchant ships, bring food from afar. Okay, maybe I was fishing for praise, but I also wanted them to know I do all this work out of obedience to scriptural principles. Eighteen-year-old Nathan answered, "Maybe it means her family looks forward to her meals." Cut short by such insight, I agreed he probably captured the primary emphasis of the verse. I had mistakenly focused on the ship and the trip; my son saw himself on the shore, waiting with anticipation and appetite.

When we create meals worth waiting for, whether they be homemade from scratch, gourmet-cooked with expensive ingredients, or store-bought and microwaved with love, we adhere to biblical standards of virtue. When the Proverbs 31 woman works in her kitchen, she envisions what her family will need and enjoy. She serves food which they will welcome like a merchant greeting his treasure-laden ship as it docks at home port after a long excursion.

Bon voyage and bon appetite! ♡

Great Ways To Organize Your Kitchen

HEATHER RICHMOND

*H*aving an organized kitchen can give you more time to be with your family and God. First of all, if you start with a list when going to the store, you won't have too many "extras" in your cabinets or refrigerator. Glance into your cabinets before you leave and you should easily be able to tell what you need. Here are some great ways to categorize your kitchen:

- Get a couple of "lazy susans" for your spices. Arrange your spices, teas and coffees on your "lazy susans" and you'll be amazed at the space you save.

- Group your soups together neatly to one side of the cabinet next to your canned vegetables, fruits, etc. Anything canned should be grouped together for convenience and easy access.

- Cereals should be put into canisters with flip-top lids. This will keep them fresh and you can see when you're running low.

- Sugars, flour, grits and other baking supplies can be put into canisters with snap-on lids for freshness.

- I bought most of my containers at a local dollar store. It was fun putting pretzels, cookies, pastas and other snacks into containers. This made my life so much easier since running out of snacks in my house is an emergency.

- Organize a snack drawer at a low level, making access easy for children. They can pick out healthy "on-the-go" snacks. This drawer in my house contains raisins, granola bars, packaged peanut butter crackers and plastic bags full of popcorn and pretzels.

- Keep cabinets, drawers and the refrigerator wiped down and clean to avoid buildup of bacteria. Doing this makes my kitchen smell fresh and clean.

- Consolidate your ketchup, mustard and mayonnaise into one container for each.

- Keep bread and potatoes in the refrigerator for freshness.

The key to an organized kitchen is to keep things catergorized, consolidated and in containers. Once you start you will see what you have and what you need. Proverbs 16:3 says *"Commit to the Lord whatever you do, and your plans will succeed."* Pray that God will give us the creative ideas needed to make our households happy places. Put some praise music on, invite the kids to help and praise God for all of the extra minutes you're creating by being organized. ♡

Food For Thought

JANET STEDDUM

*M*y husband, half in jest, recommends staying home as a means of saving money. He says we get into trouble the moment we start the car. I couldn't agree more!

Here's some "food" for thought as you approach the arduous task of grocery shopping.

GOAL:
To purchase the MOST NUTRITIOUS FOOD at the LEAST COST in the LEAST AMOUNT OF TIME.

Strategy:

Plan meals a month at a time (yes, you can). Benefits include: less stress from last-minute "scrambling" for a meal; better balance and variety; and less cost and waste.

Create a shopping list (output of step one).

Shop once a month for non-perishables (two or more stores), weekly for perishables (spending less than 15 minutes in the store).

Create a "price book" listing the non-sale price of items you purchase regularly. This will instantly tell you which store has the best price for a given product so you can shop accordingly.

Use ads in conjunction with your price book to locate exceptional buys, and bulk buy these items when possible. Remember "loss leaders" (items advertised on the front and back pages of the circular, sold at a "loss", and designed to get you into the store).

Coupons: Easy does it! Would you purchase the product anyway? Most coupons are for "new" (read: repackaged/expensive) items.

Question your buying habits: "My mother always bought brand x, so I will too." Could a generic product fit the bill? Better yet, can you do without it?

If you apply wisdom, tailoring these suggestions to meet your specific needs, you'll be pleased with the results. Go ahead and start your engines. ♡

Lifting The Load Of Laundry

BONITA LILLIE

HAVE YOU EVER FACED A MOUNTAIN OF LAUNDRY

THAT MAKES YOU FEEL DOWNY IN THE DUMPS

AND YOU KNOW IT WILL TAKE MORE

THAN AN ARM & HAMMER TO GET

THE JOB DONE?

YOU WISH SOMEONE WOULD

JUST WISK IT ALL AWAY.

WHEN YOUR HEART STARTS

TO SINK

YOU HAVE TO BE BOLD.

TURN THE TIDE

AND START A NEW TREND.

PUT SOME BOUNCE IN YOUR STEP,

GIVE IT YOUR ALL

AND DO IT WITH CHEER.

YOU HAVE SO LITTLE TO LOSE

AND SO MUCH TO GAIN.

WHEN YOU ADD THAT FINAL TOUCH

AND SNUGGLE INTO YOUR NICE, CLEAN CLOTHES

YOU WILL FEEL JUST FAB-ULOUS!

DO YOU GET MY DREFT?♡

Lord Of My Life And My Checkbook

RENEE SWOPE

*I*t was January of 1992. I'd been a Christian for three years, I was single and well into my "career." Yet I had little to show for it except a balance of $10,000 in debt. Somehow, when I'd given my life to the Lord, I'd forgotten to give him my credit cards and checkbook. As Proverbs 22:7 warns, I had become a *"slave to my lenders."* But I had been bought with a price and knew the Lord didn't want me to belong to anyone but Him.

A 12-week financial Bible study was being offered through my church so I signed up. Much to my surprise, I found out the Bible includes over 2,300 verses that refer to the handling of money — obviously this area of my life was very important to the Lord. During that first meeting we read I Chronicles 29:11 *"Everything in heaven and earth is yours. Yours O Lord, is the kingdom."* My heart was opened as I realized all my "stuff" really belonged to God and that I needed to give it back to Him. One of the first homework assignments was to make a list of all of my possessions in the form of a deed and then sign it over to God. By acknowledging Him as owner, I felt free to move on.

After establishing proper Lordship in this area of my life, I had to deal with the core issue of self-control. Although I owed my lenders a large sum, I had continued to purchase unnecessary things. The Holy Spirit convicted me that it was time to stop spending and pay back what I owed. The first steps were to stop buying clothes, limit my eating out and focus on needs instead of wants. I then made a plan to double my loan payments so I could avoid prolonged "slavery" and the accrual of interest. A year and a half later, I was debt free. It wasn't easy! Without the Lord's help and promises, I could not have done it. My strength was in Philippians 4:13 *"I can do all things through Jesus Christ who strengthens me."*

By the end of 1993 I was married and faced a whole new challenge — family finances. It had been much easier to determine my personal goals when I was single, but now I needed to be united with my husband, J.J., and what he thought our goals should be. It wasn't easy at first because our spending was very different. To him, getting a paycheck meant we needed to decide what we should buy next. To me, it meant paying off the credit card in full, paying bills early and then seeing if we had money left over to go to eat at Taco Bell. I had become <u>very frugal</u> and I drove J.J. crazy at first. We had to find a balance. Our desire was for unity because we knew that's what God wanted. Psalm 133:1 says that "*... it is good and pleasant when we live together in unity, for there the Lord bestows His blessing.*" We wanted God's blessing so we decided we needed to be reading off the same sheet of music. For us that meant going through the financial Bible study together.

The key to staying united has been good communication and proper planning. Past arguments have taught us that it's important to sit down and set goals early, before a problem arises. We plan time to get away and evaluate our budget and write out our short and long-term financial goals. During that time we also reflect on our current standard of living and prayerfully consider our anticipated standard for the future.

Couples need to decide who is best for the job of balancing the checkbook, paying their tithe, paying bills, keeping up with a budget, etc. We made a family decision that I am best suited for these tasks since my schedule allows more flexible time and I have the gift of administration. Plus, I really enjoy it. However, my husband knows everything that is going on and fills in for me when needed. When our money is tight, I ask him to pay the bills so he can share the burden of knowing what the balance of our checkbook is. We have an "administrative night" bi-weekly to evaluate our bills, review household paperwork, etc. If J.J.'s traveling, I bring the important issues to his attention.

For other couples it may be different. Often one spouse isn't interested in finances and the other wants to be in full control. I just encourage couples to be united in their understanding so that both are aware of what's going on in case of an emergency or sickness. It is a large burden for one person to carry and should be shared. ♡

Experience Is The Best Teacher

KELLY HOWE

As a teenager from an upper middle class family, I did not understand the concept of a budget. I worked part time through high school and college and all my money went to support my clothing and make-up habit. Malls loved to see me coming! Then came the fateful day — the day that changed my life forever: my first pre-approved credit card arrived. Needless to say, I had no self-control. It was like "free" money. I had no concept of having to pay it off. Within six months I was at my limit, behind on my payments, and receiving collection notices in the mail. My parents, realizing what a valuable lesson I was about to learn, let me squirm. Finally, after many sleepless nights, I went to them and admitted I was in over my head. They paid the debt, but I had to sign a note promising to pay them back. I got a full-time job that summer and they sat down and helped me work out a budget. That experience prepared me more for adulthood and married life than any college course ever could.

When I got married, my husband and I sat down and worked out a budget together. "Together" is a very important word. I realized God placed us together for a reason. His strengths complement my weaknesses and vice-versa. Our budget had to be realistic and workable. Many couples think if they don't write it down, it won't be spent. But clothes wear out, cars break down and you will go out for an occasional dinner and a movie. Make sure to allow room for these items in your budget. A budget doesn't have to be complicated or time consuming, but it does have to be honest.

The envelope system endorsed by Larry Burkett of Christian Financial Concepts, has worked well for us. We take the money we have budgeted for each category and put it in an envelope. Some sample categories we use are groceries, personal care, gifts and entertainment. When the money in the envelope is gone, we quit spending. It's that simple. Sometimes this takes a lot of self control. No going out to dinner on the money we have budgeted for Aunt Ethel's birthday present! If you are nervous about keeping that much money in your home, adjust it to bimonthly, or weekly. We also have a separate savings account in which we deposit a set amount monthly for car insurance, repairs, taxes — anything that comes up during the year that isn't paid monthly. Our set bills (mortgage, car note, utilities, and phone) are paid directly out of our checking account. Find the average of your utility and phone bill and budget for that amount.

This is our plan but we have had our share of setbacks and problems. Early in our marriage we decided to put our charge card in the freezer in a block of ice to keep us from using it. This was a good idea in theory, but we weren't addressing the problem — our lack of discipline. Needless to say, when our freezer went out and the credit card thawed, we had a problem! We have since learned, however, when this system is used correctly, there isn't a need for a credit card. Your needs have been anticipated and planned for. If you are in the process of paying off a credit card debt, remember two things:

Make sure to budget for your payments.

Be patient — you didn't run the bill up overnight and you won't pay it back overnight either.

Above all, remember the words of Proverbs 16:3, *"Commit to the Lord whatever you do and your plans will succeed."* Happy budgeting! ♡

CHAPTER *Seven*

The Beauty of Motherhood

"HER CHILDREN ARISE AND CALL HER BLESSED ..."

PROVERBS 31:28

So This Is Motherhood

BONITA LILLIE

It's ironic that I would be so challenged by motherhood. For as long as I can remember, I've wanted to be a wife and mother. Although I took the career path for a season, I always longed for the day I would be married and home with my babies. I pictured myself married to Mr. Right, living in an immaculate home with a house full of perfectly behaved children. Of course I'd be an energetic, loving, caring mother who never spoke an unkind word. That bubble burst the day I stepped into motherhood.

By the time my son was born I'd labored 29 hours and been awake for 44! I was exhausted in every way and looked forward to those luscious hours when I would "sleep while the baby slept." Unfortunately, the baby never slept more than 1-1/2 hours at a time for the first whole week of life. I was certain I would die from sleep deprivation. This was the first of many shocking realities of motherhood that I would discover.

During this time, when one by one of my idealistic pictures faded away, I became discouraged and depressed. God seemed a million miles away until I stumbled across Psalm 34:18: *"The Lord is close to the brokenhearted and saves those who are crushed in spirit."* Brokenhearted? Crushed? That was me! What a comfort to know that God was close to me even when it didn't feel like he was anywhere to be found. That scripture carried me through those first months as I adjusted to my new role and lifestyle.

I'm pleased to report that the Lord is still close and has remained so every moment of this journey called motherhood. It's been nearly four years since those dreadful first days. I'm now the experienced mother of a son and a daughter. I admit that my house is rarely tidy, my children are imperfect as I am and I've made many mistakes in parenting. Yet even though I've never reached the goals that I felt were trademarks of a "good" mother, I've grasped what's truly important — to love my children. ♡

Stop And Smell The Roses

CAROLE BALDWIN

I had just about lost it. Somewhere between the sticky kitchen floor and the cookie crumbs in the cracks of the van seat, I had almost lost it. It's very easy to lose, you know. There is always another meal to prepare or clean up after, library books to return, a basketball practice to get to or homework to supervise. In fact, it's almost a wonder that I found it again.

It took a dream about the death of a family member to remind me to open my eyes to the life that is bursting around me. What good would the endless hours of practicing violin with my daughters be if I never enjoyed the music they were making, or appreciated their struggle to achieve? Was I waiting for my youngest to leave for college to realize I'd lost the time to tickle her belly or play "Candy Land" with her?

My children's delight when I join their game of hide and seek, their endless efforts to be ballerinas with my necessary participation as their audience, their rapt attention when I tell a story, their eager desire to share a neat new shell they just discovered — how long will these moments of needing and wanting me last?

As long as there are parents and children, there will be food to fix, messes to clean up, activities and lessons to get to and math flash cards to drill. Hopefully there will also be kisses on a ticklish belly, cuddles on laps at story time, bike rides together and time to just sit and talk. The Lord has given us such a short time to enjoy our children. After all, unlike home videos, we can't rewind real lives. ♡

I Saw You Today

ANONYMOUS

I saw you at the grocery store today. Oh, you didn't see me. You wouldn't have known me anyway — for I am a stranger to you. But there you were in your slacks and T-shirt, pushing your little girl in the cart, groceries piled around her. You went down the aisle choosing the items on your carefully planned list (I bet you're having to watch your budget!). I stopped at the other end of the aisle and, without your awareness, I watched you.

You chatted back and forth with your little one and then impetuously reached over and placed a light kiss of affection upon her little precious cheek.

Quietly I lifted my heart to the Lord and thanked Him for you and asked Him to bless you.

I left you then and continued my own shopping only to see you again down the next aisle. This time your long, lovely hair was tied in a ponytail and you wore neat shorts and sandals. Your little boy sat in the top of the cart with his older brother holding down the bottom rack. As you rushed down the aisle, I heard you tell them they could set up the swimming pool on the deck when you got home if they promised to be good.

Again you were unaware you were being watched. But I quietly observed and again lifted you and your family to the Lord.

No, you don't know me — neither do I know you, but I love you and admire and respect what you are doing.

For you see, I am an older woman. My years of living your lifestyle have long since passed. In fact, I have grandchildren the ages of your children. I do remember those years of never-ending demands — children, husband, housework, all the things that now consume your every waking moment. I also remember struggling with the feelings of uselessness, the moments of wondering if anyone ever appreciated my many sacrifices, or even noticed. I remember that there would be days, and sometimes weeks and months, when I would completely forget my purpose of staying at home with my children.

I suppose your "stand" to be a stay-at-home mom must meet with a greater lack of understanding today than mine did many years ago ... because today you are in the minority. Society tells you it is important for you to be in a career that is self-fulfilling. It tells you to keep up with the Joneses, that every home needs two incomes to survive.

Yes, society is against you … but the good new is, God is for you!

I watched you today and you did not know … but guess who else is watching. If watching you gave me warm fuzzies, just imagine how the Lord must feel! Oh, my dear lady, God loves you so much! How you warm His heart. Your decision is exactly His plan.

I think He would say to you, "My child, my beloved daughter, you are so precious to me. I love you so deeply that I have entrusted to you my very greatest responsibility and honor of discipleship: that of being a mother. You are the pastor of a 'great,' although small, congregation. I have placed my dearest possessions into your hands, my little babes. Care not if those around you understand or appreciate … only look up to Me. I am always and forever watching over you, as you tenderly and lovingly watch over them. Be not discouraged, for I am with you."

And from me to you — thank you. You are paving the way, by your example, for a new generation with morals and values that have long been displaced and forgotten. You are our hope for tomorrow … our shining star on the horizon.

You may see your task as mundane drudgery at times, but I see you as the warriors on the battlefront — as Sarah, Hannah, Esther, Mary, Martha — God's chosen handmaidens. I see you as saints! ♡

A Badge Of Honor

NANCI SMITH

I just wanted to share a wonderful experience of God's love for me as a mother.

A friend recently told me that she asks the Lord to bless difficult situations and use them for her good. Just the other day I was having a really difficult time — complete with a screaming 2-month-old, a whining 22-month-old, laundry piling up, dirty dishes overflowing, etc. When my baby spit-up on me for the fourth time, instead of "falling apart", I prayed for the Lord to bless the situation — never imagining how He could use it for my good.

To do His work as mothers, we must get dirty.

As I looked down at my filthy sweats, covered with spit-up and sticky fingerprints, a sudden peace came over me. The Lord spoke to me in a still, small voice saying I should wear this like a badge of honor because sacrifice is never pretty. I envisioned our Savior on the cross, covered with blood and spittle; not a pretty sight to the world, but beautiful to believers because of what it means. To do His work as mothers, we must get dirty. Now the dirtier I get, the messier I look, the more blessed I feel! ♡

Mining For Gold In The Heart Of Your Child

LYSA TERKEURST

Moms, have you ever thought of yourself as a gold miner? In the life of your child you are just that. When a miner heads into the mine looking for gold he has to move tons of dirt to get just a little gold but he doesn't go in looking for dirt ... he's looking for gold.

That's the way it is with our children. Every child has little nuggets of gold inside just waiting to be discovered but there may be lots of dirt that has to be moved. Just remember, the more gold you look for, the more you will find.

My mother is a gold miner in my life. She has had to look past a lot of dirt but she is willing because she has seen gold underneath. When I was a child she saw past my snotty nose, childish ways and insecure feelings to recognize a precious creation with special God-given talents and abilities. Now I pray that I can be a gold miner in my children's lives.

I want to help them discover that God has uniquely designed them for a significant purpose. As a mother I must never forget that I could be raising a future president of the United States, a future pastor or pastor's wife, the future mommy or daddy of my grandchildren ... and the list goes on and on. I wonder if the mother of Moses knew that her son would be used to help deliver Israel. I wonder if Susanna Wesley had any idea two of her sons, John and Charles, would cause a sweeping revival that saved England.

Remember, moms, on those days when you feel as though you have blown it:

Lord, help us as mothers to never forget the eternal significance of raising a child.

Anything worth having is worth working for. Motherhood has a lot of mountain top experiences but wherever there is a mountain there are valleys. Hang on ... you are doing the greatest job there is. The pay isn't great and you won't get much vacation time but the fringe benefits are the best!

There is no greater feeling for me than when I see my children pray and I know that I taught them how to talk to God. Or when they say, "I love you, Mommy," and I know that in their eyes, I am one of the greatest people in the world.

Lord, help us as mothers to never forget the eternal significance of raising a child. Help us to mine the gold you've placed within their hearts. Help us to see these little ones as you do and let us not grow weary. Thank you, Lord, for the great privilege and honor of raising these little people for whom you have great plans! ♡

Nuggets Of Gold

RENEE SWOPE

After reading "Mining for Gold In The Heart Of Your Child" in the Proverbs 31 Ministry newsletter, I found myself looking for "golden" attitudes and actions in my 4-year-old son, Joshua.

The article came at the perfect time. While running errands recently, I noticed Joshua wanted to buy something new at each store we visited. To pacify his requests I told him I would make a chart with stars he could earn for different ways he obeyed Mommy and Daddy. We would then count his stars at the end of the week and let him pick something to buy or do according to the number of stars he had accumulated. He was excited and asked me daily if I had made his chart.

I must say, I felt hesitant about making the chart because I did not want to teach Joshua to measure his value by his performance. I grew up thinking that if everyone in my life was pleased with my behavior and accomplishments then I was valuable. My heart was a bottomless cup that could never be filled. Unfortunately, after two weeks, I still had not made the chart.

After reading Lysa TerKeurst's article, my perspective changed. She described how we as mothers can be gold miners in our children's lives. "When a miner heads into the mine looking for gold, he has to move tons of dirt to get just a little gold but he doesn't go in looking for dirt ... he's looking for gold. That's the way it is with our children. Every child has little nuggets of gold inside just waiting to be discovered but there may be lots of dirt that has to be moved. Just remember, the more gold you look for, the more you will find."

I now had new inspiration for the chart. Instead of stars, why not use nuggets of gold? Why not get a book to teach Joshua about gold mining and explain that I want to be a gold miner looking for nuggets of gold in his heart? What an encouragement it would be to know his mommy was looking for treasures in him!

I was encouraged to see how much of what my husband and I want to teach Joshua could be included in the chart. We want Joshua to know God has given him qualities that make him special. Our categories include golden attributes as well as actions and attitudes. His special attributes are a compassionate heart, hard working hands and a desire to be a great helper. We also want Joshua to know he is obeying God when he obeys us, so we included a verse with each category. Since God wants us to grow in ways that are hard for us, we listed areas we want to see Joshua grow in. His personality is cautious and shy so we have included a verse about being courageous with God's help. He's also been struggling with jealousy lately so we want to teach him God's perspective on that as well. We will pick a verse each week that we as a family can memorize and apply in our everyday lives.

We plan to review the chart every couple of days during dinner or at bedtime and talk to Joshua about the "golden treasures" we have seen in his heart. Then we will give him a gold nugget (made of foil sprayed with gold paint). I am sure when I find a big chunk of gold, I will get excited (just like a real gold miner would) and talk to him about it right then. To teach Joshua about delayed gratification we will incorporate a list of how many nuggets he needs to save to buy a new toy or to go somewhere special.

Joshua is a visual learner so I believe this will be a great teaching tool. However, like his Mom, he is driven to please and gain approval so we must always remind him that we see "gold" in the heart of who he is, not just what he does. Sometimes he asks me why I love him and I say, "Because you are my Joshua, there is no one like you. You are my gift from God. No matter what you do I will always love you." We even sing a song to him that our pastor taught us. It goes like this:

"I love you when you're happy, I love you when you're sad,
I love you when you're feeling good or even when you're mad.
I love you, I love you, I really, really love you ...
I love you, I love you, I really, really love you ...
I really, really love you!"

I share this because I want to encourage you to do the same. It is vital that we as parents lay a godly and unconditional foundation for our child's sense of self worth.

A chart is a great way to visually praise children and encourage them to choose to do the right thing, knowing there will be an eventual reward. It can teach wonderful lessons, but it doesn't compare to the unconditional hugs and praises of a loving mom or dad. In fact, we plan to use it to teach grace (undeserved favor) as well. On some of those "not-so-golden days," we might just go out for ice cream to create a "golden" memory instead! ♡

Each Day Is A Gift

CHERYL BESSETT

*P*ast year I gave birth to a wonderful, healthy, baby boy. This was our second birth, and much to my delight, I experienced none of the previous bouts with postpartum depression as I did with my first child. After my first pregnancy, I was extremely depressed and spent most of the day crying or lamenting over the "loss" of my former life. I was totally unprepared to meet the challenges set before me as a new mom, and I did not understand the havoc that consumed me by the lack of sleep compounded with rampant hormones. My husband is the most patient and tolerant man I know, and even that was of little comfort.

Often while we are fanatically searching for hope, the joy set before us fades. I was looking for peace, and instead of recognizing His light in my life, I hid in the darkness of worldly compromise. Instead of embracing my new role as a mother, I ran from it, often laying my new baby down to cry while I cleaned the back porch or rearranged the closets. I refused to take the opportunity to sit with her soaking in the sweet smell of her breath on my face, or enjoy the warmth of her body next to mine. I confused motherhood with a "doing task" rather than a "being task". So here I was, mother of one, wife of Mr. Wonderful, trying to understand where I went wrong. It took me nearly two whole years to come to the joy. Then one day I looked into my daughter's eyes, and I knew what I had come to mean to her.

Often while we are fanatically searching for hope, the joy set before us fades.

These delicate babies that God gives us are totally dependent upon us to teach them what comfort, satisfaction and joy are ... what a tremendous job! And what a terrific responsibility. Unfortunately I focused on the overwhelming responsibility of the job rather than the job at hand. Strangely enough, to her I am a source of delight, satisfaction and even joy. Her father and I are the charmers who make her smiles appear, kiss the boo-boos and have the key to her young heart. God has been teaching me some amazing lessons. I hope that I, in turn, can encourage other new moms to discover the joy in their children early. Most women do feel overwhelmed after giving birth, but don't let it get in the way of loving your babies. Enjoy the briefest season in your child's life while it lasts. There will always be leaves on the back porch to sweep and messy closets to clean, but there won't ever be a single day in your child's life that you can relive.

"If you, then, though you are evil, know how to give
good gifts to your children, how much more will your
Father in heaven give good gifts to those who ask him!"
Matthew 7:11 ♡

Practice Hasn't Made Me Perfect

KIM DOEBLER

Perhaps "practice makes perfect" rings true for you, but not for me. I relate to, "That which I do not want to do I do all the more." Let me share a few examples where perfection has eluded me.

This morning I decided patience was an area I needed to perfect. Unfortunately, it ended up being the day my daughter emptied the Kleenex box, salivating on each individual tissue. While I cleaned up from her rampage, she plucked the little tufts off my beautiful heirloom quilt. Only then did I find out she had eaten too much breakfast. She left a new design all over our mattress. No need to get into the details of my feelings; let's just say that perfection was not attained and patience is a goal for another day.

I have also failed to achieve many of my idealistic hopes in child rearing. For example, my husband and I were going to help our daughter by not talking about things like monsters or the boogie man. At the time of this serious discussion, we didn't think we would actually cross this bridge until she was older. Perhaps her friends would be the first to expose her to monsters. How wrong we were. Who knows where it started, but today she is often referred to as the drool monster, smile monster and giggle monster. I guess monsters don't just live under beds anymore.

Then there was my resolve to greet my husband lovingly each evening by looking perfect when he returned from work. How hard could it be to shower, get dressed, put on makeup and perfume, and comb my hair by 5 p.m.? A 14-year veteran of the workforce before becoming a stay-at-home mom, I assumed these habits would continue in my new vocation. Again I failed. Many evenings I hoped he wouldn't notice I didn't have on make-up ... AGAIN.

The most alarming example of my failure to achieve perfection was the time I arrived home from the mall with a nice black angora cardigan sweater. I modeled it for my husband. I was sure he would be in awe of how I perfected practicality and style at the same time. The words that flew out of his mouth surprised me: "Where did you get that sweater? It makes you look like your mother." My mother is quite beautiful; that was not the issue. The fact that she is 25 years my senior was. I do not want to dress like my mother.

Is it any wonder why the word "perfect" has been banned from our home? For some reason it has been easier to delete "perfect" from our vocabulary than "monster". Yes, "practice makes perfect" has a nice ring, but I prefer a revised saying, "practice helps improve." Hopefully. ♡

Missing Faces

MARY ELLISON

I was in the 11th grade — dressed in lavender bell bottom hip huggers, bubble knit short sleeve top, Dr. Scholl's wooden sandals and a blue bandanna tied around my head of long stringy hair. No, it wasn't "casual day" at school. This was the acceptable attire for teens in the 70s — except for days when there was a special assembly for awards or recognition.

As I sat in homeroom, the Principal came over the intercom and announced, "There will be an unscheduled assembly at 11:00 this morning to recognize those students who will be inducted into the National Honor Society."

Ah, I thought, so this is why so many of my friends are dressed a notch above the norm today. Their parents got the traditional warning call the night before and made sure their hair was washed and the frayed jeans stayed in the drawer.

Four hundred teens found seats in the darkened auditorium. The Principal made a speech of commendation from the podium. "We are here to recognize those students who have achieved academic excellence, upheld high moral principles, and represented our school positively in the community. Will the following students come forward when your name is called to receive a certificate and a candle to be lit by last year's inductees."

Mrs. Smith called each name and I watched several of my friends walk across that ominous state. Then to my mingled horror and delight, I heard my name. "Mary Ellison." Delight at the honor. Horror at my shabby appearance. Why hadn't my parents warned me?

Standing as a weed among flowers on the stage, I panned the back of the room where proud beaming parents snapped pictures and pointed out their prodigy to others standing on tiptoes to catch a glance. Even though I held a candle in my hand, the light in my heart went dim, as I realized my parents were not there again.

Later I discovered that my dad had received the call from the school the night before — the call that would have made more parents explode with excitement and pride. But, he forgot, and forgot to tell my mother. And even though they both worked just blocks from the school, they were not there — again. Just a few steps would have made a world of difference to me. For more than a candle and a piece of paper, it was their approval that I desired above all. But their continued absence at my events echoed in my mind that I was unimportant and held very little value in their eyes.

Going to my older brother's athletic events had been a weekly family outing. But for the six years I was a cheerleader, my parents never came to a game to watch me "perform." After all, I reasoned, he was a boy and well, I was just ... I wasn't sure what I was. But I knew I was not important. At school plays, field trips and class parties, it was always the other moms who took the pictures that fill my scrap books.

I don't want anyone reading this to think "this is a bitter woman," for I am not. But I want you to know that the pain of a parent's absence, the pain of a lack of interest in a child's activities and accomplishments, can leave scars that last a lifetime.

As a teenager, I accepted Jesus Christ as my Lord and Savior. Yes, He saved me from spending eternity in hell. But He also saved me from a lifetime of feelings of inferiority, insecurity and inadequacy. In my 30s I began to understand for the first time, my true value in Christ. I learned that I am chosen and dearly loved, that I am the Bride of Christ, that I am the salt of the earth. It was hard to believe that my heavenly Father loved and accepted me, because many times one's perception of their heavenly Father is a reflection of their relationship with the earthly parent. But through many years of struggles, I finally grasped these valuable truths.

My charge to you as mothers and fathers, is to be available for your children. Is there a school play? Be there. Is there a track meet where you have to sit three hours to see your child run a 58-second race? Be there. Is there an awards assembly where your child walks across the stage to receive a ribbon, a plaque, a trophy? Be there.

The time we spend encouraging our children will be one of the best investments we will ever make. We will not be able to be at every event, but they need to know that they are a priority in our lives. And remember, in this mission called parenting, it is better to build children, than to repair adults. ♡

In this ministry called parenting, it is better to build children, than to repair adults.

Worry, Worry, Worry

JULIE REIMER

"Will all your worries add a single moment to your life?
So don't be anxious about tomorrow. God will take care of your
tomorrow too. Live one day at a time."
MATTHEW 6:27,34 (TLB)

According to many moms, children should be potty trained by a certain age. As a daughter who respected the advice of two experienced mothers now grandmas, I attempted to bring my now 3-1/2-year-old son Noah into the world of potties at the same age my husband and I were trained. Over the past 1-1/2 years, we have tried EVERY bit of advice, trick or suggestion available with absolutely no success. Some people shake their heads or whisper behind our backs, but the simple truth is that Noah will be the one to decide when he's ready. No amount of worrying will change his mind, but the worries have caused anxiety and frustration for me.

Today I looked out at the young maple planted on the day Noah was baptized. Its leaves are the last on our block to grow into autumn's glorious colors before falling to the snowy ground. As I gazed at the leaves, I realized that this tree which symbolized Noah's life as a young Christian also held meaning for his journey through life. Although the tree colors and sheds its leaves later than other trees, it does so nonetheless; it simply has its own time schedule. Similarly, Noah will certainly be potty trained someday soon; he's just doing it on his own schedule. Instead of worrying over his lack of conformity, I need to appreciate the delightful things he says, his love of the Bible and his enthusiasm for life.

This was just another instance which reminded me that there are times in my motherhood journey when I need to take a step back and remember that each of my children is unique and special in his own way. Often I find myself caught up in the well-intentioned advice and experience of others or catch myself comparing my children to other children I know. Instead, I should remember Jesus' words about living one day at a time and cast my worries aside. Without those worries, I can certainly live my days with the happiness and enthusiasm of my son! ♡

A Mother's Work

CAROL MADER

IT TOOK ALL OF ME, AND MORE

TO CARRY YOU

TO DELIVER YOU

TO HOLD YOU

TO NURSE YOU

TO DISCIPLINE YOU

TO NURTURE YOU

TO GUIDE YOU

IT WILL TAKE ALL OF ME, AGAIN,

TO FREE YOU.

225

Can Everything Come In?

BONNIE COMPTON HANSON

Knock! Knock!

Sprawled on my knees on the kitchen floor, wiping up yet another peanut butter and jelly mess under the kitchen table, I groaned. Oh, no, not another interruption! Finally, after a week of rain, this morning was a sunny enough day to shoo my three preschoolers out of the house. If I could just manage to get everything halfway straightened up before I called them back in for lunch. Maybe even find five minutes for myself. And now the door.

I was already hating my interrupter. Go away! Quit bothering me! And why in the world are you knocking, anyway, instead of using the doorbell? Trying not to slip on my newly mopped floor, I ran angrily to the door, all ready to greet yet another salesman with, "No thanks, we don't want any." Yanking open the front door, I stared up at where the salesman's eyes should be but the eyes, all 20 of them, were way down at knee level. For there stood not only my three little boys, but every other child in the neighborhood as well, all smiling expectantly. "Hi, Mom!" my oldest chirped brightly. "Can everything come in? I told them you wouldn't mind, because they're our friends."

I stared back at his eager eyes then at 20 muddy shoes and my newly mopped floor. I laughed and said, "Tell you what. Everyone's welcome to come around to the back yard the outside way and then we'll have some lemonade and cookies. Okay?" More than okay, of course, and soon they were all playing happily on the swing set and getting muddier than ever.

Yes, come on in, my sons. May my door be always open to you and your friends for lemonade and cookies, tea and sympathy, and hot chicken soup even if it means scuffing up a newly polished floor.

In this same way your Heavenly Father's "door" of love, help and comfort will be ever open to you to help you meet joyfully and expectantly all the "everythings" that will come to you in the wonderful years ahead. ♡

Mother's Day Confession

NANCEE SKIPPER

MOTHER'S DAY
A DAY SPENT PRAISING ME.
IF ONLY I COULD MEASURE UP
TO THE "SUPER MOM" I'M SUPPOSED TO BE!

I LONG TO BE THAT MYTH,
OF EVERY YOUNG ONE'S DREAMS,
BUT I'M JUST ME WITH ALL MY FLAWS,
STRUGGLING WITH SELF ESTEEM.

I WORRY ABOUT THE MISTAKES I'VE MADE.
I WONDER HOW THEY'LL SURVIVE.
"IN SPITE OF ME," I'M TOLD THEY'LL FLOURISH,
PERHAPS THEY'LL EVEN THRIVE.

THROUGHOUT THEIR DAYS I'VE BEEN THERE,
BANDAGING ALL THE VITAL PARTS.
DEAR LORD, FOR THE TIMES I'VE FAILED THEM,
PLEASE HEAL THEIR FRACTURED HEARTS.

AND THOUGH I AM NOT WORTHY
OF THESE PRAISES I CONFESS,
BECAUSE YOU'VE BLESSED ME RICHLY,
IN YOUR STRENGTH, I'LL DO MY BEST. ♡

A Successful Mother

SUZY RYAN

What will my children recall of their mother? After time sifts through the marathon of life, what memories will champion the winner's circle of their impressionable minds?

Will they remember the discipline? I pray they only hear me say, "I love you too much to allow you to choose disobedience."

Will they remember their mom, green-faced, holding her breath, while cleaning vomit off their beds? I long for them to just savor the warmth of my hug as I gently rocked them back to sleep.

Will they remember looks of exasperation because they wanted to show me the rocks that they found? Surely only my departure from the dishes to discover more treasures will remain important.

Will they remember the countless times I said "no" to Power Rangers, when every other child on the block enjoyed unlimited time gaining "morphin power"? How can they forget about the excitement experienced while playing Go Fish, Legos and PlayDough instead?

Will they remember the countless times heading to the grocery store instead of time with friends? Hopefully, their stomachs will prompt them of the laughter and abundant goodies we shared while cruising the aisles of the store.

Will they remember me frantically rushing everyone out the door without using my "indoor voice"? Maybe memory will only acknowledge the fun songs we sang while driving the carpool to church.

How will my three cherubs remember me? Oh please, Lord, as a woman who modeled godliness, so that they will accept and depend on You. I beg You to filter out the many mistakes I made during their development. Allow them to see a glimpse of Your love through me.

If they choose to fear and serve You, Jesus, then I am a successful mother. ♡

A Mother's Passover

SHARON JAYNES

It was mailing night for The Proverbs 31 Ministry newsletter. The room was pulsating with energy as 10 young mothers and one not-so-young mother got instructions for collating, stamping and bundling newsletters by zip codes and states. I had just joined the Proverbs 31 Ministry staff and mailing night was a new experience for me.

Everyone got situated in their little work space in the founder's den, with piles of papers, stamps and mail boxes surrounding them like a fortress of sorts. Then "Part II" of the evening began; the real reason for the meeting. No one said, "Now let's begin Part II." It just kind of happened. And I was reminded of a kind of ritual that occurs when mothers of 2-year-olds are in a room together. I felt like I was at a Passover Seder, remembering the days of captivity.

It began with one mom saying, "Meredith has started having temper tantrums! I just don't know what to do with her!" Then the room buzzed with, "Meredith! You must be kidding. She's always been such an angel!" The advice on how to handle the situation sprung forth from mothers around the room. Meredith's mom was reassured that she could indeed handle the problem and that her angel was not turning into a devil.

Another mom complained, "I'm having trouble with potty training. Those M&M rewards just aren't working." That was followed by, "You think you've got problems? Mary Madison has been smearing the contents of her diapers on the walls again."

There had been frustration with kids clinging to mommies at church, little Ashley pulling sister Hope's hair out in handfuls and ear infections for the tenth time. Each time a frustration was voiced, the listening moms jumped in to reassure and give tips that had worked for them or for someone they knew with a similar problem. Whether this advice would work or not had nothing to do with anything. Each mom got the frustration off her chest and she felt better hearing that someone else had problems too!

I just sat there listening and stamping, hoping no one would notice that I was not giving advice or sharing my mothering problems. Finally, I had to interject some words of wisdom. "Well, I have a 12-year-old." That comment brought gasps from around the room from ladies who didn't know my age. Then I continued, "And when my son was 2, one of my favorite verses was Luke 2:1, *'And it came to pass.'*" And so it does.

Many people laugh at the struggles of a mom with a 2-year-old. They think, "Wait until your child hits 14. Then you will have big problems." But I beg to differ. The truth is, as children age, the struggles are fewer in number but greater in magnitude. It's the confrontations every five minutes that wear on the parents of toddlers.

That night I was taken back 10 years, to a different time. It was like the Jews celebrating the Seder, eating bitter herbs, unleavened bread and horse-radish (now there's a meal that will get your attention!) to commemorate their time of captivity. We moms who have passed through the Red Sea of toddlerhood need to remember the diapers, the whining, the tantrums and the endless laundry. I was not going to sit there with these mothers of toddlers and say like so many, "Enjoy these years. They go by so quickly. Your child is whining 'Hold me, hold me' now. But in 10 years you'll be begging them to let you hold them!" All of which is true, but not what they needed to hear.

So that night I sat in silence and listened, and remembered. I had eaten my bitter herbs. Preschool years are precious, but wow, are they exhausting; spiritually, physically and emotionally! So when your children leave the toddler years and you find yourself saying, "You were such a sweet baby. Things were so much simpler back then. Oh for the good ol' days," I suggest that you go sit in a room full of moms of 2- and 3-year-olds and remember. Don't say anything, just listen. Better yet, I know several moms who would be more than happy to let you borrow their precious angels for a day, just to refresh your memory.

This and additional inspirational stories by Sharon Jaynes can be found in her book "At Home With God — Stories Of Life, Love and Laughter," published by Honor Books. Release date: Fall 2000. Used in this work with permission from the publisher. ♡

Moms: Get Your Muscles Moving

L Y S A   T E R K E U R S T

Exercise. Does the very word conjure up feelings of guilt and dread? Well, it certainly used to for me. I can tell you with all honesty that today I actually enjoy both exercising and the benefits I get from working out. What caused this amazing change in my attitude toward moving my muscles and getting in shape?

First of all, it took a lot of prayer. It's important not to limit Christ to just the religious compartment of our lives. I believe the key to becoming a dynamic Christian is giving the Lord control over every aspect of your life. You see, the more you change, the more you can be an instrument of change in the lives of others. So, I pray daily for the Lord's help, remembering I can do all things through Christ who strengthens me (Phil 4:13). Now, because I have changed, the Lord can use me as an instrument to help encourage others to take better care of themselves.

The second attitude changer in my life was my very encouraging husband, Art. He has always been active and has the body to show for it. He always has plenty of energy and a very positive attitude. I read in a fitness magazine that studies have shown that depression and fatigue are often the result of not getting enough exercise. Art encouraged me to develop a realistic work-out plan and then stick to it. He helped me set some short-term and long-range goals which we wrote down to chart my progress. Art became my accountability partner and learned what did and did not motivate me.

The last big attitude changer was getting educated. I have always had a fear of the unknown and because I didn't know a lot about the human body and the benefits of exercise, I always feared trying to get started. However, when I got educated on the facts, knowledge itself became a motivator. Here's a simple version of what I learned:

- One pound of fat equals 3500 calories
- It is a safe and realistic for my body to lose 1 lb. per week until I get to my goal weight
- I can exercise off 350 calories per day x 4 workout days = 1400 calories

- I can cut my calories by 300 calories per day x 7 days = 2100 calories
- 1400 calories + 2100 calories = 3500 calories per week or 1 lb. lost per week

It's important to remember to consult with a physician before starting any type of diet and exercise program in order to learn what is safe, effective and realistic for you. I went to a local YMCA facility and consulted with a fitness pro who helped me figure out my aerobic heart rate training zone and how long I needed to do certain aerobic activities to burn the necessary number of calories. Because I have small children, I invested in a stair master to use in my home. I plan my exercise time around my children's nap times. You'll have to develop a plan for the most realistic way for you to find time to exercise.

Let me encourage you to start today on the road to a healthier, happier, you. Don't make excuses, make progress. Let this be the year you become an instrument of change in the life of others. Trust me, if I can do it, so can you! ♡

Called Of God

AUTHOR UNKNOWN

CALLED OF GOD
TO SERVE HER LORD,
'TWOULD SEEM A
LOWLY PLACE;

CALLED OF GOD
TO DRESS A DOLL AND
WASH A DIRTY FACE,

CALLED TO TEACH
A BABY'S LIPS
TO SPEAK THE
SAVIOR'S NAME

AND TO THE QUICKLY
GROWING CHILD GOD'S
HOLY WORD PROCLAIM.

CALLED TO DISCIPLINE
WITH LOVE
THAT SMALL FEET
GONE ASTRAY

MAY LEARN A LOVING
GOD ABOVE
EXPECTS THEM TO OBEY.

CALLED OF GOD
TO INTERCEDE
BEFORE THE THRONE
OF GRACE

TILL EVERY CHILD
SHALL SERVE THE LORD
IN HIS APPOINTED PLACE. ♡

Help Lord, I'm Going To Be A Stepmother

JANETTE BABCOCK

Five years ago, if anyone had told me I was going to be a mother of four I'm sure I would have laughed in their face! One husband, two teens, one preteen, one "terrible two" and one cat later I'm laughing, alright ... but for a slightly different reason — sanity!

A few years ago I thought life could not get any better. I had just purchased my own home, been promoted at work and finally felt settled. To top it off, my relationship with the Lord seemed to be at the most solid point ever of my barely less-than-30 years. (I guess that's when all the warning bells and whistles should have been ringing in my ears!) To make a long story short, I was sandbagged into a blind date. It turned out to be the "date-of-a-lifetime" and in six short weeks, I was engaged. My only dilemma was my fiancé came bearing "gifts" ages 10, 8 and 6 years old! I thought about the only two stepmothers I knew of: Cinderella's stepmother, and Snow White's stepmother. Well, I sure didn't want to pattern myself after them. I tried to think of a biblical stepmother and only came up with Bathsheba (David's wife) and she definitely wasn't a good example. I prayed for insight, took a deep breath, and decided to dive right in ... how hard could it be anyway? I had a little experience with my "children", the cats. I figured there could not be THAT much difference between the two. Both had to eat, sleep and liked to play.

The long awaited "introduction" quickly arrived and I anxiously met each child. I wondered what they thought about me and my home. Most of all, was I "acceptable" in their eyes for their dad? We made it through dinner amazingly well. I was just starting to relax as dessert was served (strawberry shortcake). I had planned to have dessert in the family room, hoping it would provide an informal atmosphere. I served Rick and his children first and was on the way into the room with mine when tragedy struck. The littlest spilled her entire plate on the carpet. Strawberries, sauce, shortcake and whipped topping lay in a heap at the bottom of her feet. Four pairs of panicked eyes now were fixed on me. Without thinking, I returned to the kitchen for cleaning supplies and cleaned up. Once the spill was taken care of, we made her another plate together. The rest of our evening passed smoothly and as they left, each gave me a big hug.

As I cleaned the kitchen, I reflected over the evening. I had prayed for guidance on how to be a stepmother and in a fleeting moment I had, without thinking, simply done what I had seen my own mother do countless times with me. The Lord suddenly revealed to me that I didn't need to look any further for a stepmother example. He had already provided the best example I would ever need. I have followed my mother's lead many times since that evening four years ago. Yet, as in most blended families, issues arise that my mother never had to deal with (remarriage, new siblings, custody/visitation, ex-spouses and many more). During those times I continue to look to the Lord for direction, solutions and comfort. He has been faithful and provided far beyond what I ever imagined!

"For the Lord is good and his love endures forever;
his faithfulness continues through all generations."
PSALM 100:5 ♡

The Long Road Home

BONITA LILLIE

What do you do if you have an internal desire to be a stay-at-home wife and mother, but your circumstances aren't lining up with your desire? Let's face it, a lot of women would love to come home, but are simply unable to do so.

Personally, this is an issue I've struggled with for years. Having grown up as a latch key kid, I was determined that I would be home for my children. This matter was settled in my mind until the birth of my first child. Suddenly, I was faced with two major obstacles. First, my financial contribution was vital to our survival. Because of our financial situation at the time, my husband didn't agree that I should be at home full time. The result was that I continued working a few days a week.

This issue created a lot of conflict within me and within our marriage. I felt like God had forgotten me. I became angry with Him and my husband, and disillusioned with the whole idea of family. Thankfully, the Lord helped me overcome these feelings and adjust to the situation. He also rekindled my hope of staying home full time.

I'd like to share some of the principles that helped me the most and I hope these will benefit those of you in the same boat.

Know that God is faithful.

Even though I couldn't have my heart's desire exactly when I wanted it, God was faithful to provide what I needed along the way. Part of His provision included a wonderful, Christian baby-sitter and the ability to choose my own hours at work.

Practice good stewardship.

My husband and I scoured the Scriptures to make sure we were following God's commandments concerning money. We also sought out new ways to invest, save and recycle. Not only did we learn to appreciate what we have, but by applying what we learned I was able to drastically reduce the hours I work.

Submit to your husband.

This has been my most difficult area. It isn't easy to go against your desires and what you think is best in order to submit to another fallible human being. As I look back, though, my submission benefited our family greatly. Because I continued to work, my husband didn't have to get a second job, so he had free time which he used to develop a wonderful relationship with our children. Also, he had time to pursue God's wisdom concerning how to increase his income.

Pray.

Mark 11:22-25 gives us the assurance that our prayers will be answered if we don't doubt. This is easier said than done when you are facing impossible circumstances. Dig into the word of God and find verses that pertain to your situation. Pray, stand on those verses and watch God move.

Never give up!

My first child is 4-1/2 years old now. I'm still a working mom. It's been a long road, but I refuse to give up and I believe this year is my year to come home! Maybe it's your year, too! ♡

I Miss My Momma

MATT OSMAN

This article was written by Matt Osman and published by The Daily Tarheel, a student newspaper at the University of North Carolina at Chapel Hill. It was shared by his mother, Desiree'.

Now settle down out there. I can already hear some of my friends starting in with the "your mom" jokes. Granted, I realize those never grow old, but I really do miss my mom. Besides, I'm secure enough to say it. Does my mom miss me? I can't imagine that she would. I'm sure she doesn't miss me beating on my sister or being told that she is wrong. I remember when I first left for college. I wanted nothing more than to assert my own independence. "Oh, yeah, this is the life." Finally I was away from home, with no chores to do, the freedom to do what I wanted.

Call me a momma's boy, but the good old days when Mom used to fix me peanut butter and jelly sandwiches are starting to look better than ever. While the reality of "senior-ness" is still setting in for me, the memories of the past are only becoming more vivid. Granted, my memories are probably glorified accounts, but I love talking with my mom after dinner. I can never hear the same stories enough.

There was the time when as a 3-year-old I picked some chewed-up gum from a gravel ash tray at the mall. My mom, displaying an amazing quickness, threw me down and proceeded to dig it out of my mouth. Despite my kicking and screaming, this was only the beginning of a long line of battles I was destined to lose. Another time, my mother and I engaged in a battle of iron wills over the issue of potty training. Although I was only 2, I'm sure that my mother's love was severely tested that day. At the end of that hellish day she literally threw me at my father when he walked in the door from work.

Like all familial relationships we had our fair share of ups and downs, the larger part of the downs coming because I had way too big a mouth for my own good. As convinced as my mom is that I have been scarred for life with some of our past warfare, I love her still. And the best part of it all is that I know that she loves me. She gets worried when I am sick and prays for me when I am stressed out. She is deeply interested in my future and wants nothing but the best for her baby boy.

I hope to always hold that place in her heart. I was the first born, the eldest son. I'm the one they watched the "Muppet Show" and "Monday Night Football" with when I wouldn't sleep. My mom tells how she would hold me in her lap and with my little arms mimic the referee on television. One day I hope to hold my son and teach him how to signal a touchdown.

One of the best things about my mom is that she has never tried to hold on to me so tight that I couldn't move. Never have I needed to cut the so-called apron strings to gain my freedom. In her infinite motherly wisdom, she gave me freedom rather than smother me with her June Cleaver impression. When I left for school back in August, my mom walked me to my car. After giving me a big hug, she said something I will never forget. She said, "I don't want you to grow up, I just want you off the payroll." Gee, Mom, thanks for the sentiment. I don't enjoy being a sponge, but there's no sense in arguing the truth that I am. Sure, I worked my token summer job to pay for my "expenses," but it really boils down to the hard work and love of my parents who have blessed me with a college education.

When I turn 21 I know that any chance of regaining the safety and security of my mom's love will be lost forever. Of course she will still love and care for me, and at least the knowledge of that carries me through the hard times. I hope she realizes that I really do love her, even if all I ever bring home from school is dirty laundry and sleep deprivation. But even in this age of independence, I really do.

I miss you, Momma. ♡

CHAPTER *Eight*

Holidays and Everydays

Healthy Resolutions That Last

LAURIE ELLSWORTH

*I*t's estimated that 95% of all resolutions made each year never come to pass. Even if folks start out committed saying, "Okay, this year I AM going to be successful with managing my weight, my temper, my organization skills ..." — they rarely stay on track past the first few weeks. They end up feeling more guilt because they failed once again to make good on that illusive resolution. What a sour way to begin the new year — already defeated!

Christian sisters, God has called us to live victorious lives where we are conquerors, upheld by His powerful right hand. He understands when we don't have enough willpower to lose weight or be in perfect organizational order. He isn't disappointed when we are weak, only when we fight the battle in our own strength. One of the reasons resolutions fail each year is because we often forget that God wants to be a part of them. What about letting Him choose your resolutions for you this year? Instead of making up a long list of ways you need to strive for perfection, let your loving Father gently guide you toward His plan for you.

Last year I was going to work on developing better organizational skills, but I heard God's wise voice say, "You could probably get all of your filing done each week if you'd stop watching daytime TV." Ouch! That hurt, but I took it to heart and switched from TV to Christian radio. A year later, my office is always orderly and my mind and heart are being more influenced by godly values.

As a fitness educator, I receive a lot of inquiries this time of year about weight loss and getting in shape (the number one resolution, according to a poll by USA Weekend). It's a joy to tell people to take it to God first and hear what He has to say.

Then, if God agrees with them that losing some weight would make them healthier, I offer these guidelines represented by the acrostic **WELL:**

Water — Drink at least eight glasses every day. If we don't get enough water, we are much more likely to get fatigued. Too little water may stimulate our hypothalamus (thermostat-like brain center) to increase our appetites. Our body cannot function without water and since God designed our bodies to protect themselves, they will accept water from food as a source. That means that you could be eating more food than you need and the result could be an increase in stored fat/weight gain. Not drinking enough water has a powerful effect on your body so drink enough of it and let it work to your advantage.

Eat by the Food Pyramid — Most of the food you eat should be rice, pasta, bread, cereal, whole grains, with six to 11 daily servings. Fruits and vegetables should be the next most chosen food with three to five daily servings of each. Consume two servings of meat each day, preferably chicken or turkey, and two dairy servings. Limit sweets and fats.

Lift your heart rate by exercising aerobically five to six times a week. Three to four times a week isn't enough to make a huge difference. Aerobic exercise means anything that keeps your heart rate elevated consistently for at least 20 minutes, including walking, bike riding, a dance class, stepping machine, swimming, etc. Use the "talk test" to determine how hard you should be working. You should feel like you need your mouth open for air, but can still carry on a conversation. If you can say four or five words and then feel the need to take a breath, you're likely to be in the correct range. If you are pregnant, remember that all your exercise should be low to non-impact, and don't get too warm because even though you can sweat, the baby can't.

Lift weights to maintain a high metabolism and toned muscles. Many women tend to leave the iron pumping for men, but it is crucial to your success in maintaining a healthy weight. Start with small two- to three-pound hand weights and use a safe exercise video to find out what works for you. Any of Kathy Smith's videos are extremely safe. Becky Tirabassi uses Christian music, and the Buns of Steel, Arms of Steel, etc., series is very good, too.

Resolutions are meant to improve us, make us more loving, more fit, more godly, more faithful. And while I agree that we do well to strive for those attributes, this year my biggest resolution is to daily surrender my goals and weaknesses in prayer. I desire nothing more than to hear the Lord's voice assure me of His love and acceptance and mercy. And I know that it is there, at the feet of my precious Savior, before the throne of the Almighty, that I will be renewed and empowered to see me as He sees me: precious, holy, set apart, esteemed.

What a way to begin the New Year. Already victorious! ♡

A New Year's Tradition

BETH McKNIGHT

Several years ago we had a New Year's Eve party where we "prayed in" the new year. We prayed ahead of time about whom to invite. We invited a large group, many of whom did not know one another, and left it to the Lord to select the group.

Just the right number of people came, and just the right blend. We gathered about 9 p.m., after church services, and had time to socialize before beginning to pray, around 10:30 or 11 p.m. We also read Scripture aloud.

After midnight, I served a light breakfast of mock-cheese soufflé with fruit salad and banana nut bread. Some people left, and some stayed and talked until the wee hours.

It was a warm, positive way to begin the new year with cherished friends. ♡

Special Ways To Say Happy Valentine's Day

VICKIE PHELPS

*A*re you tired of giving the same old valentine cards every year? Try one of the following ideas, which is sure to put a sparkle in someone's eye! Choose a new way to say, "I'm thinking about you," on February 14.

- Send a card or letter to an elderly neighbor or relative, offering to do a service for them during February. Supermarket trips, baking and letter writing are just a few examples.
- Take cuttings from your large plants and make several smaller ones. Tie a red bow around the pot and you have a nice valentine to give to plant-loving friends, for your husband's office or a child's bedroom.
- Prepare your favorite candy or cookies. Divide into small quantities and distribute to the postman, hairdresser, etc.
- Make special crafts (with your children, if they're old enough) to distribute to senior citizens in your church or civic group.
- Compose a valentine letter using red paper or white paper with red designs. Send to friends and relatives, informing them of what's happening in your family. Use valentine stickers to decorate the paper and seal the envelope. A great project for kids!
- Invite a special friend to lunch at her favorite restaurant.
- Create you own valentines by purchasing blank note cards and writing your own verse. The same verse can be used in more than one card, since different people will receive them.
- Plan an open house for Valentine's Day. Have fun decorating, then invite friends and neighbors over for simple snacks (appetizers, heart-shaped cookies, punch and coffee). ♡

246

Easter Truths vs. The Easter Bunny

MEG AVEY

It is not often that one finds the barometer of the civilized world inside a card store on a glorious spring day. Mind you, I did not enter my local major market share card store with the intent on changing the attitude of the majority. However, something struck me as odd when in the pursuit of Easter cards I could not in all the hundreds of choices laid before me find one without cute bunnies, adorable chicks or bouquets of flowers. All I was looking for was the true meaning of Easter in something suitable for mailing. When I finally went up to the desk and inquired, I was told I needed to be looking at the area marked "religious." Hmmmmmm, kind of sounded strange to me that the non-religious section was so large they did not need to be specific, yet anything relating to Jesus' resurrection was relegated to one row at the end. My young son, noticing his mother muttering under her breath, said in a stage whisper heard throughout the store "Don't these people know the real Easter story?"

Heaven became our birthright though we as sinners have no rights.

Later that day I wrestled with that innocent question. Just what do people think Easter is all about? There were times when Easter was the most holy of seasons. There were no gifts, elaborate baskets or mountains of chocolate to help us through the celebration. There were constant reflections on the incredible gifts Jesus gave to us which are the keys to His house. Heaven became our birthright though we as sinners have no rights. Jesus' birth is a reason to celebrate and we only have to look around to see that it has become quite a large celebration. Yet, if Jesus did not accept the burden of the cross and feel the loss of His father's presence, there would have not been the triumphant end to death in the resurrection. Read Ephesians 4:7-16 to see what Jesus meant for His followers to do after the cross.

Have we turned so far away as believers that we not only accept what is happening but also participate? How many of you have children in schools that allow all the trappings of Easter as long as there is no reference to Jesus? As believers we need to be careful where our focus is. I have heard Christian parents tell me they would rather not include Jesus' death on the cross for fear of scaring their children. You must take age into consideration but I think all can hear some version of the entire story. Whatever it takes, we need to share with our children the true story of Easter so that they can understand the importance of Jesus' death and resurrection.

Do I mean that there will not be a single chocolate bunny in my house? Speaking as a confirmed chocoholic, of course there will be, but my children will also have something more important waiting for them Easter Sunday. They will know that a very long time ago God so loved us that He gave us His son and that His son gave us the right to join Him in heaven for all eternity. Not only does that last longer than any Easter basket, it doesn't add inches to your waist.

Father God, thank you so much for the eternal gift of Jesus. Heaven's doors are open for us by the sacrifice of your beloved son. We as sinners don't even deserve to be doormats, yet you have made us equal heirs. Humbly Lord, we accept your ever asking love. ♡

Ideas To Celebrate New Life At Easter

LYDIA E. HARRIS

Easter is a season of triumphant celebration, rich with meaning and new life. Easter can also be a time of family fun, surprises and an opportunity to witness to others. While choirs prepare "Christ Arose" and pastors prepare Easter sermons, what can we do to prepare our families for Easter? Try these ideas to add new life to your Easter celebration.

Making an Easter Cross

Is your Christmas tree shedding needles in the back yard? Then here's the perfect use for it.

After Christmas we trim the branches from our Christmas tree and save the trunk. At Easter we cut off the upper one-third of the trunk and nail or wire it to the lower two-thirds, making a cross. This teaches children the connection between Christmas and Easter: Christ was born to die. You can decorate the tree with homemade tissue paper or silk flowers, leave it plain and rustic, drape it with purple fabric, or add a grape vine wreath to represent a crown of thorns. We display our cross beside the fireplace in our living room. It stands as a ready witness and helps us share the Easter story with others.

After Easter we're reluctant to discard our special crosses, so they accumulate in the wood pile. One Easter we displayed three different-sized crosses. The larger cross in the center represented Jesus' cross, with smaller crosses on either side. As I told the story of the two thieves, our grade-school-aged son studied the crosses and asked, "Which cross belongs to the good thief?" I chuckled, thinking it's never "good" to be a thief. But his sincere question provided the opportunity to teach a lesson of our choices, God's forgiveness and new life in Christ.

Baking and Sharing at Easter

We naturally think of giving to others at Christmas, but Easter is another opportunity to teach our children to give. Do you have a favorite recipe? Why not prepare it as a family and make a surprise delivery to a neighbor, hurting friend or elderly person during Easter? Here are some ideas to try:

oatmeal cookies molded into Easter eggs and decorated with frosting; sugar cookies cut into crosses and decorated with sprinkles; chocolate no-bake cookies shaped into nests and filled with green coconut "grass" and jelly bird eggs. For an inexpensive "basket," use empty plastic produce containers from berries or tomatoes decorated with paper handles. Fill them with Easter grass and homemade goodies.

Did your mother make you an Easter basket as a child? Baskets filled with treats delight young and old when discovered on Easter morning. Everyone loves a surprise. Be sure to give one to your husband, too. Consider a basket of fresh fruit as a healthy alternative to sweets.

Some families prepare special foods at Easter. My mother baked paska, a lemon-flavored Russian sweet bread. Even in her 80s, she baked it every year. One Easter when Mother was hospitalized she insisted, "I have to get home and bake paska." There's a great paska baker in heaven now, but I continue the tradition of baking it for my family. We frost the loaves and decorate them with chopped walnuts or colored sprinkles strewn in the shape of a cross.

Easter Symbols

What are the symbols of Easter? Bunnies, baby chicks and Easter egg hunts? Children need to hear the true story of Easter. Family Life Today has prepared a carton of 12 colorful resurrection eggs. Each plastic egg contains a meaningful object related to Easter (e.g., nail that pierced Jesus' hands and feet) along with a booklet explaining these symbols. Look for these eggs at your local Christian bookstore.*

Watching bulbs grow is another way to illustrate new life. Help your child "plant" a sweet potato in a jar of water. Poke in toothpicks on each side near the center so only the lower half of the potato rests in water. Watch the new life sprout and grow.

Easter Greetings

Friends may anticipate cards at Christmas, but why not surprise them with an Easter greeting? Easter is a natural time for surprises. That first Easter held the most wonderful surprise of all — an empty tomb. Share the real meaning of Easter by sending a few surprise cards. Buy them or make them with your children. Save the fronts of pretty floral cards and cut them into crosses. Crosses can also be made from construction paper. Cut them double, hinged at the left to open. I like to write the words from John 11:25-26 inside: *"Jesus said to her, I am the resurrection and the life. He who believes in me will live, even though he dies; and whoever lives and believes in me will never die. Do you believe this?"* This verse presents the clear meaning and message of Easter and allows me to witness to neighbors and friends. Is there someone who needs your love and witness this Easter?

Each Easter I recall the greeting my father taught me as a child; the one he learned in Russia as a boy. Dad exclaimed, "Christ is risen!" and I joyfully replied, "Christ is risen indeed!" Why not proclaim this message of new life in your home this Easter? ♡

For ideas on creating your own Easter Story in Eggs read the next article, "Hatching The Easter Story."

Hatching The Easter Story

SUSAN YOUNT AND SIDNEY DUNLAP

Most Christians celebrate Easter with tremendous joy, knowing that our Lord's redeeming love on the cross, His crucifixion, death and resurrection, are our source of life now and forever. Most Christian parents desire above all else that their children know and understand the love of Christ, and accept the gift of salvation made possible through the Easter story.

Our challenge is communicating the Easter story and the awesome truths inherent in our Christian heritage in ways that our children will truly understand. Relying on the power of prayer and the Holy Spirit, we can share the Easter story using effective learning techniques.

Here is one way you can lay an Easter foundation with your children: make "Hatching the Greatest Treasure: The Easter Story in Eggs." You can use a six-egg story (which we recommend for preschoolers) or a dozen-egg story, depending on the attention level and development of your child.

To make "The Easter Story in Eggs":

1. Spray a half or whole egg carton with gold paint.
2. Glue faux jewels on the outside of the dry carton.
3. Fill the carton with plastic eggs.
4. Using a permanent marker, number the eggs 1-6 or 1-12.
5. Review the Easter story in scripture (John 3:16, Matthew 26-28, Mark 16, John 19-20), keeping in mind ways you can illustrate the story.
6. Decide on the six or twelve points and corresponding objects from the Easter Story that will relate to each egg. (For a 12-egg story, those objects might be a Bible opened to John 3:16; bread and a wine cup; silver coins; a soldier figurine; a crown of thorns and a square of purple cloth; a cross; a nail; a sponge; white cloth and a stone; cloves; an angel; and emptiness.)
7. Purchase and/or make the objects.
8. Fill the eggs with the objects.
9. Write a script using the Easter story from Scripture, assigning a number to each point, corresponding object, and numbered egg.
10. Practice the story until you are comfortable ... then GO TELL THE GOOD NEWS to your child or children.

Begin by saying that you are about to share the greatest treasure in all creation, the Easter story. This is a story of GRACE (God's Riches at Christ's Expense) ... a story of joy. Also begin with egg number one reflecting the source of this story ... the Bible, God's true Word. Get excited as you share John 3:16, God's love and Jesus' desire for us to live forever with Him!

The last egg will be empty like the tomb, because Jesus lives. He rose from the dead, so we are free to love Him and other people. Be sure to wish your children a Happy Easter and give big hugs! Then invite them to tell you the story. Invite them to share the story with a neighbor, friend, or anyone else. Remember ... Jesus said that a child will lead them!

Offer to share the Easter story with your child's preschool or Sunday School class, or during a children's church sermon. Educators are very receptive to the learning principles employed in Hatching the Greatest Treasure. Sharing the Easter story teaches storytelling techniques, including progression and sequencing, as well as reading cues (symbols, object association) and preparedness (sorting, classifying, if you let them explore the eggs and reassemble them). Handling the items contributes to fine muscle development. Shapes, colors and numbers can be reinforced during egg play, and children gain verbal skills as they retell the story.

Enjoy watching your children learn the Easter story, share the Good News and experience God's grace in many ways through this learning tool.

Caution: Young children should be supervised while handling the egg set. Small objects, sharp points and breakable plastic present safety issues. ♡

Decorate With Easter Crafts

JEAN SOYKE

*E*aster is perhaps the most exciting holiday in the life of a Christian. What joy to know that Jesus died and rose again to bring about our salvation! The following crafts can be used to help your children express the joy of the Easter story or to share its message with others.

1. **"Stained glass" cross** — Have your child draw a large cross in the middle of a piece of black construction paper and cut it out (with your help, if necessary). Discard the cutout and save the outline. Cut two pieces of waxed paper, each approximately 8 x 11 inches. Let your child use a vegetable peeler to shave old crayons over one piece of waxed paper, lightly covering it completely.

   Place the other sheet of waxed paper on top, then put the waxed paper "sandwich" on top of a wad of newspaper. Place three or four more sheets of newspaper on top and press with a warm iron. (NOTE: DO NOT ALLOW YOUR CHILD TO USE THE IRON WITHOUT YOUR PERMISSION AND SUPERVISION.) Remove the waxed paper "sandwich" and have your child staple or tape it to the back of the black construction paper. Hold it up to a window and watch the spring sunlight as it comes through the "stained glass."

2. **Triptych** — Help your child cut a manila folder in half crosswise, from the open edge to the fold. Discard the half with the tab. Have your child separate the front and back of the remaining piece. Help him round the top of the back piece to form an arch shape. Cut the front in half crosswise and make two arch shapes, each half as wide as the back piece. Have your child use crayons to draw a picture of the Easter story in each section. Attach the two smaller arches on either side of the large arch with tape. Bend the side pieces to that the triptych is able to stand. (NOTE: Rubbing a light coat of vegetable oil over the pieces before attaching gives the triptych a rich, translucent look.)

3. **Egg carton "lilies"** — Separate the sections of an egg carton (preferably Styrofoam; you can also use white tempera paint on cardboard cartons). For each section, cut deep "V" shapes in each side, creating

four points in the corners. Poke a small hole in the bottom of each "lily" and run a green pipe cleaner through it. Twist the end of the pipe cleaner inside to hold the "lily." If desired, glue or staple green construction paper leaves or Scripture verses onto the pipe cleaners.

4. **Pysanki** — This is an eastern-European method of dyeing Easter eggs. While this is traditionally done with hot wax and blown eggs, you can provide your child with a white crayon and hard-boiled eggs. Have your child draw an Easter design on a piece of scrap paper and decide what colors he or she would like in the design. (Your child might choose an Easter symbol such as a cross, a Chi Rho, a butterfly, a lily or a crown.) Next, the child lightly draws the design on the egg with pencil. The part of the design that is to be white is traced over with white crayon, then the egg is dipped in the lightest color of the design, such as yellow. After the egg has dried, the part of the design that is yellow is traced in white crayon, and the egg is dipped into the next darkest color, such as orange. Continue the procedure until the egg has been dipped in the darkest color you have available (usually blue, dark red or purple). When dry, the crayon can be scraped off or removed with a paper towel slightly dampened in hot water.

5. **Stick Puppets** — Have your children draw the different characters from the Easter story no larger than five inches high — Mary, Peter, John, Jesus, the angels, etc. Cut out the figures and glue them to craft sticks. Your children can now use their puppets to tell the story.

Easter is a time for rejoicing. May your home be filled with joy this season as your children decorate it with their homemade crafts. ♡

Sweet Colors Of Easter

JANET GOTT

RED IS FOR THE BLOOD HE GAVE,

GREEN FOR THE GRASS HE MADE;

YELLOW FOR HIS SUN SO BRIGHT,

ORANGE IS FOR THE EDGE OF NIGHT.

BLACK IS FOR THE SINS WE MADE,

WHITE FOR THE GRACE HE GAVE,

PURPLE FOR HIS HOURS OF SORROW,

PINK IS FOR OUR NEW TOMORROW.

A BAG OF JELLY BEANS,

COLORFUL AND SWEET;

IS A PRAYER! IS A PROMISE!

IS A SPECIAL TREAT!

EUNICE ELLEFSON

This poem, which appeared in an Amish newspaper, is a wonderful way to teach children the real meaning of Easter. Make ahead a daily treat for your child using sandwich bags. Put in one or two jelly beans of each color, tie with ribbon and have them ready the week before Easter. As you say each line of the poem, you and your child can share the different colors. By Easter morning, each jelly bean will have a new meaning.

This was so much fun for our family that we wanted to share it with others. We took enough to our church for the Cherub choir practice and the children's Sunday school classes. Imagine our surprise when the high school and junior high classes came downstairs eating jelly beans and reciting the poem!

If you want to share this or let your child make a daily treat, here's how. Put paper liners in a cupcake tin. Sort the jelly beans by color. Using one color at a time, let your child put the jelly beans in the liners. Repeat for the seven other colors, making sure each liner contains all of the colors before bagging. Place the full liner into a sandwich bag. Make copies of the poem, punch a hole in the corner and attach to a ribbon when tying the bags shut.

You have been teaching "naturally" — language arts, one-to-one counting, color identification, sorting, methodology, the meaning of Easter and sharing. Jelly beans are a terrific investment. ♡

My Father, My Hero

VICKI LANE

My father passed away one Sunday in December, 14 years ago. He suffered a heart attack while directing the choir at church. It truly was "the day I cried endless tears." The words of this poem came to me while driving the car several weeks after he died. I've never shared it with anyone. It seems a fitting tribute for Father's Day. My father was and is my hero. He taught me all the important things in life. He was a remarkable man and I miss him. Happy Father's Day, Daddy! I love you!

HIS HAND WAS VERY LARGE
AND HERS WAS VERY SMALL
SHE WAS VERY LITTLE
AND HE WAS VERY TALL.

HE WAS SO STRONG
THE TALLEST MAN SHE KNEW
AND HE REMAINED SO
EVEN THOUGH SHE GREW.

HE WAS ALWAYS THERE
HE KNEW JUST WHAT TO SAY
WHEN SHE HAD A HURT OR CARE
HE'D MAKE IT GO AWAY.

HE TAUGHT HER SO MANY THINGS
MORE THAN HER HEART COULD CONTAIN
ABOUT LIFE — LOVE — DREAMS — SONGS
SO EVEN WHEN HE'S GONE, IN HER THESE THINGS REMAIN.

SHE NEVER KNEW WHAT SADNESS WAS
'TIL THE DAY SHE CRIED ENDLESS TEARS
BUT EVEN THOUGH SHE COULD NOT SEE
HE WAS THERE AND CALMED THOSE AWFUL FEARS.

SHE'S MUCH OLDER NOW
BUT IN A WAY — STILL VERY SMALL
HE WAS JUST A MAN — A FATHER
BUT SHE'S SURE, THE GREATEST MAN OF ALL. ♡

The Gift Of A Father's Love

LYSA TERKEURST

My dad is not blood related — he came to be my dad when my mom got remarried. Our family had been through a messy divorce and I didn't want to trust any other man, especially not enough to call him dad. I tried everything to get him to go away. I remember telling him once that my mom didn't really love him, she was just marrying him for his money. This, of course, was not true. Deep down inside I wanted so desperately to feel loved, but my hurts ran deep and I felt unlovable.

I remember the Christmas before he and my mom were to be married. He gave me a small gold ring with my birthstone in it and told me that he loved me. That event started a slow process that would eventually chip away at the walls around my heart. He took me camping with the Girl Scouts, helped me get through algebra, showed me how to save enough money to buy my first car with cash, made me write an essay on the importance of safe driving when I had my first fender-bender and he told me I was beautiful even on bad hair days. I still have a letter he sent to me in college reminding me to do my best in life, but keep life in perspective. He also told me that it didn't mean I was a failure even though I was failing economics. After all, he had almost failed one of his law classes and now the school invites him back to teach that very class.

My father met me at each stage in my life and actively participated in my struggles and triumphs. He didn't give me life but he gave me love. Remember, fathers, to take the time and effort to love each child as God loves you. You are the best example of Christ in your child's life. I wasn't able to fully understand Christ's love until my dad showed me how a parent's love should be. ♡

The ABC's Of Honoring Dad On Father's Day And Every Day Of The Year

LYDIA E. HARRIS

Father's Day is a perfect opportunity to teach our children the biblical command of Ephesians 6:2,3: *"Honor your father and mother"* — which is the first commandment with a promise — *"that it may go well with you and that you may enjoy long life on the earth."* The promised outcome for obedience — a long, happy life — is certainly what we want for our children. Here are some fun ways to help them honor their fathers and grandfathers.

A. **Affirm Dad with banners, cards and notes.** Banners can be purchased, computer-made or designed by the kids. Hang banner on the front door "World's Best Dad Lives Here." String together Dad-sized paper footprints; write appropriate slogan on footprints, e.g "Dad, we want to follow in your footsteps" or words of appreciation about him. Trace children's hands onto paper and list things Daddy does for them with his hands (e.g., fixes broken toys). Alternately string hands with hearts telling why he's loved.

Cards, homemade or purchased, express love, honor and respect. Cut cards shaped like neckties, first-place ribbons, or the letters D-A-D connected. Create collage cards using pictures from old magazines. Write messages or acrostics for DAD, FATHER, or GRANDPA inside. Use descriptive words for each letter (e.g., D-devoted, A-admirable, D-daring).

Notes add surprise to Dad's life. Hide messages in unexpected places (e.g.) in his Bible, shaving case, pillow, briefcase). Tuck notes in his suitcase when he travels. Make a balloon bouquet with affirming notes inside. Place a note in each balloon before blowing it up. Play the lively game, "You're the best Pop." Dad must "pop" balloons to find messages. Affirmations inside could include compliments, memories, prayers, etc.

B. **Bless him with prayer.** Plan a special time of prayer as a family, thanking God for Dad. Include a scriptural prayer from Ephesians 3:16-19,

Numbers 6:24-26 or a favorite passage. Pray daily for your husband and teach your children to do the same. Pray for godliness, wisdom and strong family relationships. If you don't pray for him, who will?

C. **Crown him "King for a Day."** Place a paper crown on his head and treat him like royalty. Serve his food on a special plate, decorate the table with a centerpiece made by grouping pictures of him at different ages and add a sign, "Love is spelled Dad." Wait on him and don't allow him to do any work. He won't object, I promise.

D. **Delight him with father-child dates or planned outings.** Make coupons describing the date (e.g. sports event, concert, movie, out for ice cream cones, flying kites — whatever Dad enjoys and is appropriate for the child's age). These events create happy memories and father-child bonding. He wouldn't mind a coupon for a date with his wife, either.

E. **Entertain Dad with songs, skits, slides, or games.** These show him he's special and provide wholesome family fun. With younger children, write a song about him using a familiar tune. Grade-school aged children may enjoy acting out a short skit, "This is your life," or narrating a slide show about Dad. Play charades, dramatizing some of his interests, hobbies or special attributes. One game our children enjoyed playing was, "Beat the socks off Dad." Together they'd wrestle him to the floor, trying to pull off his socks while he protested and resisted. Eventually he'd let them succeed. They still laugh about these fun times with Dad.

F. **Favor him by fixing his favorite foods served in his favorite place.** Does he prefer breakfast in bed? An outdoor steak barbecue? An elegant meal? Or dining in a special restaurant? If possible, let children help prepare the food, set the table, draw placecards and "wait" on Dad.

G. **Give him gifts to show love and gratitude.** Suggest ideas for what Daddy likes and shop together for the gifts. Children could make coupon gifts for doing his chores for a day or week (e.g., take out the garbage, let out the dog, help wash the car). If he enjoys reading, consider a Christian fathering book or magazine as a gift.

H. **Honor Dad all year through, not just on Father's Day.** Honoring means more than cards, gifts and family fun. It includes obedience and attitudes of the heart. Teach your children to obey their father and speak respectfully to him, correcting them when they don't. Support your husband in child-rearing goals and allow him to exercise his God-given authority. Set a good example for your children through the love and respect you show your husband, their dad, and their grandfather, your father.

These are a few ABC's to get you started honoring Dad. Adapt them for your family or create your own. As your children learn to honor their father, they'll learn to honor you, their mother, as well. Teach them to obey God's command and they'll reap God's promise of a bright future: "... *that it may go well with you and that you may enjoy long life on the earth.*" ♡

Looking For God On Vacation

SHARON JAYNES

One summer my family visited the San Francisco area for vacation. My heart's desire and prayer was that we would see God's handiwork and be reminded of His greatness as we ventured out like three eager explorers to discover new aspects of His creation.

We traveled south along the shoreline and were amazed at the 150-foot regal cliffs that rose from the earth and pushed heavenward with waves splashing at their feet. Then we traveled north and drank in the beauty of acres and acres of vineyards on grassy rolling hills in the Napa Valley wine country. We stood under 1,000-year-old, 260-foot redwoods and were dwarfed by their towering branches.

But the most amazing sight of all was in a place called Alcatraz. There in the middle of the San Francisco Bay, just a mile and a quarter from the sights and sounds of the beautiful city, sits a rock island, known by some as the "Devil's Island of America." From 1934 to 1963, Alcatraz was a prison where the country's most corrupt, incorrigible criminals were housed. Al Capone and Machine Gun Kelly were just a few of the more colorful residents. Today, visitors can wear headphones and hear ex-prisoners tell about their life behind bars with no hope of ever being free. As I stood in a place called "the hole" which was used for solitary confinement, I tried to imagine what it would be like to live in total darkness with no other voice but my own. It was a depressing place of hopelessness and despair.

But as I rounded the final corner of the tour, I saw the most amazing sight: a white haired, 80-year-old grandfather with laughing blue eyes and a wide smile that spread across his wrinkled face. A line formed as tourists stood waiting for him to sign his name and number on his autobiography, *Alcatraz: From the Inside*. This precious man before me was Jim Quillen, ex-prisoner #AZ586, who spent 1942 to 1952 behind bars in this prison that was built to house the most dangerous criminals of his day. I looked into his eyes as we spoke. This was not the face of a dangerous man. What had happened that had changed his life?

I didn't have to flip many pages in Mr. Quillen's book to find the answer. In it he wrote, "It was only through the grace of our Lord Jesus Christ and His intercession that my life of hopeless incarceration was averted. His help and forgiveness permitted me to obtain freedom, family and a useful and productive place in society." I went back over to Mr. Quillen and sat by his side for a minute or so. Then God spoke to my heart, "You prayed that you would see My handiwork and be reminded of My greatness. This man is some of My best work."

On my trip to San Francisco I saw regal cliffs, rolling vineyards and majestic redwoods. But when I looked into Jim Quillen's eyes, I saw God's most incredible masterpiece, a changed life.

As you travel with your family, whether to the shore, the mountains or even simply to the neighborhood park, ask Him to show you something of Himself in a new and fresh way.

This and additional inspirational stories by Sharon Jaynes can be found in her book "At Home With God — Stories Of Life, Love and Laughter," published by Honor Books. Release date: 2000. Used in this work with permission from the publisher. ♡

When I looked into Jim Quillen's eyes,
I saw God's most incredible masterpiece,
a changed life.

Summer Fun For Kids

COMPILED BY PROVERBS 31 NEWSLETTER TEAM

Whatever the age of your child, summertime can seem overwhelming. The routine of school, play groups or other activities disappear, leaving you with lots of free time. The following ideas have been contributed by our subscribers through the years. We hope they help you find constructive ways to have fun and keep your children busy during the summer!

- Take the kids on an outing: Water parks, children's museums, children's movies (summer passes sometimes available), amusement parks (season passes are often less expensive if you live close by), state parks, or the library are fun places to spend the morning or afternoon.
- Pretend you are at the beach: If its rainy outside, fill the tub up with water, toss in a couple of beach toys, turn on a tape of wave sounds and pretend you're at the beach. If it's nice outside, do the same thing in the wading pool.
- Paint with matchbox toy cars: Roll wheels in a water-based paint, then roll on white paper, using different colors and designs.
- Make fruit pizza: Use a pre-made sugar cookie dough or make your own, roll out on pizza pan and bake at 350 degrees until light brown. Layer icing (1/2 tsp. vanilla, 8 oz. cream cheese, 1 box confectioners sugar, 1/2 stick margarine blended together) on top of dough. Place fruit in circles on icing. You can use grapes, blackberries, strawberries, kiwi, oranges, etc. Cut like a pizza and enjoy. ♡

Tips For Summer Vacations

MARY ELLEN BIANCO
AND JENNIFER McHUGH

As we plan those fun summer trips, being prepared is the best way to start. Our families have traveled extensively and through trial and error we have learned how to be efficient and organized.

The first decision to make is where and when to go on your vacation. The age of your children should be your primary consideration. A theme park is great for children over 3 years old, but if they're any younger, a beach vacation or something less structured would be better. A toddler might be overwhelmed at a big amusement park. Older kids always want to be on the go, so a spot like Myrtle Beach, with a variety of activities, would be a good choice. Of course, keeping within your budget is an important goal.

Managing young children on vacation can become a greater challenge than normal and often you will come back more exhausted than when you left. There are breakable things within easy reach and new dangers such as brick fireplaces, un-gated stairs, sharp table corners, etc. A solution for some families is to hire a babysitter to go along. It is so nice to have an extra pair of hands when traveling on the road, stopping for a picnic and even getting the kids to bed at night. This is a great solution — even if you don't have a lot of money. Usually a teenage girl will go for next to nothing if you offer her "free time" on the beach, a free game of miniature golf and pay for her expenses while on the trip. Check with the homeschooling association in your area or ask friends for referrals. Be sure to spend some time with them to see if they are compatible with you and your family beforehand.

What to pack? A first-aid kit that includes syrup of ipecac, acetaminophen, bandages, cough medicine and antihistamine, sunscreen and lip balm. Prescription medication should be easily accessible. Bring your pediatrician's number and insurance cards in case of emergency. If you are stopping for the night, pack pajamas, toiletries and a change of clothes in a small bag so you don't have to unload the whole car. Other items to pack are sunglasses, hats, special toys, blankets or pillows, diaper wipes (for sticky fingers), paper towels and window shades for the car. Bring along

socket covers and other safety supplies if you have an infant or toddler. If
you are staying at a hotel, the amount of clothes you need will vary. If
laundry facilities are available, you can pack less. Bring a sweater or light
jacket, since you never know what the weather will be like. One outfit with
long pants or a pair of tights will keep little legs warm. A small umbrella is
also a must — it will fit in a diaper bag or suitcase.

Whether you travel by car or airplane, plan to bring toys or games along.
A cassette tape player, books, crayons, coloring books, pencils, paper and
small figures tend to be our family favorites. When driving, stop frequently
to let your children stretch their legs and change places to reduce boredom.
Simple, healthy snacks and drinks will also keep you going between stops.
You might want to bring a small cooler along for formula, milk or juice.
Try to keep on schedule with meals and snacks for young children. They'll
be much happier and so will you.

If you're travelling by airplane, help reduce pressure in your child's ears
during takeoff and landing. Have them drink something, or chew gum to
equalize the pressure. A pacifier will even work. Let your child get up and
move around occasionally. Bring along some of their favorite snacks too.
It will make the plane ride a lot more enjoyable.

Remember that safety should always be your top priority. Keep children
in their car seats or seat belts at all times. When you arrive at your destination, take the time to find fire escapes and look for dangerous balconies,
stairs, etc. Protect them from sunburn, accidents and injury by always
being aware of your surroundings. We start each trip with a prayer and we
end each trip thanking God for protecting us. It's a great way to teach your
children to depend on Him always. ♡

Prayer Walking With Children

A WONDERFUL HALLOWEEN ALTERNATIVE

MARY LANCE V. SISK

During a Billy Graham Crusade in my city, three of my grandchildren, ages 7, 9 and 11, helped me reach out to my neighbors by putting together informational packets about the crusade. Together, we prayed over the packets and then my husband, Bob, helped the children hang one on the doorknob of each home in my neighborhood. We all had great fun doing this and the children returned full of joy. When I asked them what was the most fun, the grandchildren wholeheartedly agreed that standing in front of each home to pray for our neighbors was the very best part!

Five weeks later, these same grandchildren were to spend a few days with us while their parents were away. As Halloween fell during one of those days, Jonathan, the 7-year-old, came to me with an idea. He said, "Mommo, we want to dress up like angels and walk around your neighborhood to pray for your neighbors!" I thought this sounded wonderful, so on Halloween night Bob and I accompanied our three "angelic" grandchildren as they went door-to-door in my neighborhood — not to trick-or-treat, but to pray for each home, and give a blessing and a little bag of treats they had prepared! My neighbors were absolutely delighted, the children were warmly received and God was honored. What a wonderful way to turn Halloween into a blessing! ♡

A Box Full Of Blessings

BONITA LILLIE

ast Thanksgiving I started a blessing box, an idea I found in the November 1995 issue of *The Proverbs 31 Ministry* newsletter. Whenever God blessed me or my family in any way, I wrote the blessing on a slip of paper and put it in a children's shoe box. I quickly learned that my view of God was much too small when the box was full to overflowing in less than four months.

I'm amazed at the goodness of God. It seems I scarcely prayed for a need before it was met. In fact, many of our blessings were neither prayed for, nor needed, but stemmed from God's tender loving care. We faced several unusual trials this year and truly came to know that, *"Many are the afflictions of the righteous, but the Lord delivers him out of them all."* (Psalm 34:19 NKJV) Each family member also experienced personal "victories and fulfilled goals.

quickly learned that my view of God was much too small

God used the blessing box to teach me two very important principles. The first is the principle of the open hand, a hand that freely receives and freely gives. As I began to realize just how blessed I really am, I had an increased desire to be a channel God could use to help others. The second principle I learned is that of the grateful heart. As I slipped each piece of paper into the box, I grew more thankful. The more I expressed this to God, the more the blessings increased. I'm looking forward to the best Thanksgiving Day ever. This year I won't have just a vague sense of thankfulness, but a box full of tangible evidence of God's goodness to me. ♡

The Gift Of A Grateful Heart

MEG AVEY

As mothers we have all been in the same situation: dealing with a child who demands <u>another</u> toy, whines for <u>more</u> candy or complains when only allowed to stay up 30 minutes longer. How can they be so ungrateful? Can this behavior be changed? As the holiday season approaches, here are some ways to help your children appreciate what they have been given.

First of all, look at your own behavior. Do your children see a grateful person who thanks God for all she has? Or do they hear prayers that contain complaints, such as, "Thank you God for this house, but we really wanted a bigger one"? Do you confuse what you need with what you want? Read the Bible to understand the difference. Exodus shows that Moses had the same struggle with his band of ungrateful Israelites. Also, Colossians 3:15-17 speaks of thankful hearts. Try the following suggestions to teach thankfulness:

- Pray daily for God's help in this area.
- Devote more of your prayer time to thanking God. During family devotions, have everyone pray with thanksgiving, instead of just asking God for help.
- Use "please" and "thank you" often, especially with your children.
- Require your children to say thank you and to write notes for all gifts received. Even pre-schoolers can draw a picture.
- Limit gift purchases for special events. Offer other rewards such as hugs, food treats, a trip to the park, etc.
- Volunteer as a family. Go to a food bank, homeless shelter or children's hospital to help others. Discuss what the children see and how they could help change the situation.
- If a child complains about a toy, take it away for a while. Explain that you will keep it unless they appreciate the toy as it is.
- God is so generous to us, His children. He gave us the ultimate gift — Jesus.

Thank you Lord for all you do for us. Help us to turn our eyes away from ourselves and towards you. ♡

Organizing Your Holidays

PART I: PREPARING FOR THANKSGIVING

LYSA TERKEURST

*Y*ou are probably all too familiar with the hustle, bustle and stress that usually accompanies the holiday season. While I can't guarantee the following information will be the end-all answer to your anxiety, I can promise that it will help you get on the road to organization for the holidays. Tasks have been broken down to help keep your preparations manageable and leave time for what's really important. So, if you want a Thanksgiving with time for giving thanks and a Christmas with time to focus on Christ and your family, read on ...

November Week 2:

* Hold a family planning meeting and decide what your Thanksgiving and Christmas will look like, where you'll celebrate each and who will be invited. Create a master calendar to keep track of school functions, office parties and travel plans. Set up a holiday budget that fits within your family's means. Include holiday food costs, decorations, gifts, gift wrap, cards, postage, date night costs for holiday functions, travel expenses and any other relevant expenses. * Invite your Thanksgiving guests. Written invitations are not necessary although they can add a special touch. * Plan your Thanksgiving dinner menu. If it will be pot-luck style, you should be in charge of the turkey, stuffing, gravy and drinks. Guests can bring the vegetables, salads, rolls, cranberry sauce, sweet potato soufflé, desserts and any other family favorites. * Purchase your Christmas cards. * Pull out your Christmas card record and start updating it.

November Week 3:

* Plan your Thanksgiving centerpiece. A piece of festive fall fabric down the center of the table with a pumpkin, Indian corn and other fall vegetables grouped in the center is easy and attractive. Add silk ivy and candles for the finishing touch. *Use a ribbon to tie a Bible verse around each guests' napkin. During your Thanksgiving dinner, have each person read their verse and share what they are most thankful for this year. *Take an inventory of your serving pieces, platters, china, silverware and glasses. Arrange to borrow any extras needed. If your meal is going to be casual, purchase disposable products this week. * If you will be a guest at someone else's home, purchase a small hostess gift. New kitchen towels, muffin tins, gourmet coffee or scented bubble bath are thoughtful and useful. * If you are going out of town, arrange to have someone care for your pets and pick up your mail. * Buy Christmas wrapping supplies: paper, ribbon, bows and lots of tape. * Make your Christmas shopping list, complete with sizes, gift ideas and your budget. * Purchase any Christmas presents that need to be shipped out of town.

November Week 4:
* Check your menu for last-minute details and buy food.

Let's Talk Turkey! Frozen turkeys are best thawed in the refrigerator for five hours per pound. After the turkey is thawed, wash it well and pat dry with paper towels. Preheat the oven to 350 °. Clean the cavity. Save yuckies for gravy or throw away. Salt the cavity and stuff with dressing if desired. Rub the outside of the turkey with pure olive oil. Then slide your hands between the skin and the meat on the breast to break the membranes and rub olive oil on the breast meat underneath the skin.

Emilie Barnes' slow-roasting method is the best way I've found to cook a turkey. It takes longer but requires a lot less attention because you don't have to worry about basting the bird. Put the turkey breast down in a roasting pan uncovered. Cook for one hour at 350° to destroy bacteria, then turn the temperature down to 200° and cook three times as long as moderate roasting. For example, a 20-pound turkey normally takes 15 minutes per pound to cook and would take five hours. This slow roast method takes three times as long therefore cooking time will be 15 hours. A smaller turkey usually takes 20 minutes per pound, so an 11-pound turkey cooked at moderate roasting would take three hours and 40 minutes. Slow roasting an 11-pound bird will take three times as long which equals 11 hours. Emilie says, "Although the cooking time seems startling at first, the meat is amazingly delicious, juicy and tender." When your turkey is done, a meat thermometer should register 185° F in the thickest part of the thigh and juices should run clear when pierced.

*Lay out your serving dishes and utensils. Place a 3x5 card in each dish listing the food it will hold so as guests arrive they will know which one to use. * Set your table a few days early. Set glasses and dishes upside down to avoid dust. * Make a pick-a-chore basket. Write assignments for your guests to help you with on 3x5 cards. As they arrive, have them pick one. Be sure to include filling glasses with ice, clearing the table, dish-washing crew, drying crew, dessert servers, coffee servers and dessert cleaner-uppers. * Be the kind of hostess everyone will be thankful to be around. Keep Christ and a thankful attitude the focus of the day. *After your Thanksgiving dinner is over take a long hot bubble bath. *Wrap your gifts for out-of-town loved ones and get them in the mail next week before the big post office rush. * If you enjoy the after-Thanksgiving sales, get a jump on your Christmas shopping. Don't forget your list! * If you observe Advent traditions, get out all necessary supplies and replenish as needed.

Happy Thanksgiving! ♡

Organizing Your Holidays

PART II: PREPARING FOR CHRISTMAS

LYSA TERKEURST

opefully you found the tips for Thanksgiving preparations in Part I of this article, useful and stress-reducing. Get out your calendar one more time and start planning your way to a peaceful, organized, Christ-centered Christmas.

December Week 1

* Start your advent calendar and candles. This is a great time for family devotions. Have special Christmas devotions during your quiet times.
* Pull out your Christmas decorations and start early this year. Hang a wreath on your front door, string outside lights and put up your tree. We decorate ours early so we'll have more time to enjoy it. It's also nice to have a place for wrapped presents. * Try to finish your Christmas shopping and start wrapping your gifts. We use plain white paper decorated with hand prints, drawings of angels and other Christ-centered pictures and stamps using precut sponges from a craft store. We top our gifts off with colorful ribbons and bows. This is a fun family night project! * If you are planning a Christmas party, send out your invitations. * Finish your Christmas cards and get them in the mail.

December Week 2

* Review your Christmas activity calendar along with invitations you've received and make sure to RSVP in time. * Finish your shopping. If you like the last-minute rush then save your stocking stuffers for week four of December. * Keep up with your gift wrapping. * If you are having a Christmas party finalize your preparation plans. Start gathering your supplies. * Finalize your plans for Christmas Eve dinner, Christmas day breakfast and Christmas lunch. Invite your guests and make out your menus. Don't forget the pot-luck option. If you are going to someone else's home for one or more of these meals, offer to share the cooking load by bringing a dish or two. * If your Christmas tree isn't finished yet, make a fun family night out of decorating it.

December Week 3

* Remember to keep the true meaning of Christmas in your heart, espe-

cially as you get down to these last couple of weeks of holiday preparations. Hebrews 13:2 says, *"Do not forget to entertain strangers, for by so
doing some people have entertained angels without knowing it."* Entertain
some angels this week as you and your family do something for the less
fortunate. * Bake your Christmas cookies with a Christ-centered theme by
telling your children the Christmas story as you cut out the different shapes.
Bundle them up with cellophane and ribbon and these cookies make a wonderful gift for neighbors, your postman and trash collectors. Type or write
out the most important parts of the Christmas story below and underline the
cookies as they relate. Punch a hole in the paper and tie the story to the
cookies. What a creative way to share the gospel!

*An <u>angel</u> brought the glorious news that a savior had been born. Wise
men and shepherds followed a bright <u>star</u> to the manger where Jesus lay.
They brought precious gifts much like the <u>gifts</u> we have under our <u>tree</u>. The
best gift of all that day was Jesus. God sent his only son that whoever
accepts Him into their <u>heart</u> will have life everlasting and go to Heaven.
Let the <u>bells</u> ring out this holiday season as we celebrate Jesus' birthday
and God's greatest gift to us.*

* Finish your gift-wrapping and deliver gifts to friends and neighbors.
* Double check to make sure you have plenty of film, video tape and
batteries. * Check your shopping list and purchase any last-minute gifts you
may have forgotten. Keep some Christmas bags on hand for these. * Make
sure you and your family are recording every gift you receive so thank-
you's can be written. A "Gifts Received" record is handy. It includes space
to record the gift, the family member who received it, the giver and a place
to check when the thank you is sent.

December Week 4

* Look over holiday menus and make out your grocery shopping list.
* Buy your food and purchase a few extras to help stock your church's
charity kitchen. * Make final plans for your Christmas meals. Set your
table in advance. Don't forget candles and a centerpiece! * Lay out your
serving pieces and utensils and label them with 3x5 cards like you did at
Thanksgiving. * Make a birthday cake for Jesus and have a party for Him.
* Make the Christmas story real to your children. Every year my children
and all the cousins dress up as the Biblical characters from the Christmas
story and the kids act out the story while Grandma reads it and daddies
video tape this precious time. * Take lots of pictures of all of these precious
memories! * Don't forget to save a little money for the after-Christmas

sales — the best time to buy decorations, cards, wrapping paper, etc. for next year.

I hope these ideas help to organize your holidays, giving you time and energy to really enjoy them with your family. Don't get overwhelmed by feeling like you have to do everything listed here. Pick out the things that will work for your family and use this time line as a way to make it all manageable. Have a wonderful holiday season. May Jesus and His love be more real to you this year than ever before! ♡

Pray Upon A Star

CARALYN M. HOUSE

Last year, yearning for a more spiritual way to countdown to Christmas, my children (ages 7 and 9) and I made 25 paper stars, approximately four to five inches in diameter. We decorated one side of each star. On the back we wrote the name of someone for whom we wished to pray. Each day, they took turns drawing a star from the basket. We would pray for that person at every meal and bedtime. Then we would hole-punch each star, string a ribbon through it and hang it on our tree. What lovely decorations they made!

When we took our tree down, we mailed each star to the person whose name it bore, with a note explaining what we had done. My children and I were touched spiritually and many of the prayer recipients told us that was the best Christmas gift they received. ♡

Creative Gift Giving

BEVERLY CARUSO

he following column is from a question one of our subscribers sent in for Beverly Caruso, who was featured in the 1996 newsletters.

Q   I'm one of those blessed women whose husband handles the family finances. Because I am a full-time homemaker, I have no independent source of income. This is normally not a problem for me. However, it's awkward saying to my husband, "I need some money so I can buy you a gift." What can I do?

A   After reading your question, my mind traveled back in time. Thirty-some years ago I was close to our baby's delivery date. I wanted to earn the money for my husband's Christmas gift. I spent a day or two working on the Christmas tree lot of family friends. I got a range of reactions from our amazed, and amused, customers. I still remember my sense of fulfillment and satisfaction when Pete opened his gift. The next week our first son was born.

There are several avenues of action for wives in your position:

- By budgeting carefully, you can set aside several dollars from each week's grocery fund. This might need to be an all-year effort in order to have money for birthdays, wedding anniversaries, Christmas, Valentine's and Father's Days.
- Use some of your set-aside money to purchase materials in order to make a one-of-a-kind gift for him.
- Make something and sell it at a profit, then purchase a gift.
- There are unlimited ways you can earn small amounts without neglecting home responsibilities, such as: baby sitting, walking dogs or doing errands for busy working women.
- Have a garage sale and earn the money by selling your unused items.
- Barter with someone. It may take many individual barters to come up with just what you want. For example, you might type for one friend, who will baby-sit for another, who makes just the Bible cover your husband has been admiring. Don't overlook your talents or your possessions when forming your list of available resources to barter with others.

A look at Scripture indicates that Bible women were resourceful in their use of time and resources. You can be, too. As Proverbs 31:24 states: *"She makes linen garments and sells them, and supplies the merchants with sashes."* Take the time to plan what money you need for gifts and how to earn it. You'll be so proud of what you've accomplished. ♡

Good News And Clean Laundry

ANNA M. O'BRIEN

My mother works in the laundry department of a Catholic hospital in New York. The department is located deep in the bowels of the building. In the summer months, fans whir from above in a futile attempt to alleviate the suffocating heat. Some, including my mother, have succumbed to heat exhaustion.

By Christmas, the inferno has become a faint memory. The joy that the upcoming holidays bring bursts forth as the hospital dresses itself up with all the trimmings. One year, the administration sponsored a departmental door decorating contest with a "candy cane" theme. The women and men of the laundry room rose to the challenge with enthusiasm. Their creativity was, appropriately, Christ-centered. "... *at the name of Jesus every knee should bow ...*" (Philippians 2:10) the laundry room's entrance proclaimed. The focus of their display was a picture of Santa Claus bowing down in homage to the baby Jesus and this unique perspective of the traditional holiday treat:

- A candy cane is more meaningful than just a tradition of Christmas. It can remind us of Jesus.
- Its shape is like a shepherd's staff. Jesus said, "I am the Good Shepherd."
- Its wide red band reminds us that Jesus shed His blood for our sins.
- Its narrow red stripes remind us that *"By His stripes we are healed"* (Isaiah 53:5).
- Its wide white bands remind us of purity. For by His death we were made pure.
- Its peppermint flavor is similar to hyssop (Psalm 51:7), which was used in biblical times for purification.
- Its taste is sweet as it is sweet to walk with Jesus.
- Turn the candy cane upside down and it becomes "J" for Jesus.

Their display was a hit! Passers-by commented on its spirit. Others assured the laundry workers that they were sure to win first prize. But when my mother came home and announced that they had taken second prize, I detected a trace of disappointment in her voice. I am certain, however, that the Lord's face shone down upon that little laundry room — truly a more glittering prize. His light shone so brightly that it attracted all who crossed its path. For those few weeks, the laundry department at Mt. St. Mary's Hospital of Lewiston, New York, did more than just pump out clean linens and surgical gowns. It trumpeted out the Good News of Christmas in much the same way that the angels' horns blared on that Most Holy Night. All who heard that sweet sound will never again look at a candy cane in quite the same way.

We are all called to be messengers of the Good News, and we must be prepared to seize the opportunities as they present themselves. Our daily lives must always be decorated like the doors of the laundry room, so that all who cross our path can see that Christ's light burns in our hearts. ♡

Pictures With Baby Jesus

JEANNIE MARENDT DeSENA

Cherie Shelor of Winston-Salem, NC, decided that instead of dragging her children to be photographed with a shopping-mall Santa each year, she would photograph them with baby Jesus. So she set up a photo backdrop near a local mall in the parking lot of a Christian store. Her children dressed up in colorful robes, donned gold cardboard crowns and knelt in a hay-covered shed to have their pictures made with baby Jesus. Family members paid $1 each for the Polaroid shots and took flyers with candy canes and biblical quotes on them. (From the *Charlotte Observer*, December 5, 1995)

This is a great way to teach your children about the real meaning of Christmas. You could take the pictures at home, or get some neighbors together to start an annual event. ♡

An Advent Event

S U S A N   Y O U N T
(W I T H   S P E C I A L   T H A N K S   T O   T R A C E Y   B E C C O N E)

*L*ast fall, a friend and stay-at-home mom shared a great idea for a Christmas tradition: The "Advent Angel." The purpose of the Advent Angel is to shift some attention off of Santa Claus and teach our children about the waiting, watching and always being ready elements of Advent. The latter purpose also underscores our eager anticipation of Jesus' second coming as well as His birth.

The Advent Angel leaves small unwrapped gifts throughout the house with little notes any time between December 1 and 25. Time of day, frequency and location of gifts should vary to keep those little (or big!) ones eager, watching and ready to find a special surprise. The gifts can be symbolic (gold foil wrapped chocolate coins for the King or pieces of a nativity scene) or simple (candy bar or hair clip). My favorite gifts are ones that can be incorporated into a rhyme focusing on Jesus for the Angel's note (i.e. "A miracle you now can see; But the Greatest One is yet to be" to accompany the videotape, *Miracle on 34th Street,* or "Reminder, Reminder, of He Who is Kinder" to accompany a note pad). The Angel's notes can rhyme (I start all of mine with "Hark the Herald Angel brings, Little things on golden wings" on the front of the card) or simply write "To (your child's name), From your Advent Angel."

The experience can be as simple or complex as you wish and age appropriate. I encourage you to make it fun. Let the joy in giving match the joy in receiving to the full glory of God!! I would recommend that you have the same friend, relative or neighbor write the notes (all at once if you are organized) for consistency on paper that you would not normally use (like red and green construction paper). Above all, enjoy, and you'll soon find yourself waiting, watching and eagerly anticipating your child's "Advent Event." The scripture *"and a little child will lead them"* will take on new meaning once again!!! But, hey, moms and dads, remember children come in all ages. You might even have your own Advent Angel!!! ♡

Celebrate Christmas In Every Room

VICKIE PHELPS

*H*ere are some suggestions for creating a holiday atmosphere all through the house during the Christmas season:

Greet guests in a greenery-filled entry. Fill and arrange baskets or large vases with holly, poinsettias or your own house plants in the entryway.

- Use pine cones to fill a basket near the hearth. Add a bow for color.
- Display Christmas magazines and books on the coffee table or near the sofa or easy chair.
- Hang holiday decorated towels and pot holders in the kitchen. Add a basket of gourmet coffees and teas to the breakfast table.
- Decorate small artificial trees in the children's rooms using their favorite keepsakes or small toys. Be sure to include decorations that tell the Christmas story.
- Use red bows or holly to decorate the piano or other musical instruments. Place seasonal music around the instrument.
- Plan to use inexpensive holiday place mats and napkins on the dining table every day during December. Select another set for Christmas dinner.
- Place scented holiday candles in areas too small for an arrangement, such a window sills or occasional tables.
- Display holiday soaps and towels in the bathrooms. A small gift purchased especially for a guest and left on the vanity adds a festive touch.
- Arrange Christmas cards you receive on a fireplace mantle or attached to the doorway or refrigerator door.
- Place small bowls of potpourri in hallways, guest bedrooms and closets. Keep out of reach of smaller children.
- Display holly or mistletoe over the doorway leading into each room and on windows.
- Arrange a nativity scene in a prominent place and as a focal point for all the decorations. ♡

Lighting Christmas Candles

VENUS E. BARDANOUVE

"*I* know our children have a hard time thinking of something to buy us for Christmas," I said to my husband. "We, like many grandparents, have very few needs." Even though we are blessed and amply provided for, we know this is not true of countless others in the world. Therefore, some months before Christmas last year, we wrote our family and friends, expressing our appreciation for all they had done for us in past years but asked them to do a "new thing" for the upcoming holiday season.

"This year we are asking you to begin planning to make our next Christmas a special time for us and others," we wrote. "We suggest you give a gift in our name to a charity, person, organization or any cause that helps meet a need in the world. Then send us a card telling what you did. We will open these messages on Christmas Eve, and hope that your gift, in our name, will 'light a candle' in a dark world."

Christmas came, and what joy we had as we opened many cards and letters under our tree. And what a variety of responses, as varied as the people who sent them! Concrete blocks were given to Habitat for Humanity in our name. A 9-year-old girl and a 6-year-old boy received a book through the Reading is Fundamental Program. Someone gave to the Nicole Brown Simpson Charitable Foundation to help battered women's shelters and promote educational programs on spouse abuse. A flock of chickens and "share" of a pig was another of our presents, given to a third-world family through the Heifer Project International. My daughter knew of an East Indian missionary family of five studying in the U.S. with many needs. She joined her church in donating many useful items. A granddaughter's family had become acquainted with a couple returning to Japan as missionaries and gave them a donation for their work as our Christmas gift. A friend knew of a 70-year-old woman in Montana who has a ministry to needy in her town at a nearby Indian reservation. She provided clothes for many, once taking 50 coats, 70 new outfits and a truckload of frozen and canned food to the reservation. She received a donation for her work in our name, too.

There were several gifts to buy Christmas meals for the homeless and needy. One was to an organization that goes into homes of disadvantaged people and helps them develop skills that will aid them in handling their lives. At Christmas, they went into these homes with supplies and helped the families make cookies, rather than taking boxes of cookies already baked. The idea of Christmas sharing inspired others. A group of my daughter's friends in another state became interested in our request and contributed clothes, toys, books and other gifts to a safe-house for the women and children who were living there on Christmas Day.

> ur Lord said, "I tell you the truth, whatever you did for the least of these brothers of mine, you did for me"

Christmas is over. We received no new slippers, candy, cosmetics or books, but the gifts we received warmed our hearts in a special way. What a glorious Christmas it was! And what wonderful gifts we were given! Our Lord said, "*I tell you the truth, whatever you did for the least of these brothers of mine, you did for me*" (Matthew 35:40). The gifts were given in our name, but may He accept each of them as given in His name, too!

And next Christmas? After thinking about all the small candles burning in the darkness this past holiday, how could we ask for anything other than more candles? ♡

Enjoying God's Presents

LYSA TERKEURST

"Don't you love the thrill of receiving a beautifully-wrapped gift? You shake it and examine its shape, wondering what lies beneath the paper, ribbon and bow. Have you ever opened just such a gift only to be disappointed because the gift was something you needed but not necessarily something you wanted? Sadly, when God sent His Son, the greatest gift this world has ever received, that is exactly what happened. The people were disappointed and ultimately rejected Jesus because, though He was exactly what they needed, He wasn't what they wanted. They desired a mighty king to take over and rule. Yet, God knew they needed a Savior so that is whom He sent.

This still happens today with gifts from God. The one who loves us with a perfect unconditional love always knows what is best for us. The problem is sometimes our definition of best and God's definition of best can be quite different. There are things that I have prayed about and either received a totally different answer than I expected or what seemed like no answer at all. What I have come to realize is that God is always at work around me and in His timing, will answer according to His perfect plan. My choice is to either wait on God's best and accept His way or go my own way and suffer the consequences.

Sometimes God's plan and His timing are hard to understand. I like that popular Christian song that reminds us, "when you can't see His hand, trust his heart." You can always be assured that God loves you and wants the best for you. However, in order to trust God's heart you've got to know His heart. The only way to know Him intimately is to get in His word and apply it to your life. His word is filled with promises of hope, provision, strength, victory and love.

Let me encourage you to take time to open God's word and enjoy God's *presence* as well as His "presents" this glorious Christmas season. Here's a poem that has helped me get ready for Christmas inside and out.

Ready For Christmas

"Ready for Christmas," she said with a sigh. As she gave a last touch to the gifts piled high ...

Then wearily sat for a moment to read, til soon, very soon, she was nodding her head.

Then quietly spoke a voice in her dream, "Ready for Christmas, what do you mean? ..."

She woke with a start and a cry of despair. "There's so little time and I've still to prepare.

Oh, Father! Forgive me, I see what You mean! To be ready means more than a house that's swept clean.

Yes, more than the giving of gifts and a tree. It's the heart swept clean that He wanted to see,

A heart that is free from bitterness and sin. So be ready for Christmas — and ready for Him."

Author Unknown,
Reprinted from
"The Greatest Christmas Ever" ♡

Merry Christmas!

BONNIE COMPTON HANSON

Years ago, as Christmas approached, a homesick young couple was out on the road, headed for a strange city. But when they arrived, all the places to stay had "no vacancy" signs out. So they had to spend Christmas Eve in a rundown, smelly old barn. No turkey. No fruitcake. No Christmas tree, decorations, cards, parties, family get-together. Nothing! Except love. For that night Mary and Joseph had the most joyous Christmas ever known as they welcomed into this world God's Son, the Savior of mankind.

Every year about this time we all panic. Christmas is coming — and there's so much to do! How will we ever get it all done? Here are some time, energy and sanity-saving ideas to help you prepare and enjoy a Christ-honoring Christmas this year:

Meditate on the true meaning of Christmas each morning before you begin your day.

Estimate your expenses. Begin with a total dollar amount that won't put you in debt. Estimate non-gift expenses such as tree, cards or wrapping paper and subtract from your budget. List all those you need to buy gifts for and divide the number into what you have left in your budget.

Refrain from grandiose schemes. If a large gift is needed for someone, maybe several in your family can pitch in and buy it together.

Review what you already have on hand to use. Pull out last year's unused cards and decorations. Check bulbs. Consider loving, homemade gifts: jelly, needlework, baby-sitting vouchers, gifts of your time.

You must be organized. Your daily responsibilities won't stop for Christmas.

Calendars are indispensable. Keep one on the refrigerator or by the phone to note all parties, practices and programs. Make plans early and say no to some things.

Help. Let your family help you. Even little ones can help decorate and wrap gifts.

Remember the Reason for the Season. Helping in a shelter, convalescent hospital, school or youth center can help you show Christmas as a time of giving as well as receiving.

Invite friends for informal times of fun instead of big parties. Pop corn, decorate Christmas goodies, make candy apples, go ice skating, take a hay ride, sing Christmas carols, have Bible study times, watch videos. Why not potluck?

Shop Smartly. Stick to your lists and check off when something's bought. Wear comfortable shoes. Once home, wrap, label, put away or under the tree as soon as possible.

Traditions are half the fun — and it's never too late to start one!

Mail everything early in sturdy, well-wrapped containers with the correct postage.

Ask for assistance from your family, relatives and friends and take short-cuts. Children would just as soon have hot dogs or spaghetti.

Savor this joyous time; it'll soon be past.

MERRY CHRISTMAS! ♡

I Always Burn My Candles

VENUS E. BARDANOUVE

*"Who said Christmas trees have to come down at the
last of December, anyway?"*

It was getting near the end of January and my house was still decorated for Christmas. I had not had time to begin packing away all the lovely decorations. As my husband and I sat in our living room and enjoyed the lighted tree, the nativity set and other lovely trimmings, we realized how much more we appreciated them than we had in busy December.

People who came into our home also seemed to soak up the seasonal — or out-of-season — beauty. Our artificial tree is decorated with handmade white and gold Chrismons (Christ monograms). Each ornament has a symbolic meaning in our Savior, and we and others now had more time to think about them.

"I may not take my tree down until Easter. Well, at least not until Valentine's Day," I said, savoring the freedom to make such a statement. "We enjoy it during these quiet winter evenings." Daring to do as I wished, not as others might think I should, gave me a sense of lightness and freedom. As I grow older I realize that I don't always have to be bound to traditional ideas. I can do as I like in small ways that please me and are not important to others.

I remember Jesus said, *"... if the Son makes you free, you will be free indeed."* (John 8:36 RSV) I know he spoke of a deep truth — freedom from sin. But such loosing frees us from all bondage, fears, anxieties, ideas and traditions, too. My daughter recently told me about an interesting woman she met in a gift shop. They both were admiring some special candles, and Katie commented, "These candles are so beautiful, but I would never burn such lovely ones." The lady said, "Not me. I had a cancer scare last year. Now I use my good china, wear my good clothes, use my best perfume and I always burn my candles."

I have thought about the wisdom of this woman who was savoring life in small ways — a lesson learned when it seemed to be slipping away from her. Jesus said, *"... I came that they may have life, and have it abundantly."*

(John 10:10 RSV) Abundant life! Free! Free from sin! Free from bondage! And free to enjoy the world — its people and its beauty! Why do we often hold it too tightly, treat it miserly, refusing to live in daily enjoyment of the beauty around us and in ourselves and others?

I'm glad I have discovered that I can leave my tree up as long as I wish, and I am going to try to remember to "always burn my candles." ♡

My Gift To Jesus

LYSA TERKEURST

*T*his year I started my Christmas shopping early. No, I didn't search the malls with a perfectly planned gift list to ensure that everyone in my family would receive their heart's desire. I searched within myself to find a gift to give Jesus that would meet His heart's desire. My gift to Jesus this Christmas has changed my life and the lives of many others. You see, I gave Jesus the key to my heart, my whole heart, even my deepest darkest secrets that I always swore I wouldn't let anyone else see.

I have been a Christian for almost 20 years, but I was not free. I have been a slave to feelings of worthlessness, doubt, fear, anxiety, depression and anger. Oh, I put on a perfect smile and kept all of the bad stuff locked tightly away. I attempted to encourage my fellow Christians and win the lost by making everyone think I was perfect. Finally, after 20 years of this charade, I read Neil Anderson's book *Victory Over the Darkness*. I'll never forget getting to page 45 and reading a list that told me who I am in Christ. Tears streamed down my face as I realized that my life has nothing to do with what others think, but everything to do with what God thinks.

I am a child of God, holy and dearly loved. My job as a Christian is not to show everyone around me how perfect I am, but how perfect Christ is. I need to let people know that I am a real person who has had many bad things happen to her. I have also done some terrible things, but I know Jesus, who is the truth, and *"the truth has set me free"* (John 8:32). I consider it a joy that I have had and will continue to have various trials, because I know that the testing of my faith produces endurance. Yet *"let endurance have its perfect result that you may be perfect and complete, lacking in nothing"* (James 1:4).

It's kind of like making a cake. If we took the ingredients, one at a time, and ate them we would not like to eat cake. I mean, who wants to sit down with a tall glass of milk and two cups of flour? Each of the trials we face in our life, though distasteful when looked at individually, will help us become perfect, complete and lacking in nothing when mixed together using Jesus as the recipe for our lives.

My gift to Jesus this year is to let Him have everything in my life to use for His glory, that I might be a bridge over which many may walk from the darkness into His light. ♡

Epilogue

SHARON JAYNES

*W*e have been on an incredible journey looking at the Proverbs 31 Woman and the people that she loves. Let's take just one more peek at this treasure of a lady.

Verse 10 begins, *"An excellent wife, who can find? For her worth is far above jewels."* (NAS) The NIV calls her *"a wife of noble character."* But I personally like the Amplified Version that says, *"a capable, intelligent, and virtuous woman."* Then there's the Revised Standard Version that just says, *"a good wife."* The Hebrew word that's translated, "excellent" or "virtuous," can also mean "wealthy, prosperous, valiant, boldly courageous, powerful, mighty warrior." Now that's a lot better than just "good!"

But you know, there's one word that I could not find listed in Proverbs chapter 31 — the word "perfect." And what a relief. Yes, the Proverbs 31 woman is a pretty incredible ideal. She's an awesome standard of excellence. But it never says she was perfect. She probably had days when she yelled at her kids for misbehaving. She probably had days when her husband kept quiet and didn't praise her at the city gates. And occasionally, I think she had days when she worked with her hands, but it wasn't in delight.

And why do I think that? Because even though she was excellent and virtuous, she was a fallen woman who needed a Savior. And so do we. I can remember when I first heard that I was a "sinner." I didn't really like that word. But then I read that "sin" was an old archery term that meant the distance between the bulls-eye and where the arrow actually landed on a target. To sin meant to "miss the mark." It still means that today. To sin means to miss the mark of God's perfect standard.

And because of that sin, we have been separated from God. But He has provided a way for us to be joined back together with Him. Read over the following Scriptures and consider what God has done for you.

1. *"For all have sinned and fall short of the glory of God."* Romans 3:23
2. *"For the wages of sin is death, but the free gift of God is eternal life in Christ Jesus our Lord."* Romans 6:23

3. *"But God demonstrates His own love toward us, in that while we were yet sinners, Christ died for us."* Romans 4:8
4. *"If you confess with your mouth Jesus as Lord, and believe in your heart that God raised Him from the dead, you shall be saved; for with the heart man believes resulting in righteousness, and with the mouth he confesses, resulting in salvation."* Romans 10:9-10
5. *"Whoever will call upon the name of the Lord will be saved."* Romans 10:13
6. *"There is therefore now no condemnation for those who are in Christ Jesus."* Romans 8:1

If you have never accepted Jesus Christ as Lord of your life, what better time to do that than right now. Simply say the following prayer and receive the greatest gift of all time.

> "Dear Lord,
> I confess that I am a sinner and need Your forgiveness. I believe that You sent Christ to die for my sins and that He rose from the dead. I want to turn from my sins and follow You. I now invite You to come into my heart and be Lord of my life. I want to trust and follow You for the rest of my life. Thank you for saving me.
> In Jesus' name.
> Amen.

If you prayed that prayer for the first time today, we would love to hear from you. God bless you in your continuing journey to become, a Proverbs 31 Woman.

Charm is deceitful and beauty is vain, but a woman who fears the Lord, she shall be praised.

CHAPTER *Nine*

365 Ideas To Make The Year Special

COMPILED BY MARYBET HUDSON

January

1 **Happy New Year!** Ask the Lord what resolutions you need to make this year.

2 Read Psalm 51. Ask God to restore to you the joy of a life lived in His service.

3 Plan a get away weekend with your husband this month to do a "marriage tune-up".

4 Clean out your closets today. Give away anything you haven't worn this last year to a ministry or charity.

5 As a family, take time to commit this year to the Lord and thank Him today for all He will do in the coming months.

6 Listen more than you speak today. Read and meditate on James 1:19 all throughout your day.

7 Let your children record a new message on your answering machine for each month of the year.

8 Rent a movie your husband has been dying to see. Let the kids skip a nap so they will go to bed a little early.

9 Get all of your tax records out and get organized early this year.

10 Let the kids illustrate Bible stories as you read them aloud.

11 Write all birthdays, anniversaries and special occasions on your new calendar.

12 Make popsicles with the children by putting juice in paper cups and inserting straws. Put them outside to freeze.

13 Ask your husband what you can pray for his job today. Tuck a note of encouragement in his lunch or car.

14 Throw blankets over the table and chairs to make a big tent and eat dinner underneath it tonight.

15 Examine your heart. If you need to forgive someone, do it today. Matthew 6:14-15

16 Spend time as a family praying together for your church leaders and teachers.

17 Start a memory book for your parents. Write down special memories and add them to the book throughout the year.

18 Learn to say "I love you" in as many languages as possible. Quiz each other at dinner.

19 Plan a family scavenger hunt around the house with prizes for all.

20 Invite all stay-at-home moms in your neighborhood over for coffee. Pray for how God may use you to minister to them.

21 See how many things can be done in one minute. Time the kids as they do push-ups, sit-ups, pick up toys, etc..

22 Pray for your husband. 1 Corinthians 1:4

23 Shovel a neighbor's driveway as a family service project.

24 Do you know a local hero? Let your newspaper know.

25 Try a new recipe tonight. If you like it, plan to make it again for a friend.

26 Take advantage of technology. Send a message of love to your husband and far away family by e-mail or voice mail.

27 Learn a new skill or homemaking tip. Check out books from the library for ideas.

28 Grow an aloe plant. They aid in healing minor burns.

29 Take your children to a museum or indoor play area. Invite a friend to meet you there.

30 Take a care package of diapers and/or baby things to a local Crisis Pregnancy Center.

31 Invite a single-parent family over for a meal today. Offer to watch the kids while mom or dad takes a break.

February

1 Memorize Psalm 139:14 with your children. Talk about how God has created each person uniquely. Pray for wisdom in raising the unique children He has blessed you with.

2 Make a double batch of muffins or cookies today. Leave some on a neighbor's doorstep as a surprise.

3 Call your husband at work for no other reason but to say, "I love you." Plan a surprise date for tonight.

4 Roast some nuts together, and then shell and eat them by the fire.

5 Help your children learn a new skill such as riding a bike, baking a cake, fixing a flat tire.

6 Pray through the newspaper with your children. Explain how the events affect children just like them.

7 Write ten things you love about your husband. Give a copy to him and then post the list where you can see it and thank God daily for him.

8 Pamper yourself tonight! Treat yourself to a facial, a hot bubble bath and read your favorite magazine from cover to cover.

9 Make your child's favorite cookies or snack in the shape of a heart.

10 Get out the old family photos and play "Remember when?"

11 Three days until Valentine's Day. Now is the time to make your plans and gather your supplies!

12 Lincoln's Birthday Get a book from the library and read about our 16th President.

13 Send a "tender loving care" package to a college student you know.

14 Valentine's Day Say a special prayer of thanks for all of the valentines in your life. Later, serve pancakes filled with chocolate chips and red food coloring.

15 Encourage your husband to take a day off work this month and just spend the day doing things your children enjoy!

16 Fast from something today: a meal, a habit or whatever God lays on your heart.

17 Mending day! Have the children help you sew on buttons while you repair clothes. If children are too young, have Dad help tonight.

18 Surprise your husband for lunch. Wear his favorite perfume and a dress he likes. Tuck a love note in his pocket while you are together.

19 Help your child wash his bike or car. Show that you care about the things that are important to them.

20 Take the kids to a flea market and give them one dollar to spend. See what treasures they find.

21 Read Matthew 11:28. Spend time with our Lord in prayer and just relax in His presence. Let Him refresh you for the week.

22 Washington's Birthday Honor our 1st President by praying for today's President.

23 Send an orange to work with your husband. Include a note telling him you want him to stay healthy.

24 Exercise with a friend. Perhaps you could go on a prayer walk around your neighborhood.

25 Now is the time to begin planning and planting your spring garden. Make a cup of hot tea and enjoy looking through gardening magazines and catalogues.

26 Choose a good deed for today.

27 Read Psalm 90:12 and Ephesians 5:15-17. Make the most of your time today.

28 Obtain a large appliance box for a clubhouse and let the kids decorate it.

300

March

1 Discover what your prayer life with your husband can become. Ask the Lord what He wants you to regularly pray about together.

2 Just for one day be June Cleaver. Greet your husband at the door all dolled up with a charming attitude.

3 Talk to your family about your summer plans. Find out now what everyone wants to do and begin planning.

4 Relieve a caregiver who needs a break.

5 Make today a work day around the house. When the work is done, break out the pizza and games.

6 Teach your children telephone manners. Role play telephone conversations with them.

7 Ask your husband what respect means to him and ways that you can show him respect as a father and husband.

8 Do something to decrease your stress level.

9 Make a necklace with the children using O-shaped cereals for a portable snack.

10 Be a courteous driver. Remember that you are setting an example for future drivers – your kids!

11 Invite an elderly person over to share stories from the "good old days."

12 Let the kids investigate their world with a magnifying glass.

13 Read Matthew 6:25-34. Now turn your worries over to God.

14 Spend time gazing into your husband's eyes. Tell him again how much you love him.

15 Make or order Chinese food and eat with chopsticks.

16 Let the kids tuck you in bed and tell you a bedtime story.

17 St. Patrick's Day. Put green food coloring in your food today – green pancakes or mashed potatoes!

18 Give thanks for your health and your family's health.

19 Call your church and ask if you can donate flowers, perhaps for Easter.

20 Children love receiving mail. Send them a letter or sign them up for a book of the month club.

21 Count ten blessings and help your children do the same. Post the lists to look at over the next week.

22 Deliver a batch of homemade cookies to your husband and his co-workers.

23 Pray for your children's friends today.

24 Learn a foreign language by putting a tape in your car and listening to it during your errands.

25 Donate to a home for unwed mothers.

26 Create a kite out of newspaper and small dowels. Take your kids to fly the kites.

27 As you do your houshold chores this week, make a point not to grumble in the monotony.

28 Make an encouragement package for your pastor.

29 Review fire safety with the family. Have a fire drill and tell the children where to meet you outside.

30 Hug as many people as possible today.

31 It's the anniversary of the Eiffel Tower. Try your hand at making crepes.

April

1 April Fools Day. Play a fun prank on the family today. Perhaps ice cream for dinner with spaghetti for dessert?

2 Mail a love note to your husband, either to home or the office. Mark it "Personal and Confidential."

3 Stay focused and don't major on the minors.

4 Read Matthew 6:28-30 and buy an Easter lily to brighten up your table.

5 Set some goals for getting fit and eating right. Explain to your kids the importance of good health.

6 Only 9 days left …. Are your taxes prepared?

7 Start some new Easter traditions with your children. Perhaps you could invite their friends for an Easter egg hunt.

8 Pray for each child in your family today.

9 Go for a rainy day walk with an umbrella.

10 Give your child a small plot of ground for his own garden. Teach him about new life through plants.

11 Go visit the police station and give kids tips on safety.

12 Swap out babysitting with a friend. Dress up and meet your husband for lunch.

13 Make a Spring centerpiece with the children. Set it on the table for dinner tonight.

14 Make a box of easy craft things that Dad can do with the children when you are out.

15 It's tax day. Serve a poor man's meal of beans and cornbread.

16 Practice makes perfect. Practice patience today towards those around you.

17 Take some time to consider what books God wants you to read.

18 For an elegant treat, dip strawberries in melted chocolate. Yum!

19 Minister to your minister. Write an encouraging note, send some flowers, or just call to say, "Thanks."

20 Make snacks of celery with peanut butter and feed each other. "God loves a cheerful giver."

21 Pray for your neighbors. Tell your children how God has answered prayers in your own life.

22 Secretary's Day. Send a care package to your husband's secretary or to a secretary at church.

23 Take one child on a special "date" today. Then plan another date with another child.

24 Read Proverbs 2:1-5. Hide a treasure for the kids to find. Don't make it too easy.

25 Invite Jesus to dinner and set a place for Him.

26 Let the children write a message to Dad with sidewalk chalk.

27 For insurance purposes, make a video of your home and all your valuables.

28 There is nothing that can happen to separate you from the Father's love. Read Romans 8:38,39.

29 Make a pan cookie and cut it into puzzle piece shapes. Let the kids enjoy themselves as they put it back together.

30 Say "yes" to Jesus today.

May

1 Start each morning by exercising with the kids. Take turns leading.

2 Hide clues all over the house. Make your spouse find his way to a surprise at the end of the hunt.

3 Sing praise songs to the Lord. Talk about how important it is to praise God.

4 Create a collage of your children's pictures for their grandmothers for Mothers Day.

5 "Blessed are the peacemakers." Talk with your family about how peace would change our nation.

6 Mail a thoughtful note to your mom everyday this week.

7 Play beauty salon with your girls. Teach them how beauty comes from the inside, too.

8 Don't expect your husband to read your mind. Tell him what you need.

9 Ask each member of the family to pick a number between 1-10. Give that many kisses.

10 With the children, make a list of 25 things you love about Daddy.

11 Praise God for His gift of nature. Plant a tree or two to help keep the earth clean and alive.

12 Invite a teenager to join your family for pizza.

13 Have your children help with some "Spring cleaning" – shake their stuffed animals in bags filled with baking soda.

14 Go for a walk with your husband and enjoy the beauty God has created.

15 Play a game as a family – Pictionary, cards, hide and seek, etc. Laugh and have fun.

16 Early breakfast! Wake up everybody with praise music, coffee, omelets and chocolate milk.

17 Borrow your husband's appointment book long enough to add a few special "appointments" he can look forward to.

18 Play charades and act out your favorite Bible stories.

19 Don't limit God today. Read Matthew 19:26. All things are possible with Him.

20 Ask your children, "What makes you feel special and loved by me?" Really listen and pray about their answers.

21 Celebrate the giver of life and give back to others. Make a point to donate blood this month.

22 Write a note to the kids and tape it to the back of the cereal box.

23 Let the children set up an art gallery of their work for Dad to tour when he gets home.

24 Pray for your children's future (or present) spouses.

25 Visit a petting zoo.

26 Pray Ephesians 3:16-19 for your husband.

27 Listen to your favorite hymns on the way to church.

28 Have an "Around the World Party" and have each person bring cookies from a different country.

29 If you don't have time to write a letter, send a postcard.

30 Lift someone's spirits with a kind word or deed.

31 Make ID pictures of your kids and place them in your wallet. Update them annually.

June

1 With your children's help, plant an herb garden and you will have fresh herbs for cooking all summer long.

2 Write a love letter to your husband telling him how much you appreciate his help around the house.

3 Give God your best today. Read Psalm 37:5.

4 Read a biography of someone you admire.

5 Write a note of encouragement to your children's teachers. Thank them for all of their hard work this year.

6 Let the kids stay up late and sleep in tomorrow. Play hide-n-seek and other favorite games.

7 Ask your husband what he enjoys doing most. Get a sitter and go do it.

8 Pray for families with small children as they prepare for worship. It can be hard to get little ones to church.

9 Take the family for a ride on a city bus.

10 Use old 2-liter bottles as bowling pins and let the kids bowl inside. Weigh the pins down with water or sand. Add streamers or confetti for color.

11 Help your children write a Father's Day letter to their grandfathers. If they are too little, help them make a cassette tape.

12 Invite neighborhood kids and their moms over for a Splash Day in the back yard. Set up water games and have them each bring a water toy.

13 Cover a wall in your children's room or the garage with an old bed sheet or butcher block paper and let them create their own mural.

14 Look for the good in everyone you meet today.

15 Show your children how to disagree agreeably.

16 Find the number for your local poison center and post it near every phone.

17 Look for ways to show respect for your husband this week.

18 Rearrange your kitchen to make it more user friendly.

19 Help your children design Father's Day cards for Daddy.

20 When changing the sheets, sprinkle baby powder under the bottom sheets to make them smell nice.

21 Cut strips of construction paper and teach the children how to weave.

22 Hug your husband for no reason today. Hide a message expressing your love for him to find.

23 Be spontaneous. Don't make any plans today.

24 Pray for couples in your church who are expecting a child.

25 Fill buckets with water and let the children "paint" the driveway or porch.

26 Insert popsicle sticks in bananas. Brush them with honey then roll them in nuts or sprinkles and freeze them for a cool summer treat.

27 Go through your old, untried recipes and find a new one to try out.

28 When it is time to pay bills, thank God that you are able to do so. Commit all needs to Him as well.

29 Pack a car safety kit with first aid supplies as well as important phone numbers.

30 Do a good deed for a widow or widower.

July

1 Challenge your kids to a water fight. Finish with cold slices of watermelon.

2 For a quick centerpiece, fill a large crystal bowl with water and float a magnolia flower in it.

3 Relax in the tub tonight. If you've had a little too much sun, add some baking soda for a soothing soak.

4 Independence Day. Let the children decorate a sheet cake with a flag design using whipped cream, cut strawberries and blueberries. Yum!

5 Many children and teenagers are attending camp during the summer. Pray for those you know and send a card or a small treat.

6 Give the children plastic water bottles to decorate and then carry with them to prevent dehydration.

7 Make an encouragement calendar by writing scriptures, quotes, jokes, etc., on 365 index cards.

8 Make pancakes or waffles and double the recipes. Freeze the extra for future breakfasts.

9 Fill a jar with Chex mix, nuts or other goodies. Tie with a ribbon and send to work with your husband.

10 Make a movie for faraway relatives that depicts ordinary life at your house.

11 Give yourself a break from cleaning the kitchen and grill outdoors tonight.

12 The year is almost halfway over. If you haven't already, schedule your annual physical exam.

13 Visit a pond and see how many different creatures and plants you can spot.

14 Take your husband to the go-cart track and race with him.

15 Peaches are in season. Make homemade peach ice cream this afternoon. Invite some neighbors over to enjoy it with you.

16 Take a family nap. Enjoy some rest as a family.

17 Go to a museum for the afternoon. Enjoy the air conditioning as you challenge each other to learn something new.

18 Double tonight's recipe and bring dinner to a single or expectant mom.

19 Have a praise day! Sing praise songs in the morning, pray for your day with the kids and give thanks all day long.

20 Spend some quiet time in the afternoon planning your activities for August.

21 Read Psalm 119:103. Visit a beekeeper and get some fresh honey.

22 Catch fireflies with the children and put them in a jar. Take them in a dark room to see how bright their light is.

23 Teach the children in your neighborhood a game you enjoyed as a child.

24 Share a favorite recipe with a new bride.

25 Leave your problems outside the church and really focus on worshipping God.

26 Spend an hour in prayer today.

27 Let your husband be king of the castle for the day. Crown and serve him.

28 For a low cost vacation, spend a night in a local hotel and go sight seeing in your own town.

29 Make a list of expressions of praise. Post the list in a visible spot and see how often you can use them.

30 Let the children finger-paint with chocolate pudding or yogurt.

31 Keep the dinner conversation uplifting. It aids digestion.

August

1 Go to bed early and catch up on some sleep. Fall asleep counting your blessings.

2 Is your garden exploding yet? Perhaps a local food bank or shelter could use your surplus.

3 Make sun tea while it's still summer.

4 Don't expect more from your husband than he can give.

5 Have a watermelon seed spitting contest with the neighbors. Think of some goofy prizes for the best spitters.

6 While shopping for back to school clothes for your children, pick up something extra for a child who doesn't have as much.

7 Stay in your pajamas until lunch time. Have everyone get together and read under the covers with a flashlight.

8 After shopping for new clothes, plan a fashion show for Dad.

9 Treat your children with the same respect you want them to show you.

10 Visit a butterfly pavilion. Make gelatin butterflies with cookie cutters. Be creative with candy eyes, antennas, etc.

11 Pray for your children's teachers.

12 Take a family drive in the afternoon. Explore a nearby town or new park.

13 Spend extra time in prayer for your husband today. Ask the Lord to show you how to pray for him.

14 Talk with your children about their goals for this school year. Pray with them and commit their desires to the Lord.

15 Bless a shut-in with stationary and a roll of stamps.

16 Read Proverbs 22:6. Ask God to reveal your child's unique gifts and talents.

17 Commit to praying daily for someone who doesn't know the Lord.

18 Now is the time churches are looking for people to teach children's Sunday School classes. Could you serve this fall?

19 Take your children to a flea market. Give them each a dollar to spend and see what treasures they find.

20 Challenge your husband to an old-fashioned egg toss. See how far you can toss the eggs before they break.

21 Put out a plate with honey on it. See how many flies you can trap with sweetness.

22 Go garage sale shopping. Pick up a few toys for your church nursery or clothes for those in need.

23 For one day, do things in the wrong room of the house: eat in the bedroom, and sleep in the living room.

24 Read about Paul and Silas in jail. (Acts 16:23-36). Make paper chains and act out the story.

25 Are you registered to vote? Today is a great time to register and be prepared for the fall's elections.

26 Memorize a Psalm today.

27 Invite the grandparents over for family night and let the kids make and serve the snacks.

28 Send flowers to your mother-in-law, thanking her for raising your wonderful husband.

29 Be available to your children's friends if they ever need an adult with whom to talk.

30 Get a jigsaw puzzle to enjoy on the next rainy weekend.

31 Laugh at yourself today.

September

1 Use old mismatched socks to make sock puppets.

2 Line up chairs and let your children play train as you read "The Little Engine That Could." Sing, "I've been working on the railroad."

3 Share a special childhood memory with your husband. Ask about one of his.

4 Pick up some inexpensive "goodies" – like stickers or little erasers – for your children's lunch bags. While you're at it, find a little "goodie" for your husband.

5 Teach a child a new skill – perhaps one that helps with the household chores.

6 Make the Sabbath a time of quiet and rest. Share a favorite story with your family by reading aloud.

7 Read Proverbs 6:6-8. Watch and study ants. Make an ant farm.

8 Make a tape of your children's favorite songs for the car. Or find Scripture verses set to music for easy learning.

9 Pray for the staff of this ministry.

10 Practice being content today.

11 Buy cheap dishes at a yard sale to use when you give a meal. If they don't get returned, it doesn't matter.

12 Play detective by hiding something and giving clues how to find it.

13 Start a babysitting co-op with other parents in your area or church.

14 Read Psalm 37:4 and make a family dream book with pictures to represent hopes and dreams.

15 Believe God for something and don't doubt.

16 Play-Doh was invented in 1956. Enjoy it with your children today.

17 Let your children read to you. If they are too young to read, ask them to tell you a story.

18 Relax in the tub with soft music and candlelight. Perhaps invite your husband to join you.

19 Expose your children to other races, cultures and social classes.

20 Meditate on and pray through scripture for your marriage. Prevent the weeds of strife before they come up.

21 Bless a teacher with something she wants for her classroom.

22 Take the children to a restaurant with a playground. Don't rush, just let them play.

23 Give yourself a break and have a salad bar at home tonight.

24 As a family, act out your favorite Bible stories. Play Bible charades and guess what each is portraying.

25 Go through your magazines and find recipes you haven't tried yet. Make a plan to try them next month.

26 Go on a family bike ride.

27 Pray for your child's principal, teacher and school.

28 Limit phone time. Spend it with your children instead.

29 Pray for joy today as you care for your family's daily needs.

30 Make up a secret sign that will tell your husband how much you love him without using words.

October

1 October is Pastor Appreciation Month.

2 Develop a "hospitality" outreach.

3 Say grace a new way, or let each person make up a blessing for the food.

4 Enjoy the beautiful fall weather. Take the family to a park for a picnic.

5 Don't be overcome by the challenges of motherhood. Look for the hidden treasures.

6 Help the children make a welcome home banner for Daddy to greet him when he arrives from work.

7 Visit our web site at www.proverbs31.org.

8 Election day is only a month away. Pray for godly leaders to be elected to office.

9 Collect brightly colored leaves and seal them between sheets of wax paper with an iron.

10 Hold a family worship service. You be the congregation and let the children handle the preaching and the music.

11 Pray for a single mother today.

12 Start a book swapping co-op with your friends.

13 With sidewalk chalk, make a race track for riding toys.

14 Place a bouquet of flowers on your church secretary's desk.

15 Visit a pumpkin farm and make a pumpkin pie.

16 Have the whole family rake leaves for a neighbor who needs help.

17 Do something special for your pastor's wife. Take her to lunch or give her a gift and a note of encouragement.

18 Pray for your church's missionaries today.

19 Remember, "Love keeps no record of wrongs," 1 Corinthians 13:4.

20 Let the children use a hole punch to make confetti. Save for a special occasion.

21 Encourage Dad to spend time alone with the children for the evening.

22 Make your kitchen into a "restaurant" complete with a menu to choose from.

23 As a family, memorize one scripture from the sermon on Sunday.

24 Pray and ask the Lord how He would want your family to be a light in the darkness this Halloween.

25 Put a note in your child's lunch telling them how proud you are of them.

26 Have a fall cleaning day. Get your house really clean before you have to start organizing for the holidays.

27 Send silk boxers to your husband at work and a note to match. Be sure to mark the envelope confidential!

28 Do yourself a favor and take a long walk by yourself. Have a long talk with the Lord as you go.

29 Begin writing your Christmas "to do" list. Plan a family picture to include in Christmas cards.

30 Get up early and cook a super special breakfast for the family. If it is nice outside, have a picnic.

31 Attend a church Fall Festival. Pray for the friends you have invited to come with you.

November

1 Are you prepared for elections? Be sure to read up on all of the people running for office.

2 Call Operation Christmas Child to find out how you can send a Christmas shoebox to a needy child. 1-800-353-5949.

3 Try to do without electricity for a day. Be creative. Thank God before bed for the blessings you sacrificed today.

4 Call and leave a romantic message on your husband's work answering machine.

5 Read John chapter one as a family. Make a list of all the things you learn about Jesus from that one chapter.

6 Try a "lying low" day and don't plan any extras for the family.

7 Before turning on the heat, replace the air filters and vacuum the vents.

8 Reminisce with your older children about their toddler days. Tell them what a wonderful baby they were.

9 Make and drink hot chocolate together as a family. Turn off the TV and get cozy together.

10 Volunteer at a soup kitchen or homeless mission together as a family. Talk about what you learned by serving.

11 The Bible's love chapter says, "Love is kind." (1 Corinthians 13:4). Think of a special way to show kindness to your husband today.

12 Write an entry in each child's journal about a trait for which you are most thankful.

13 Turn off the telephone for the day. Enjoy some peace and quiet with your family. "Be still and know He is God." Psalm 46:10

14 Share a copy of the Proverbs 31 Homemaker with a friend who really needs it.

15 Choose a color and pray for everyone you see wearing that color today.

16 After the children go to bed, give your husband a long back rub with warm baby oil. Ask him about his day and really listen.

17 Abide by the law of kindness today. Commit as a family to not gossip or speak negatively today.

18 Decorate your house for Thanksgiving. Help your children make homemade decorations.

19 Let the children create special hors d'oeurves for Daddy to enjoy when he comes home from work.

20 Declare a family workday to get your house ready for the holidays. Celebrate with pizza when the work is done.

21 Trace the children's hands and let them color handprint turkeys.

22 Pray for all of the visiting relatives over the holidays.

23 Make headdresses and string beads and let the kids be Indians for a day.

24 Give the children some magazines and have them cut out pictures of things for which they are thankful.

25 Pray for the children's program at your church.

26 Leave a note on your husband's pillow listing reasons you are thankful for him.

27 Why not make a homemade gift for Grandma? Have children dip hands (or feet) in fabric paint and place them on a solid colored apron or cloth bag.

28 Declare war on clutter. Get organized for December so you can enjoy Christ this Christmas.

29 Wrap your gifts for out-of-town family so you can mail them next week. Take a long hot bubble bath tonight.

30 Wake up happy. Claim Psalm 118:24: "This is the day the Lord has made; let us rejoice and be glad in it."

December

1 Plan with your children what they'd like to give as gifts this year.

2 To liven up the house, fill a bowl with lemons and use as a centerpiece. Later make a lemon pie.

3 Read Matthew 25:34-40. Make cards and pictures for prisoners and/or shut-ins.

4 Enjoy some special Christmas music with your family today. Make sure to teach your children the words to your favorite Christmas hymns.

5 String popcorn and hang on the trees in your yard for the birds.

6 Pray for the recipient of each gift as you wrap them.

7 Contact a homeless shelter to see if they need any donations for the holidays.

8 Deliver a batch of homemade Christmas cookies to your husband and his co-workers.

9 What are your hopes for this Christmas season? Pray that your hopes would be His hopes, your ways, His ways.

10 Gather the stuffed animals and create a nativity scene.

11 Pray for your church staff during this busy time. Ask if you can help them in any way.

12 After the children go to bed, make hot spiced cider and sit with your husband in front of a fire or the tree. Listen to Christmas music and relax.

13 Make cookies and deliver them to workers at your local fire station, police station and hospital.

14 Do the good deed you've wanted to do all year.

15 Read aloud the story of the real St. Nicholas as a family.

16 Plan the next few days carefully so that the busyness of the season does not take away from the true meaning.

17 Review your holiday menu and make a grocery list. Buy extra food for your church's charity kitchen.

18 Before bedtime, turn down each family member's bed and leave a mint with a note of appreciation.

19 Take a few minutes to unwind and reflect on the season.

20 Glue mini pretzels side to side to form a wreath. Weave ribbon through the holes and use as ornaments or to decorate packages.

21 Sing "O, Holy Night" and really listen to the words, "the soul felt its worth." Encourage your family to realize the value of their soul.

22 Start a new tradition. Read the Christmas story from Luke 2 as a family. Have each person act out a different role.

23 Make special treats for the neighbors and let the children deliver them.

24 Christmas Eve! Make a birthday cake for Jesus. Have a birthday party for him and sing, "Happy Birthday!"

25 Christmas Day! Take time away from toys and TV to rejoice in the birth of Christ.

26 Take advantage of the seasonal sales. It's a great time to pick up next year's cards and paper supplies.

27 Get started on your thank-you notes. Help the children with theirs.

28 Fill the day with laughter. Tell jokes and stories. Watch a funny movie or read a funny book.

29 Share Christ's heart. Do something kind for a stranger today to carry over the joy of the season.

30 Ask the Lord to reveal the resolutions you need to make for the new year.

31 New Year's Eve. See who can make the most outrageous party hat to celebrate the new year

The Seven Principles of The Proverbs 31 Woman

1. The Proverbs 31 woman reveres Jesus Christ as Lord of her life and pursues an ongoing, personal relationship with Him.

2. The Proverbs 31 woman loves, honors, and respects her husband as the leader of the home.

3. The Proverbs 31 woman nurtures her children and believes that motherhood is a high calling with the responsibility of shaping and molding the children who will one day define who we are as a community and a nation.

4. The Proverbs 31 woman is a disciplined and industrious keeper of the home who creates a warm and loving environment for her family and friends.

5. The Proverbs 31 woman contributes to the financial well-being of her household by being a faithful steward of the time and money God has entrusted to her.

6. The Proverbs 31 woman speaks with wisdom and faithful instruction as she mentors and supports other women, and develops godly friendships.

7. The Proverbs 31 woman shares the love of Christ by extending her hands to help with the needs in the community.

Devotional Thoughts, Prayers, Favorite Scripture

_____

_____

_____

_____

_____

_____

_____

_____

_____

_____

_____

_____

_____

_____

_____

_____

_____

_____

_____

Devotional Thoughts, Prayers, Favorite Scripture

_____

_____

_____

_____

_____

_____

_____

_____

_____

_____

_____

_____

_____

_____

_____

_____

_____

Devotional Thoughts, Prayers, Favorite Scripture

_____

_____

_____

_____

_____

_____

_____

_____

_____

_____

_____

_____

_____

_____

_____

_____

_____

_____

_____

Devotional Thoughts, Prayers, Favorite Scripture

Some of The Proverbs 31 Ministry Resources

The Proverbs 31 Woman
Annual suggested donation $15.00

This 16-page, monthly publication is a storehouse of inspiration and information. "The Proverbs 31 Woman" offers helpful ideas on spiritual growth, marriage, motherhood, home management, stewardship, friendship and much more.

The Best of The Proverbs 31 Ministry
$12.99

This book features the best articles from the first seven years of the newsletter. Chapters include articles on faith building, marriage, motherhood, friendship, overcoming trials, creating a wonderful home, holidays and a years worth of ideas for strengthening the family.

The Proverbs 31 Three-Ring Binder
$7.00

This custom designed, pink three-ring binder is the perfect place to store three years worth of newsletters for quick and easy reference.

To order, see page 319.

Being a Great Mom, Raising Great Kids
Sharon Jaynes
$12.99

A must for all mothers and mothers-to-be. "Being a Great Mom, Raising Great Kids" reveals seven key ingredients to becoming a mother whose children call her blessed. The pages are filled with heart warming stories, scriptural teaching, motivational biographies, and practical suggestions. Also included is a 14-week Bible study guide to use personally or in a group.

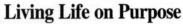

Living Life on Purpose
Lysa TerKeurst
$12.99 each

You won't want to miss Lysa TerKeurst's new book, "Living Life On Purpose" and the companion Bible study titled, "The Life Planning Journal for Women." These resources are wonderful tools to help you discover your God-given purpose and write out a well-prayed-through plan for implementing the "Seven Principles of the Proverbs 31 Woman" in your own life!

Celebrating a Christ-Centered Christmas Video
$12.95

From creating a birthday party for Jesus, to making Christ-centered Christmas Cookies, Sharon Jaynes and Lysa TerKeurst host an exciting new video that shows many ideas on how you can keep Jesus the focus of your holiday season. this 30-minute video, produced by The Inspiration Network, will inspire you and your family year after year.

To order, see page 319.

THE PROVERBS 31 WOMAN SUBSCRIPTION & RESOURCES

Name _____

Address _____

City_____ State_____ Zip_____

Phone (_____)_____ E-mail Address _____

❑ 1-year subscription ($15 suggested donation)
❑ 2-year subscription ($25 suggested donation)

Please send a Subscription to: ($15 annual suggested donation)

Name_____

Address _____

City_____ State_____ Zip_____

Phone (_____)_____

❑ Please send a gift card   Gift given by _____

❑ I would like to make a one-time gift of $ _____

DESCRIPTION	QTY	PRICE	TOTAL
The Best of the Proverbs 31 Ministry		$12.99	
The Proverbs 31 Three-Ring Binder		$7.00	
Being A Great Mom, Raising Great Kids		$12.99	
Living Life on Purpose Book		$12.99	
Life Planning Journal for Women		$12.99	
Celebrating a Christ-Centered Christmas Video		$12.95	
If you are a North Carolina resident add 6.5%			
Postage and handling			
The Proverbs 31 Woman Subscription ($15)			
Special Gift to The Proverbs 31 Ministry			
TOTAL ENCLOSED			

❑ Check enclosed. *Make payable to The Proverbs 31 Ministry*
           P.O. Box 17155, Charlotte, NC 28227

❑ Please charge to my   ❑ **VISA**   ❑ **MasterCard**

    Card number _____

    Expiration date ___/___

Signature_____

POSTAGE & HANDLING
FOR PURCHASE OF:
$0.00 to 14.99—add $3.50
$15.00 to 49.99—add $4.75
$50.00 and up—add $6.00